THE
MURDER
OF
SOPHIE

PART TWO

HOW I HUNTED AND HAUNTED
THE WEST CORK KILLER

MICHAEL SHERIDAN

SPELLING DIFFERENCES: UK V US

This book was written in British English, hence US readers may notice some spelling differences with American English: e.g. color = colour, meter = metre and = jewelry = jewellery

"The paradox of destiny: This young woman was solitary, elegant, she did not like show and took refuge in this beautiful country Ireland is. She was caught by a criminal who was the exact opposite to everything she was: obscure, barbaric, media attention-seeking. Her name should not be reduced to being a sole reference to this affair and today justice must be rendered for her."

Jean-Pierre Bonthoux
Advocate General
Paris, May 31, 2019

"Thus thee thyself in themes like these alone,
Can hunt from thought to thought and keenly wind,
Along even long and to the secret places
And drag out the truth."

Lucretius (55 BC)

"The dead are invisible they are not absent."

Saint Augustine (354–430 AD)

"For nothing is hidden that will not be made manifest, nor is anything secret that will not be known and come to light."

Luke 8.17, the Bible

DEDICATIONS

*"But O for the touch of a vanished hand
And the sound of a voice that is still."*

Tennyson

This book is dedicated to the memories of my late parents Martin and Patsy Sheridan, who inspired me in all aspects to the possibility of writing but also by their sense of justice in the society in which they lived in. And of course, their love of their children.

Also to the Bouniol family, Georges, Marguerite, Bertrand and Stephane; Pierre Louis-Vignaud and his family; to Jean-Pierre Gazeau and Marie Madeleine Opalka; to Alain Spilliaert and Jean-Antoine Bloc; and to the memory of Sophie, a light in all their lives and so cruelly taken away from them.

And to the West Cork witnesses who stuck steadfastly over the years to the cause of truth; not to specifically pick out any of them but in particular to Bill Hogan, Bill Fuller, Amanda and Malachi Reed, Richie Shelley and to the memory of the late Rosie Shelley.

Finally, to members of the Garda murder investigation team alive and dead who were wrongly and maliciously slandered and criticised over the years before being finally vindicated by numerous public inquiries and by the High Court Dublin in 2015. And who along with the Bouniol family and ASSOPH provided an unwavering voice for justice for Sophie.

CONTENTS

PREFACE

Having read *Death in December*, Michael Sheridan's first book published on the case in 2002, I came to realise the stakes and the extent of the judicial procedure surrounding the murder of my niece Sophie. This book played an important part in the decision made in 2007 to create the association (ASSOPH) to establish the truth about the murder of Sophie Toscan du Plantier, née Bouniol.

The reading of this new publication by Mr Sheridan was for me terrifying yet provided clarity. Awe at the inconceivable passivity of the DPP and of his inert reaction to the stagnation of the case in his department. Clarity on the justification of Ian Bailey's conviction for murder on May 31, 2019 by the Criminal Court in Paris.

In actual fact, this book explains the guilt of the accused much better than all other publications, by highlighting two facts. Firstly, the truth prevails when a person who is not subjected to physical or moral constraint proclaims his innocence. On the other hand, where is the truth in the shocking succession of lies by Ian Bailey? He, from the start, and with the benefit of leniency and tolerance of the DPP, continuously changed his version of events.

In addition to that, there were the lies of Marie Farrell once she retracted her statement, at the end of 2005, in the wake of a vile campaign of intimidation by Bailey in an effort to get her to change her statement. Earlier, legal threats were issued to her by him after she gave an interview to Michael Sheridan about how she lived in fear of him.

These lies were mercilessly exposed by Paul O'Higgins' defence counsel for the Gardai and the State in Bailey's failed High Court action of 2014–15.

What is to be expected now? Precisely that this book of evidence incriminating the failures of justice will make the public aware of the denial of justice in Ireland. This jurisdiction, despite a thorough and exhaustive Garda investigation, which would have resulted in a charge and trial in any other jurisdiction in the world, never made any acceptable solid arguments to justify its passivity. On the contrary, during these long and cruel twenty-three years, there has been silence and more silence.

The only exception is the well-known document entitled "Analysis of the evidence to link Ian Bailey to the Sophie Toscan du Plantier murder", not officially signed nor dated, which was pulled out of a hat before the hearings of the Supreme Court of Ireland in 2011.

This document, a one-sided accusation of the Gardai, is flagrantly biased – enough to be declared inadmissible evidence by the Irish High Court. Even to the extent of casting doubt on Sophie's words, which mentioned the name of her killer in November 1996, and I quote, "The statement of Guy Girard contains hearsay evidence only." Guy Girard, whose evidence is dated and signed, has never varied in his statement, which was direct as opposed to hearsay evidence.

On the other hand, the absurd interpretation of Bailey's confessions of responsibility for the crime to no less that eleven witnesses as some form of black humour, when not one of those witnesses experienced the confessions as anything but admissions frightening to many, which prompted the witnesses to give statements to the Garda investigators.

Michael Sheridan has accomplished in his imposing and captivating publication an extraordinary work, eminently salutary in its denunciation of the errors of justice and with the undeniable distinct demonstration of Ian Bailey's guilt.

In Ireland, Bailey suffered humiliating defeats in the libel trial of 2003 and his High Court action against the State in 2014–15, where in the latter his slanderous attack on the Garda murder investigation was roundly rejected. His complaints were also rejected by the Fennelly Commission and the GSOC inquiry. In France, eight superior court judges rejected his appeals against the 2016 indictment for murder and finally he was found guilty of the crime by the Paris Criminal Court in 2019.

Jean-Pierre Gazeau – Sophie's uncle and President of ASSOPH

CHAPTER 11
CONFESSIONS OF A
VIOLENT BEAST

Cork – 2003

On the night of New Year's Eve 1998, two locals, Richie and Rosie Shelley, had been invited to the house by Bailey. They were given the impression that it was a party which would be attended by other locals known to the host and his partner, but when they arrived it quickly became clear that they were in fact the only guests. Richie told the court he and his wife had encountered Bailey and Thomas in a pub in Schull, where the invitation was issued to go back to the house in Liscaha.

After their arrival, they were subjected to a long analysis of the murder of Sophie Toscan du Plantier by the 'expert' Ian Bailey, who produced a scrapbook containing newspaper articles and photographs concerned with the crime. All of this was most uncomfortable as the talk or lecture was being delivered by the prime suspect; a bit near the bone would have been the way to describe the scenario, which Richie noticed had disturbed Rosie so much that she wished to go home. He rang his father to arrange for him to collect them. After the call, the Shelleys were shocked to the core when the host made an admission for committing the murder.

Richie testified: "He came back into the room and seemed to be very upset. He was crying and putting his arms around me and said, 'I did. I did it.' I asked him, 'You did what?' He replied: 'I went too far.'" Richie Shelley naturally and unavoidably concluded that Bailey was talking about the murder, the sole subject of his conversation for the evening. The following night, he met Bailey in a pub in Schull and told him that he was now convinced he had committed the murder.

Rosie Shelley told the court that the encounter had a frightening effect. "He seemed to be obsessed with it. I think he had every article that was published in his file." The host's tearful admission caused her to ask her husband that they leave the house immediately. The witness was in no doubt whatsoever of the meaning of what she had heard: "I immediately recognised it was a kind of confession."

This was not the first or indeed the last of the plaintiff's admissions of responsibility for committing the crime and provided just one more insight into the character of Ian Bailey and the effect he had on witnesses who had no personal axe to grind when he made those admissions. They were frightened not by any irony or joking but by the bald impact of the confessions made in an extremely disturbed state by Bailey.

Another witness, Malachi Reed, confirmed the same effect when as a fourteen-year-old schoolboy he had got a lift home from Bailey. During the journey, he noticed the driver was preoccupied with himself, holding his head and cursing. "I did the best I could to change the subject by asking him how his work was going. He told me it was fine until he replied, "I went up there with a rock and bashed her fucking brains in."

The young boy was naturally shocked by the idea that he was travelling with a man who had just told him that he was the murderer. "I got a cold shiver, nervousness. I didn't know what to do. I kept my mouth shut for 2 miles."

Bailey asked him how he was getting to school. "I said the first thing that came into my head." He got the impression that Bailey had been drinking and was agitated and upset, which completely matched the evidence of the Shelleys. The encounter had a profound and upsetting impact on him and he did not tell his mother about the incident until the following day. When he did, there were bolts put on the doors of the house in the event that Bailey might come knocking.

Malachi Reed was asked in cross-examination whether he liked Bailey; his reply was strong and succinct: "As much as you'd like anyone who admitted to murdering a poor innocent woman." He was then asked by Jim Duggan: "Do you think he did it?" "I wouldn't be here if I didn't, to be honest."

The plaintiff's barrister in a somewhat intemperate dismissal of the evidence called it "rubbish". The young man, now twenty-one years of age, was equal to the taunt: "It's not rubbish. It's the truth. I have no reason to lie." He told the court, when asked why he had subsequently taken two lifts from Bailey, that he had not the opportunity to jump over the ditch.

His mother Irene Amanda Reed told defence counsel Paul Gallagher that her son was agitated and upset when he related the story of the lift and what Bailey had revealed in the course of the journey. "You can imagine what you would feel after an incident like this. I was absolutely terrified. I bolted the locks every night." She rejected opposing counsel's suggestion that her son might have been mistaken in the recounting of the story. "I don't think so. He was definite and absolutely terrified. And my son is not a liar."

She added that she was not surprised by the confession to a fourteen-year-old boy, as Bailey was known to do unusual things and was quite an unusual person.

Unusual and as already ventilated in the evidence of the assaults and diaries, a frightening person and violent and unpredictable. In that context, the Shelleys and Malachi Reed's evidence had the distinct ring of the truth and Jim Duggan had done his client no favours by trying to coarsely rubbish the evidence recalling a traumatic experience of a young and vulnerable boy subjected to a confession of murder that inspired fear and loathing in local people a lot more mature than Malachi Reed at that time.

Brian Jackson, a neighbour, described Bailey as a strange, bohemian type of character. "Everybody said he was a strange man. I heard his hobby was destroying religious artefacts. He had a reputation for walking at night with this thinking stick.

He mostly went out at night or early in the morning. He recalled being told by a family after a visit by Bailey that he had been smoking a joint. He told the court that Bailey had been tending to a bonfire on the Liscaha property on St Stephen's Day in 1996.

"I could see smoke. I could smell smoke. I could hear a fire crackling … I could hear the sound of walking on leaves." This evidence was corroborated by another neighbour, Louise Kennedy, who told the court that she saw the fire on the property on the same day. "I saw smoke coming from behind the studio, so I walked around the back to see what was going on. I saw a fire. It looked to me like a mattress being burned. I just thought it was unusual on St Stephen's Day. There was no one around the fire."

It was an event that the plaintiff had denied ever took place, presumably on the basis that the inference was that he was destroying evidence which he would have been under pressure to do just three days after the murder. But of course, like any person trying to cover their tracks, particularly in the cauldron of such a high-profile crime, he could slip up and undermine the credibility of his narrative.

This he did when telling the journalist Brighid McLaughlin that the fire he had previously confirmed to the journalist had taken place but now under oath swore had not occurred, had indeed happened. He dug himself into a bigger hole when complaining afterwards that he had given this vital piece of information "off the record" to the reporter.

The focus now switched to the morning of the murder, December 23, when once again the narrative already long established by Bailey and Jules Thomas would be challenged not by the murder investigators or members of the media but by the plain people of West Cork, who could not by sheer number have been part of a conspiracy against the plaintiff. The witnesses may well have had every incentive to dislike Ian Bailey but were not motivated other than to tell the truth. Their evidence was based on statements given years before the present proceedings and at least two had been reluctant to come to court.

Caroline Leftwick testified that she had spoken on the phone before midday to Bailey on the morning of December 23. He told her that a French woman who was on holiday had been killed. He was excited about the prospect of covering the murder of Sophie Toscan du Plantier for the newspapers. She recounted a conversation with Jules Thomas at a party in which she had told the witness that Sophie's body was in a terrible state.

Ceri Williams, in evidence, described the plaintiff as intimidating and while he was intelligent, he was known as being eccentric. "I don't like him. I don't agree with the beating of women. In fact, I don't agree with the beating of anyone." Referring to one of the assaults on Jules Thomas, she said that it was so brutal that she did not want anyone capable of doing that to be near her children. She said that one time late in January 1997, a local woman, Diane Martin, told Bailey to his face that he was the murderer, an accusation that received no reply.

Bailey had long maintained that he had never met the murder victim, but a former employer of the plaintiff and neighbour of Sophie's, Alfie Lyons, would beg to differ. In the witness box, he recounted that he had introduced Bailey to Sophie Toscan du Plantier when he was doing gardening work at his house in June 1995. Sophie had called to Lyons's house, a not uncommon occurrence when she was staying at her holiday home. "As far as I can recollect, I did introduce him to Sophie Toscan du Plantier. I am ninety per cent certain that I did." Though not known at the time, it would be later confirmed that local man Leo Bolger, who was doing repair work on the French woman's house, had witnessed the meeting.

Once again, in the matter of fact, however disputed, it was a mystery why Ian Bailey should deny ever having met the murder victim as far as eighteen months before the crime occurred. Nothing could possibly turn on it in relation to his possible connection to the victim in the role of the killer. Alfie Lyons, a friend and employer, had no incentive to lie any more in the matter than the plaintiff. But Bailey did just that, even when there was nothing to be gained by his denial.

Counsel and the defence team must have been happy about the progress of the trial, as nothing that came out of the mouth of the plaintiff was even the slightest bit convincing or credible in any way, and his denials were beginning to ring more and more hollow. All the local witnesses appeared both convincing and truthful. But nonetheless, there was a distance to go and at any stage the outcome of legal proceedings are notoriously difficult to predict. The most that could be said was that Ian Bailey and his case was on the back foot.

Journalist Paul Webster, who was Paris correspondent for *The Guardian* at the time of the murder, said that Ian Bailey had made contact with him about getting reporting work on the crime, boasting that he was able and in a good position to provide information in his capacity as a local freelance journalist. He made it absolutely clear that the witness said that he had talked to her [Sophie] before: "There is no doubt about that at all." The plaintiff's contention that he had never seen or met the murder victim was once more unequivocally challenged.

Alfie Lyons's partner Shirley Foster then gave more damning evidence, insisting that she had encountered Bailey on the afternoon after the murder, driving at speed to the crime scene up her laneway, as opposed to the open roadway which was his version, and she said that he had seemed in a considerable hurry. All this indicated that the plaintiff had had knowledge of the murder in advance of it coming into the public domain, and more evidence followed which copper-fastened this fact.

Eddie Cassidy of *The Examiner* had contacted Bailey to check out an incident of death in the area, and denied that he had told the plaintiff at 1.40 p.m. on December 23 that a murder had been committed involving a French national. He was not aware at the time of the phone call of the nationality involved or that it was a murder; it could have been an accident, for all he knew.

Principal of the Provision photo agency, Mike McSweeney, testified that Ian Bailey had told him that pictures of the murder scene had been taken around 11 a.m. on the morning of December

23, over two hours before the plaintiff said he first heard about the murder. As it had been claimed that the photographs were taken by Jules Thomas, this time frame was impossible, as the next witness would outline to the court.

Local John Camier told the court that Jules Thomas had been at his vegetable stall in the nearby village of Goleen around 11 a.m. on the morning of December 23 and told him about the murder. She claimed it was on Christmas Eve, but the witness was definite about the date and time, and that Thomas had also said that the victim was a French national.

Camier told Judge Moran he was under oath and he was telling the truth, and that there was no question of his statement about the incident being made under duress. "I take my own decisions and on my own conscience. I would stress the statement I made was of my own mind and my own conscience."

This gave the lie to Bailey's contention that the local witnesses had been put under pressure by members of the investigation team to give false and fabricated evidence against them. Jules Thomas had complained in evidence about how the media attention had isolated them from the community after the first arrests in February 1997, but now she and her partner were in court and under the full blaze of huge publicity, contradicting the evidence of the very neighbours whose attention they had lost by the malice of the newspapers.

John Camier had succinctly summed up his position as a witness but also that of the others; there had been no pressure applied to them and all were aware of the implications of giving evidence under oath.

The eighth day of the proceedings, December 17, commenced with Schull shopkeeper Marie Farrell taking the stand. She had been a reluctant witness, not least because she had been subjected to harassment, threats and intimidation by the plaintiff to withdraw her statement to the Gardai about seeing Bailey in the early hours of December 23 not far from the scene of the crime. There was also a skeleton in her cupboard – the identity of the man she had been with on the night of the murder and another serious matter that occurred when she and her family were living in England and which would come to dramatic light many years into the future.

Nonetheless, her version of events in relation to that night and afterwards was eagerly awaited by the media covering the trial, the defendants and the general public. If her evidence was credible then it was capable of severely damaging the plaintiff's case. A central question related to the alleged campaign of intimidation could be asked: Why did a man who had come to court as the prime suspect of the murder to "prove his innocence" feel it necessary to threaten a prime witness in the investigation with the purpose of getting her statement withdrawn?

There was an electric atmosphere in the court as the quietly spoken, rather nervous woman took the stand. She made a reference to a threatening phone call she had received just days before from a woman telling her to "keep my bloody mouth shut". There would be no prize on offer for guessing who had made that call or on behalf of whom. Marie Farrell told the court that she was a reluctant witness and had only relented after the newspapers issued a subpoena for her appearance.

The witness, gaining confidence as time passed, outlined the campaign of intimidation mounted by Bailey in an effort to make her retract her statement to the Gardai, which she repeated to Paul Gallagher and to the court that she had seen Ian Bailey in the early hours of the morning of the murder not far from the holiday home of Sophie Toscan du Plantier. The plaintiff had already under oath told the court that he had never left the home in Liscaha on the night of the murder after returning from socialising in Schull.

She had previously seen the same man standing on the opposite side of the road staring into her shop while Sophie Toscan du Plantier was browsing on the premises two days before the murder. In the following January, she had seen the same man in a local newsagent, and he was identified to her as Ian Bailey, and it was then she informed the Gardai of what she had seen.

Sometime later, Jules Thomas approached her and said Bailey wanted to meet her. At another time, Jules Thomas invited her to call to her house to record a statement claiming the Gardai wanted her to make a false statement (against Bailey).

This was the beginning of the threats and intimidation that resulted in Marie Farrell living in fear. "He was terrorising me. My life was a living nightmare. We had a small ice-cream parlour and I ended up in debt. I was so afraid to stay there because of Ian Bailey. I am afraid to let my children out because of Ian Bailey."

She said she was tortured by the man who called into her shop, opened his coat and said that he was all wired up and wanted her to say the Gardai were forcing her to make a false statement. He wondered if her shop was clean, meaning free of bugs of the recording variety. She became highly nervous of being in the shop alone and being exposed to his visits, and afraid because of his physique of what harm he could cause her.

He was becoming more aggressive because she had not retracted her statement, and on another occasion, produced detailed information about her and her partner's living arrangements in London and telling her that he was an investigative reporter. He roared at her another time, saying: "I know you saw me ... but I did not kill Sophie." He made cut-throat gestures and held his finger to his temple, as if he was holding a gun.

She was getting threatening phone calls and had to hire extra staff for the shop so that she would not be alone at any given time on the premises. Marie Farrell had grown in confidence during her testimony and was able to swat aside Jim Duggan's suggestion in cross-examination that she had invited his client to her shop. "I don't think any woman in her right frame of mind would invite Bailey to her shop when she is on her own. It is a well-known fact that he is abusive towards women."

Counsel got even less satisfaction from the witness from his suggestion that she had been put under duress to make a statement about what she had seen in the early hours of December 23, 1996 on the road near Kealfadda Bridge, namely his client.

"The Gardai didn't know me from Adam until I contacted them." Marie Farrell's reply was as assured and credible as all her evidence had been, and in addition hugely damaging to the plaintiff's case.

Another nasty, toxic and insidious side of Ian Bailey's character had been shown to the court and the public, and it was no coincidence that the object of his threats was a vulnerable woman living in fear of his cowardly bullying. The motivation for his actions was also made abundantly clear to force a principal witness to retract a statement which totally exposed the statement he had made to the investigation team about being at home the whole night of the murder as a lie. Now why would a man who protested his innocence of a crime have any need to take such a blatant and telling course of intimidation?

Even a man guilty of a crime and on the face of it getting away with it would have not simply hesitated but avoided interfering with a witness for fear of drawing attention to himself and the implications of his action. But not Ian Bailey, a slave to impulse and his uncontrolled brutal nature. The sword of justice in this trial had been sharpened once more and that afternoon would inflict another deep cut in the plaintiff's case based on the premise that he had been the victim.

His one-time friend Peter Bielecki took the stand and began to unfold a tale that in the Shakespearean phrase would make the eyes start from their spheres and each particular hair to stand on end. In May 1996, one of Jules Thomas's daughters Virginia had called to him for help and told him that her mother had been assaulted by Ian Bailey, and asked if he could bring her to hospital. He accompanied Virginia to the house, where he found a scene of horror. The youngest daughter, Fenella, was in a distressed state and as he was comforting her was distracted by terrible cries from her mother's bedroom.

"I could hear what I can only describe as animal sounds of terrible distress. Jules was curled up at the end of the bed in foetal position. Her hair was completely tousled and large clumps of her hair were missing, she had clumps of hair in her hand and her eye was purple. It was huge; a pink fluid was dripping from it and her mouth was swollen. Her face had gouges on it, her right hand had bite marks on it. It was like the soul, the spirit, had gone out of her. It was the most appalling thing I have ever witnessed."

The witness then said he drove the badly injured Thomas to hospital in Cork and when he returned, he agreed to stay in the house in case Bailey might come back and turn his attention to the daughters. He stayed for about three weeks. He slept on a sofa on the ground floor with a hammer under the pillow to defend himself if necessary, against the monster who had carried out the revolting attack. He need not have bothered; it was well known that Bailey never took on men – his violence was exclusively directed against the female of the species.

Bielecki said that he had been close friends with Bailey in the early 1990s through a mutual interest in Irish traditional music, but that this horrible incident had brought this to an end. "I thought I was a good judge of character but obviously I wasn't. From the moment Mr Bailey did what he did to Jules Thomas, I no longer considered him worthy of my friendship in any shape or form."

A horrified silence had descended over the court during the graphic evidence, during which Peter Bielecki had been overcome by emotion, apologising for the completely understandable lapse, saying: "I am sorry, this is very distressing." He could have been speaking for almost everyone sitting in the court. The exceptions were the two people directly involved. Neither Ian Bailey nor Jules Thomas displayed the tiniest flicker of emotion or indeed discomfort during the chronicle of gratuitous and sickening violence.

It could hardly have escaped any one of the furious note-takers in the box usually reserved for the jury that this incident had taken place in the same year as the murder and with the same method of what can be described as overkill – violence which far exceeds the circumstances in which it occurs and accompanied by an uncontrollable rage on behalf of the perpetrator. The words adduced in evidence from his diary would have been echoing in the same ears following the assault: "*I actually tried to kill her.*"

There are moments of revelation in trials of extreme intensity and high stakes which cut through the adversarial rituals, the complex issues, the legal imperatives and get straight to the heart of the matter. This was one during which the straightforward, honest evidence of a witness speaking the incontrovertible truth drew back the curtain of uncertainty that hangs in every court-room and revealed the plaintiff Ian Bailey, who masquerading as a victim on this stage was in fact the monstrous villain. One who told the court that he was not a man of violence but had been presented as such by the media, by the police, by the good people of West Cork who, according to him, were individually and collectively liars and fabricators.

In this passage of evidence, the real and composite Ian Bailey emerged not simply as a man capable of murder but intent upon it, compounding the horror of the act of extreme violence by refusing to part with the keys of the household car, proving the intent and forcing his partner's daughter to seek the help of a neighbour. Supposing that help was not available, then what? Were the newspapers justified in examining his role as the prime suspect for the murder of Sophie Toscan du Plantier? There was only one answer to that question in the affirmative and the minute Peter Bielecki stepped down from the witness box, the plaintiff's case was well and truly doomed.

The final witness for the day and as it transpired the case was Bill Fuller, who earlier had been accused by the plaintiff of intimidating him in the hallway earlier in the trial by saying, "I've got you now." The witness apologised for talking to Bailey and explained that he had in fact said, "You have sweat on your brow." If it was the former, a matter of the pot calling the kettle black, and if the latter, then time for a hearing aid.

Fuller recalled an encounter with Bailey, who spoke to him in the second person but referring to himself, and made what in effect was another confession to the murder, saying: "You did it.

You killed Sophie. You did it, you saw her in the Spar supermarket walking up the aisle with her tight arse. You fancied her. You went up to see what you could get. She ran away screaming. You chased her. You went too far, you had to finish her off."

Bailey had described the exact trajectory of the killing, the motive a sex crime, with rejection triggering an uncontrollable rage followed by overkill. Naturally, Bill Fuller was shocked and blurted out a reply: "Sounds like something you would say." Bailey then remarked: "Funny you should say, that is how I met Jules. I saw her tight arse, but she let me in." The witness went on to say he was both shocked and upset: "I was very disturbed and quite afraid."

So ended the extraordinary trial and there would be much to consider for the opposing counsel, who would present their final submissions to the court over the following two days. The proceedings had been characterised by revelations, twists and turns in the planned and improvised plot, and producing shock and loathing, particularly in relation to the details of the assaults carried out by the plaintiff on his partner. Like all classic trials, the closed door of privacy was thrown wide open in a manner that the plaintiff, journalists, interested parties and the public could never have imagined.

The principal role in the drama was of course played by Ian Bailey and the supporting part by his partner Jules Thomas, both of whom arrived at the courthouse, her arm clasped around his presumably to present a united front.

The violence described was remarkable not only in its brutality but also in the forbearance of the victim and the propensity of the perpetrator not to display any genuine remorse, but to blame alcohol and his partner for the horrendous incidents. Both also inexplicably played down the physical, not to mention psychological consequences of his actions in court as something that just happened.

Bailey's added propensity to feel sorry for himself rather than the victim was clear in his diary accounts. As the May 1996 incident graphically described in evidence by neighbour Peter Bielecki as part of his May 15 entry illustrated:

"Although remorse-filled sentiments and disgust floods me I am afraid for myself, a cowardly fear, for although I have damaged and made grief your life, I have damaged my own destiny and future to the point I can see in destroying you I destroyed me ..."

What did not emerge in evidence was a proper resolution of the incident from Peter Bielecki's point of view. Naturally, he hoped that Ian Bailey would never darken the door of the house again. He had, as he testified, stayed in the house in Liscaha for some weeks, protecting the victim and her daughters. One day, he answered a knock on the door to a Garda officer who told him that he had called on the instruction of Jules Thomas. Peter already knew that Jules Thomas – as she was wont to do – was seeing Ian Bailey again, but wondered why the officer had the need to call to the house and speak to him at the instigation of the victim. He spoke to the officer, who asked Jules Thomas why she had not pressed charges. She did not reply, and he told her she was lucky to be alive, and that without charges he and his colleagues could not protect her.

Before leaving, the officer warned her that Bailey would be violent towards her and possibly another woman. His prescient warning fell on deaf ears. She had made a complaint but withdrew it and again in 2001 when she was battered once more, and her partner was barred by the court from not just the house but the area. She brought him back. As the chemistry of this poisonous scenario was played out in court, it was difficult to understand how a woman would bring back into her house a man who had treated her in such a brutal fashion, not once, not twice, but three times.

But ultimately, no matter how she tried to downplay the brutality of the assaults in her evidence, Jules Thomas was clearly a victim of a cunning, controlling and manipulative man.

Bailey had insisted that his violence had been confined to one woman, as if this could be considered a virtue on his part, showing a precise, dysfunctional attitude towards his behaviour. He denied being physically violent towards his ex-wife Sarah Limbrick, but it would emerge that he was certainly abusive and in a threatening manner. Questioned by a member of the Sophie Toscan du Plantier murder investigation team in 1997, she said that he would punch the wall, turn over tables and throw the typewriter at the wall. It would later emerge that he had in fact tried to strangle her.

He would also lock her out of the apartment and was smoking cannabis, abusing alcohol and ingesting magic mushrooms. She decided to divorce him. In this process, she discovered that he had taken out a life insurance policy on her for £250,000 and forged her signature on the policy document. It would not take Sherlock Holmes to work out what plan Bailey had in his mind by taking this course of action.

On the morning of the ninth day of the proceedings, Thursday, December 18, Paul Gallagher began his final submission on part of the defence and right from the beginning of the five-hour summation went straight to the jugular of the plaintiff's case, which he proposed should be dismissed as his evidence was "wholly and utterly unreliable". His clients were justified on several grounds in naming Bailey as a murder suspect. The case, he said, should be dismissed or struck out, as up to twenty witnesses – including neighbours and friends – had totally contradicted Mr Bailey's evidence.

"We say the plaintiff's case is totally and utterly unreliable and that he sought to mislead the court in many significant respects. Every witness called contradicted his evidence in many and crucial respects, including his own witness, Mr Cassidy. The contradictions in evidence centred on a range of areas such as Mr Bailey's movements on the night of the murder; whether there was a fire in his partner's garden in the days after the murder; what details of the murder Mr Bailey knew on the morning it occurred; and claims he had confessed to the murder on at least two occasions."

Counsel pointed out that here was a witness (Bailey) who gave evidence on all those events and accused people of lying and fabricating, and significantly in relation to Mrs Farrell, intimidated her in an unimaginable way.

"A person has the right to a reputation, but no person has the right to come into this court and tell lie, upon lie, upon lie. He not only told lies, but he tried to destroy the reputation of a large number of people along the way."

Counsel said that the evidence of Marie Farrell, who said she saw him about a mile from Ms Toscan du Plantier's house at Kealfadda Bridge early on the morning of the murder, was compelling. He also pointed to the evidence of Malachi Reed, who was fourteen years old at the time, who said that Mr Bailey claimed to have murdered Ms Du Plantier with the words: "I went up there with a rock and bashed her fucking brains in." Comments by his mother when questioned about the veracity of her son's statement – "I am sorry, but my son is not a liar" – showed how strong and reliable a witness he was.

Mr Gallagher went on to say that most of the witnesses reluctant to give evidence had "no axe to grind" and had to be called to court on subpoena. He said that Mr Bailey's repeated tendency to distance himself from his confessions to the murder by insisting he was talking about "what they were saying" did not hold up. He cited evidence about the New Year's Eve party in 1998, when he had told Richie Shelley, "I did it. I did it. I went too far." Bailey said he was repeating what others said to him.

Bailey not only confirmed that the counsel had said that the conversation had taken place, but Richie and Rosie Shelley were adamant that they heard him confess to murder. He confirmed that the Shelleys believed him to be making a confession. "Mr Bailey has always tried to put another construction on the words."

When addressing the issue of whether Mr Bailey's reputation had already been tarnished by his arrest in connection with the murder and the public knowledge of his violence towards Ms Thomas, Mr Gallagher submitted: "The articles at the centre of this case, 'Sophie Man's Shame; Iil in the Hills' and 'Murder Suspect Has No Alibi' are articles that should be read in full – not an isolated phrase. Headlines or paragraphs should not be cherrypicked." The newspapers, he claimed, could use the defence of justification in publishing the articles as there was good reason to believe Mr Bailey was a suspect for the murder and also a violent man capable of murder.

This was the kernel of how this "defamation case" had been run; the defence, as I had been told by a solicitor before trial, had to prove that Ian Bailey was not only a prime suspect but also with a history of specific violence that would show that he was capable of murder. The actual articles complained of had but a walk-on part in the whole drama. None of the journalists who wrote the articles or editors responsible for publishing them were ever called by the defence.

Mr Gallagher said that Bailey was a violent man and that the assaults he had subjected his partner to were nothing less than horrific. "It is patently ludicrous to suggest that damages should be paid to a man who complains of being defamed by being called violent when that is clearly what he is." He also remarked that Bailey tried to mislead the court in relation to the violence against Ms Thomas.

"When the plaintiff was giving his evidence, he sought to seriously downplay those incidents. He clearly tried to mislead the court with regard to the true nature of those incidents. When the truth emerged in cross-examination and through subsequent witnesses it was shocking."

The plaintiff's legal team were overwhelmed with evidence of the vile behaviour and actions of their client, whose reputation had been torn to shreds by the defence, and when it came for Jim Duggan to make his submission, there was little to make an impression in any effective way. He said that the newspapers being sued had published articles which said to the man who read them that this man had murdered Sophie Toscan du Plantier.

He was shocked that journalists or editors had not been called to give him a chance to question how the articles came to be written and felt his client was subjected to a trial by ambush. Counsel was floundering or to coin a phrase, pissing against the wind or storm in this instance. The minute Judge Moran allowed in the vital evidence, the case was never going to be confined to what had been written in the newspapers but much more about the murder and Ian Bailey's involvement as a prime suspect – and a man capable of and with the opportunity to commit the crime.

There was now no reasonable chance given the length of the trial, the volumes of evidence involved and the closeness to Christmas that the judge could possibly reach a verdict until after the holiday, and that is precisely what Judge Patrick Moran proposed. He also had other cases to handle on the Circuit Court list. It was a hugely important case, the result of which would have serious ramifications not just for the parties involved but also for any future murder case. Whatever the immediate circumstances, the judge was wise to take his time. He set January 9 as judgement day but that would later be postponed, and the final date was set for January 19, 2004.

It had been an intense hearing with all the characteristics of a classical murder trial full of tension and revelations and high drama. It also, consequently, ripped apart any semblance of logic in the DPP's decision not to charge Ian Bailey. Had this been a murder trial – which in effect it was – but in a criminal court, no jury would have been detained long in finding a man who had perjured himself at such length and consistency guilty of the crime.

CHAPTER 12
THE VERDICT AND
AFTERMATH

Cork – 2004

The judgement hearing on Monday, January 19, 2004, at the Cork Circuit Court predictably was in advance oversubscribed by a huge media presence, including TV crews and reporters both national and international, radio stations local and national, and an army of print media representatives all preparing to deliver definitive coverage of the final outcome of a case that was one of defamation in name only. Ian Bailey had courted and consented to publicity in the wake of his first arrest in February 1997, and complained of it during the proceedings, but could not have imagined if it was attention-seeking then what exactly he would be facing now.

Then again, if the outcome was to his and his legal team's satisfaction, he could revel in the limelight that he had proposed in the course of the trial had ruined his career and life, and comfortably retire to the house on the Prairie in the knowledge that he would never be bothered again by the marauding wolves of the media, and put his alleged connection with the murder of Sophie Toscan du Plantier behind him for good.

There had been a fade factor from the date of the end of the trial and neither the plaintiff nor the defence could predict just how the evidence presented would impact on the mind or decision of the judge. There is no such thing as certainty in such legal matters and not even the most experienced advocates, court reporters or spectators could second-guess what might influence a judge or a jury, particularly in a civil case but also in a criminal case where circumstantial evidence is being relied upon.

So, tension on all fronts was high and when the doors of the court were opened, there was a rush to get seating mainly by the attendant media, the pressure on whom was intense, and the scribblers had to be accommodated before the general public, who were also well represented such was the high profile of the case.

The plaintiff Ian Bailey, assured of his seat, arrived without Jules Thomas – who was ill – and sat near his legal team as usual. He was well attired in court throughout the proceedings, with suit and tie appropriate for the occasion, in contrast to his previous persona of poet and bodhran player in knitted jumper and jeans.

His entrance was by dint of status less important than that of the person who now adopted by right the central role and the only role that mattered, the judge, Patrick Moran, and the whole of the people rose and sat when he took his place; settling himself, he began to read his long-awaited judgement to a hushed and attentive audience. Most thought it might be of lengthy duration given the complexities of the proceedings, but it would last for between just thirty-five and forty minutes.

The judge dismissed the defamation action against six of the newspapers and ruled that Bailey had been defamed on a lesser issue in both the *Irish Sun* and the *Irish Daily Mirror* by reporting that the plaintiff had been violent towards his former wife Sarah Limbrick, as there was no evidence offered to prove it. In the majority, the newspapers' defence of justification was fully proved and accepted by the court. He thanked the defence for providing him with overnight transcripts of the proceedings which meant he did not have to take copious notes and could observe the demeanour of witnesses.

There were, he noted, inconsistencies between Mr Bailey's version of events and those given by twenty witnesses, and on the balance of probabilities, he accepted the versions of the witnesses. The judge recalled that Ms Toscan du Plantier had been murdered on December 22 or 23 and that her body had been found on the morning of the 23rd. "The press descended on West Cork to an enormous degree. Ms Toscan du Plantier came from a well-known French family and the murder took place in a very remote and beautiful area.

"The plaintiff is a journalist and once the news broke, he became involved in reporting on the story of the murder. He wrote numerous reports, the first of December 28 and the last on February 10. He wrote for the *Star*, *Paris Match* and the *Sunday Tribune*. One can only presume that West Cork was full of rumour, reports and counter reports. I am sure the finger was pointing in various ways." The judge recalled that the plaintiff was arrested on February 10, 1997, and brought to Bandon Garda Station, where several journalists were assembled.

"When the Gardai make an arrest, they do it for a good reason because they have a strong suspicion. The plaintiff complained about the arrest, but this was not a matter for this court but authorities like the Garda Complaints Board. Following his arrest Mr Bailey was photographed and named. There was further coverage, naturally. The Gardai had arrested a suspicious person."

Judge Moran pointed out that this was not a murder case (although it had certainly been conducted like one by the defence). "There is a different burden of proof in a criminal and civil case. I was anxious this trial should not take on the mantle of a criminal trial. I'm afraid that at times it did, and I regret that. I stress it is a civil matter. Any findings of fact in this case are based on the balance of probabilities and nothing else."

The judge listed the articles complained of published in the *Irish Daily Mirror*, *Sunday Independent*, *Independent on Sunday*, *The Times*, the *Star* (two articles), the *Irish Sun*, the *Irish Daily Mirror* and *The Daily Telegraph*. He did not propose going through all the articles. The defence put forward five defences: justification, partial justification, consent, qualified privilege and contributory negligence on part of the plaintiff.

"If one is defamed, one must deal with the ordinary and

natural meaning of the words and take into account the context. The allegation of libel means that a person's standing has been reduced in the eyes of the ordinary person. The evidence in this case consists mainly of the plaintiff. Mr Bailey spent three and a half days in the witness box. He was a cool witness. He never got annoyed with Mr Gallagher. The only time he got uncomfortable was when he was giving a version of what happened within the walls of this court (the alleged intimidation by Bill Fuller).

"He told us about his relationship with Ms Thomas. He told us about how he was treated by the Gardai and being hounded by the media. He was cross-examined at considerable length. Mr Gallagher put it to him he was a violent man. He sought and used publicity. He allowed himself to be interviewed by RTE Radio on the *Pat Kenny Show*, first by researchers and then he spoke to Pat Kenny. He posed for photographs and gave interviews.

"This to me is quite unusual for someone who has been arrested on suspicion of the serious charge of murder. Normally, such people would withdraw into the background and wonder what will happen next. One can only draw from this that Mr Bailey likes the limelight, he enjoys attention and notoriety."

The judge noted that Jules Thomas was an equally cool witness. Unpleasant things had been put to her related to violence and she tended to put this under the carpet, saying it was due to drink or nothing at all. He said that the purpose of calling witnesses by the defence from the Toormore and Schull areas was to show inconsistencies and flaws in the version Mr Bailey and Ms Thomas gave of events. "The thrust of the plaintiff's case was that he was a man branded as violent towards women and branded as the murderer of Sophie Toscan du Plantier. There are other matters including that he was violent towards his wife in a previous marriage."

He continued, "The question of violence towards women is a fact. What came across as a result of questions from Mr Gallagher is that Ms Thomas suffered three nasty assaults. Mr Bailey appeared in the District Court over one of those and received a suspended sentence. Mr Bailey says that when he was violent, it takes place domestically [*sic*] and is a domestic problem. I deal with a lot of family law in this court. One rarely comes across instances of beatings. In this case we have three.

"Violence once would be unusual. Violence twice would be unusual. Three times is exceptional. The District Court gave a six-month suspended sentence because his partner said she forgave him. Otherwise, the District judge would have had no hesitation in imposing a custodial sentence. I certainly have no hesitation in describing Mr Bailey as a violent man and I think the defendants have no problem in describing him as violent towards women, plural."

Judge Moran then turned to the matter of the inconsistencies between what Mr Bailey said and the evidence of the other witnesses. He recalled the plaintiff's denial that he knew Ms Toscan du Plantier, saying he had only seen her from the window of the house of local man and her neighbour Mr Alfred Lyons, for whom he was working at the time. "Mr Lyons gave evidence that he was eighty to ninety per cent certain that he had introduced Ms Toscan du Plantier to Mr Bailey. On the balance of probabilities, I accept this evidence and that he did introduce them … it may have been a casual introduction and I accept Mr Bailey's evidence that he didn't know her to meet on the street or to have casual conversation with or to go for a drink with her."

He then turned to Marie Farrell's evidence. "The evidence of Ms Farrell, who said she didn't know Mr Bailey. The description she gave of a man seen in Schull walking on the road in the early morning; and the man she saw at Kealfadda Bridge. It was one man, that was Mr Bailey. Ms Farrell says she came here reluctantly. I heard about the 'relationship' between Ms Farrell and Mr Bailey culminating in Ms Farrell's solicitors writing a letter to Mr Bailey about his behaviour.

"On the balance of probabilities, I accept what Ms Farrell told me that the man she saw on the bridge was in her view Ian Bailey. I have to say it is evidence of identification and if it is evidence of material value, I'm not sure what standing it would have."

He moved onto the two witnesses, Ms Louise Kennedy and Mr Brian Jackson, who gave evidence about the fire on the property of Ms Thomas on St Stephens's Day.

It was not clear, he said, what was burning; it could have been branches or timber, as there was a crackling sound heard. It was clear he accepted the evidence that a fire had occurred but made no remark about the plaintiff's denial, which is probably understandable since there had been nothing but denial of every aspect of witness evidence.

He accepted the evidence of Richie and Rosie Shelley about the New Year's Eve party and the confession they heard on that occasion, and also that of Malachi Reed, though the judge thought that Bailey had been trying through bravado to impress the young boy.

Judge Moran moved to wrap his judgement up. "That is the evidence. The plaintiff says these articles portray Mr Bailey as the murderer of Ms Toscan du Plantier. I read these articles several times. I put myself in the position of the ordinary reader. They do not convey to me that he is a murderer. They do say he was a suspect and was arrested on suspicion. The articles do go on to quote what he said: 'I didn't do it.' This is given equal prominence. I take the view the plea of justification has been established strongly except for the washing of the boots, burning of the clothing and that he was violent towards his ex-wife. There is no evidence for these.

"As far as the first two are concerned, the defence of partial justification is there. I don't think these references injure his reputation having regard to the truth of the other charges. There only remains the claim that he was violent towards his ex-wife. He was defamed in regard to that and is entitled to damages of £8,000 each from *The Sun* and the *Mirror*." The judge then set a hearing about costs for February 12.

It took a little time for the impact of the judgement to be felt in the packed courtroom. Bailey closed his eyes and leaned forward in his seat. It was hard to know whether this was an expression of incredulity or disappointment. He had shown remarkable composure under fierce cross-examination and in the face of the contradictory evidence of the West Cork witnesses. Could he possibly have thought that victory would be his? Probably every litigant lives with such hope until the jaws of judgement swallow it lock, stock and barrel.

He might have fantasised about making a statement in victorious mode outside the court backed by his legal team, just like he and we had all witnessed many times on film and television. He would have seen himself as a hero who took on the might of the media not against all the odds but by right because they had dragged his name through the dirt. He could have lorded it over the members of the investigation team, the barristers, the scribblers and the public present in the courtroom. But not now.

Bailey's problem, among many others, was that he considered himself smarter than everyone else and felt that consequences played no part in his actions. The defence proved that the plaintiff did indeed possess those traits of character which were consistent with the commission of the crime, and he possessed other traits that cast serious doubt on the credibility of his explanation of his actions around the time of the murder.

There was not a flicker of emotion, no more than there had been when the details of his brutal assaults on his partner were revealed and the appalling reflections in his diaries on the incidents were ventilated during evidence, or when the defence counsel Paul Gallagher repeatedly asked him if he would describe himself as an animal. Ian Bailey was not that sort of man then and not that man now, whatever the reality of his position. Not once had he reached out and expressed sympathy to the murder victim Sophie Toscan du Plantier or her long-suffering family during the trial.

Even in death she played, beyond the grave, an ever-present role in the proceedings. The plaintiff's pity was reserved for himself but if also felt for the victim, there was no outward sign.

Bailey had avoided the media scrum before the hearing by

slipping in the back door of the court an hour and a half before the start and it looked like he was determined to avoid any contact after the defeat, which left him looking pale and gaunt. He immediately approached the desk of his solicitor, Con Murphy, and they later – after consultation – departed the court and forced themselves through the media army outside the doors, ironically with the help of Gardai, whose West Cork members and others Bailey had denigrated during the proceedings. His face was an implacable mask, showing nothing to the cameramen, photographers or reporters.

It was anything but the sort of notoriety and publicity-seeking that the judge had mentioned he sought in his summing up; the media could crowd him with impunity, no longer worried about creating a victim from the attention. By the time he reached the door of his solicitor's car, the realisation would have struck him forcibly that it was now open season on Ian Bailey.

He had tried unsuccessfully to profit from the coverage consented to and encouraged by him after he had been nominated as prime suspect to a brutal murder.

To achieve that end, he had persistently lied under oath in court, slandered members of the murder investigation team and offered pathetic explanations in denial of the evidence of local witnesses. He had ignored calls for a comment, muttering, "Not now," and was immediately driven away in his solicitor's car.

The proceedings were finally over and resulted in a humiliating and crushing defeat for Ian Bailey. He had come to court to seek damages from the very newspapers he had largely invited to interview him because the journalists concentrated on the fact of him being the prime suspect for the murder instead of providing the sympathetic portrait he hoped for and confidently expected. As the judge correctly pointed out, such a course for a man suspected of murder was highly unusual; normally, people in this position would withdraw into the background but Bailey, he observed, liked the limelight, enjoyed the attention and the notoriety.

Well, for my part in helping to expose the evidence of Bailey's vicious, aggressive and violent character – characterised by his attacks on his partner and further confirmed by his diary entries in relation to them, his narcissism, lack of empathy, degeneracy, vile behaviour and pathological mendacity – I took some satisfaction. No one who attended the hearing was left in any doubt about the true nature of Ian Bailey.

Here was a man who had not just, as defence counsel had pointed out, told lie after lie to the court, but also in his violence towards his partner had on at least one occasion concentrated on disfiguring her face and had attempted to prevent others from bringing her to hospital for treatment, and who had tried to deflect from his responsibility for his dangerous and unforgiveable behaviour by blaming alcohol and the victim for his assaults.

Behaviour that experts I had consulted would say was consistent with an out-of-control, sadistic psychopath. The court would not go into that territory, but any educated observer of the proceedings would hardly disagree. Bailey, as was well known to the defence and investigators, had in advance of his first arrest asked an acquaintance to keep his diaries, an action that speaks for itself. They had been returned and were seized during the second arrest.

The writing of those diaries was not what Bailey proposed as some kind of creative exercise – just one more lie in his ludicrous explanation – but more so classical behaviour typified in the studies of psychopaths.

Not at this time or indeed during the following day, when the exultant media – newspapers in particular – picked what flesh was left on the bones of Bailey's reputation like vultures feeding on a fallen wildebeest. The coverage was naturally extensive and all-embracing, more so than any other trial for defamation in the history of the State, and the *Irish Star* – which emerged victorious in relation to two articles – pulled no punches in its coverage of the result of the judgement.

With a front page featuring an inset picture of Sophie Toscan du Plantier and a huge head and shoulders shot of Bailey outside the court, the strapline read You boasted you killed her and the main headline read:

SO DID YOU REALLY MURDER SOPHIE?

The coverage, spread over many inside pages, went much further in connecting Ian Bailey to the crime than any of the articles he had complained of in court. The headline across pages eight and nine nailed a central issue concerning his involvement, namely the confessions he himself had made about it.

QUESTIONS THAT MUST BE ANSWERED

In six panels about that headline, under a strapline of WHY?, the questions were set out:

"Did you, as the judge yesterday accepted, tell three people that you brutally murdered Sophie Toscan du Plantier? Did you tell local Malachi Reed while in your car that you "went up there with a rock and bashed her fucking brains in"? Did you drunkenly tell Richie and Rosie Shelley while at a New Year's Eve party, "I did it. I did it. I went too far"? Did you protest you were not a violent man – when you had viciously assaulted your partner three times? Did you deny you were at Kealfadda Bridge the morning Sophie's body was found when a witness saw you there? Was a fire set in your back garden on St Stephen's Day – three days after tragic Sophie's body was discovered?"

Star correspondent Shane Phelan rightly concentrated in his piece on these highly dramatic aspects of the case, as well as other confessions to Helen Callanan, news editor of the *Sunday Tribune*; neighbour Yvonne Ungerer, wife of the famous French illustrator Tomi, whom he also told he murdered the victim with a concrete block and washed his boots in a local stream; and the graphic second-person account of his involvement in the crime to witness Bill Fuller.

It was a sober and accurate summation of the main issues raised about Bailey during the trial, including what Judge Moran politely called the inconsistencies between the plaintiff's version of events and the local witnesses whose evidence was preferred by the court but what defence counsel Paul Gallagher characterised as a tissue of lies told to the court by Bailey.

I agreed in an article for *Irish Crime* magazine, in which I posed the question of why a man who had told the judge that he had taken the action not for monetary gain but to prove he was innocent of the crime had consistently told lies to the court in the proceedings. An innocent man would have no incentive but to tell the truth while a guilty man would do the very opposite. The flagrant contradictions in his evidence echoed the adage: If you tell the truth, the story never varies.

In his own article, Paul Gill, a solicitor for the *Star* defence team, had high praise for the local witnesses:

"It is a victory for the many residents of West Cork, whose lives were irrevocably changed by the brutal murder of Sophie Toscan du Plantier at least seven years ago. They had no agenda whatsoever other than to tell the truth in court. They were subpoenaed. Their lives were disrupted. They did their duty with grace under pressure and for that they are to be enormously commended by those of us who believe in the administration of justice in this country."

The front page of *The Examiner* succinctly captured the dramatic conclusion of the trial the day before. A brilliant photograph taken by Hadyn West of the Press Association stretched across six of the eight columns of the broadsheet, depicting the haunted face of Ian Bailey in the left foreground, staring nowhere in particular and surrounded by shadowy members of the media in the background.

A radio microphone jutted over the tip of the besieged

plaintiff's left shoulder, with another one close by, and behind a camera was held aloft beside a torso of a cameraman who had obviously climbed onto railings to gain a vantage point. The man who had willingly embraced the media after his first arrest and then gagged them by issuing the defamation action had the demeanour of a person who had made a massive mistake from which he had now emerged on the wrong end and suddenly had nowhere to run and nowhere to hide.

The accompanying article was prefaced with no less than four credits from journalists who had faithfully recorded the proceedings: Liam Heylin, Michael Lehane, Niamh Nolan and Eddie Cassidy, and their combined report in the opening paragraphs read:

"*After a libel trial which bore all the hallmarks of a murder trial, Ian Bailey the self-confessed chief suspect in the Sophie Toscan du Plantier killing, lost his action against six newspaper titles yesterday.*

"*Mr Bailey now faces an agonising wait to hear who will foot the legal bill – estimated at over £700,000. The judge found him a publicity seeker and a violent man. The judgement prompted calls for a fresh inquiry into the murder of the French film-maker.*"

The newspaper reported – as many others did – that the Director of Public Prosecutions had requested a transcript of the trial to see if there was any new evidence that might ensue in a criminal trial. Under the same Haydn West photograph, the headline trumpeted the news that the DPP was to look for new evidence in the transcripts of the trial on the front page of *The Irish Times* under the by-lines of Carl O'Brien, who was the reporter on the spot in Cork; Carol Coulter, legal affairs correspondent; and Lara Marlowe, the Paris correspondent.

Even the conservative *Irish Times* had coverage that surpassed the tabloids with two full pages inside and also editorial comment. Lara Marlowe reported that Sophie Toscan du Plantier's family hoped that the DPP would bring criminal charges in the wake of the libel trial. "*We are putting all our hope in the revelations that came out in the libel trial. For justice to be done for Sophie but also for the people who so bravely testified.*" Marguerite Bouniol, the victim's mother, told the reporter and later remarked: "*There is so much precise testimony. How can it be ignored?*"

The *Sunday Independent*, which had been unsuccessfully sued by Bailey, carried a front-page piece by Gene Kerrigan and security correspondent Jim Cusack with the headline:

REVIEW COULD LEAD TO
BAILEY MURDER CHARGE

The story revealed that the DPP James Hamilton had taken personal charge of the Sophie files and the testimony in the libel case, especially that of Bailey. It said that it was highly unusual for the director to take such a personal interest in a case. But, of course, the outcome of the libel case warranted such attention, in addition to the media campaign, which put pressure on the DPP to take some action. There were many questions to be answered and considerable doubt about the reasons given in an internal report for not bringing the case to trial. The Garda team and authorities always believed they had established a prima facie case to answer, as the article pointed out:

"*Senior Garda sources believe there was compelling evidence in the file given to the DPP after a year-long investigation in 1997 particularly arising from testimony of witnesses who gave evidence during Bailey's libel case. There was further evidence of Bailey apparently telling lies.*

"*It is known that Bailey was away from the couple's house for most if not all of the night in question. He was seen by a witness on a road near the Du Plantier house at around 3.30 a.m. and local people knew that Bailey had a highly eccentric and disturbing habit of roaming the countryside at night – sometimes reputedly in the nude.*"

The Examiner's sister newspaper the *Evening Echo* outlined what the DPP and the Gardai were expected to concentrate on in their respective examination of the transcripts:

> *Inconsistencies in Ian Bailey's evidence and statements, particularly information from local woman Marie Farrell which contradicts his evidence about where he was on the night of the murder.*
>
> *Evidence from three witnesses that Mr Bailey confessed he murdered Ms Du Plantier.*
>
> *Mr Bailey's personal diaries submitted to the court for the libel action will be examined.*
>
> *Evidence from 14 witnesses contradicting Mr Bailey's evidence will be examined.*
>
> *Evidence from witnesses that Mr Bailey had information within hours of the murder which could only have been known by the killer. The DPP is believed to be particularly interested in Mr Bailey's response in court to these allegations.*

The newspaper's reporter Deirdre O'Reilly travelled to West Cork and Schull to get reaction from people on the ground and confirmed that a cloud still hung over the area as a result of the lack of resolution of the murder case. A citizen of Schull summed it up: "This was the first murder on the Mizen Peninsula since the foundation of the State. People are angry that Schull and the Mizen will always be associated with this. It's going to be hard to show all the things that are so good about the area. This overshadows everything."

Another expressed how the murder had affected the community: "People are tired of it and everyone wants closure. There is such a dark cloud over Schull and Goleen today and we hope to God it will be lifted soon. While people are down, there is some hope that justice will be done. People are wondering if the killer will be brought to justice, but we are hopeful."

Ann Mooney, who had covered the case from the beginning and produced brilliant reporting of the libel trial, gave me her reaction: "The libel trial was astounding, and evidence presented during the proceedings had never come to light before. I thought you could not have made up some of what was said but as the case unfolded and a number of people said that Bailey had told them that he had killed Sophie, I began to wonder why he had not been prosecuted in Ireland for the crime. There had been many other murder cases dealt with and prosecuted which seemed a lot more based on circumstantial evidence than this one."

Previously clarification of matters contained in the original Garda file submitted to the DPP in February 1998 had been sought by the DPP and followed by a re-examination of the investigation material, was submitted in March 2001. The DPP on November 7 of the same year decided that a prosecution of Ian Bailey would not be sustainable based on the evidence presented.

Despite the hope and expectation of the Bouniol family and the media, the request for the transcript of the trial proved to be a fruitless exercise for the simple reason that the DPP's 2001 decision not to bring Ian Bailey to a criminal trial was based largely on the premise that the suspect was telling the truth and many of the other witness evidence was not credible.

It did not impress the DPP that the opposite was proved in the libel trial and that the prime suspect had consistently lied throughout the proceedings and had also intimidated a principal witness. The flawed and prejudiced report would be even more stringently tested in future court proceedings and again would be found wanting.

It was not new evidence that the DPP should have been looking for but testing the evidence that had been successfully presented to the Circuit Court and accepted by the judge against the criticism of that evidence in the report and most particularly focusing on the credibility of Ian Bailey, which had been lauded and accepted in the report but totally destroyed by the merciless cross-examination of Paul Gallagher, one of the most accomplished practitioners at the bar and a future attorney general.

CHAPTER 13
MARIE FARRELL
JUMPS SHIP

Cork/Paris/Dublin – 2005–11

The prime suspect was down for a while but not out. He had failed to enrich himself from the media case but there was a far bigger pot of money at the end of the legal rainbow in the coffers of the State. He got the wheels moving in October 2005 when he lodged a complaint to the Garda Commissioner Noel Conroy alleging Garda misconduct in the investigation. Assistant Commissioner Ray McAndrew was appointed to investigate the complaint.

I agreed to be interviewed by review team detectives in relation to Marie Farrell. I told the detectives that I believed that she had told me the truth about Bailey's intimidation of her in great detail that could not have been invented.

The previous year, Bailey had got the services of well-known Cork solicitor Frank Buttimer, who reacted to Marie Farrell's interview by me by writing her a letter asking her to desist from making false accusations of intimidation against his client Ian Bailey. Some exchanges followed with her solicitor Ernest Cantillon, who said that the action would be vigorously defended and a countersuit issued if Bailey did not desist in misbehaviour against his client.

The prime suspect was back in business and did not have to rely on his wits or aggression to pursue his agenda; he was now being represented by a top solicitor from Cork city who had taken over his case from his original lawyer Con Murphy, who was elevated to the bench and sadly later died.

Things would get even better, with an extraordinary develop-ment which nobody could have predicted and proving a timely and considerable boost to Bailey's action against the Gardai, against whom he wanted revenge for the perceived humiliation heaped upon him by the arrests and the consequent casting him in the role, as he perceived it, of the killer by the media.

Sometime in 2005, there was what could be described as a row between Marie Farrell and her Garda handler, which according to her began after he mentioned the civil suit being taken against Bailey by the Bouniol family and he advised her she might have another day in court in that action. She blankly refused, saying that if she was put under pressure, she would go to Frank Butt-imer and tell him what went on. There was a sign that the most important witness in the murder case was beginning to crack.

Perhaps understandably, she had admirably maintained her wit-ness statements over the years since, despite a vicious, unrelenting campaign of vile threats by Ian Bailey which had added considerably to the normal stresses of her somewhat precarious existence. The exposure to the insidious evil attention of a generally dishevelled and odious drunk cannot have been easy to bear. Everyone has a breaking point, but the question is what to do next.

In April 2005, the woman who the Gardai considered a key witness in the crime investigation contacted Frank Buttimer by telephone. She identified herself as Marie Farrell, which was a surprise to the solicitor considering the acrimonious correspon-dence over the intimidation subject. He told her that as she was a State witness, he did not want to engage in any questionable or improper conduct. She insisted that she wanted to say certain things and he agreed that he would take a statement. He invited her to make an appointment and made a note of the five-minute conversation.

He did not hear from her for a couple of weeks and then she rang and made an appointment. The meeting took place in the solicitor's office in Cork on May 10. Over two hours, he talked to her and wrote down the details of her statement. They met again at the office on June 7, when further conversations and note-taking took place, and on July 27 at a car park in Clonakilty, the subject of which meeting Buttimer later recorded in a typed memo.

Marie Farrell withdrew her statements made to the Gardai in relation to Ian Bailey and said that she had been coerced by Gardai to make false statements implicating Bailey in the murder. He had never intimidated her in the manner that she had complained of to the Gardai.

The solicitor contacted Bailey, who was according to him relieved and hopeful by this turn of events. No doubt the prime suspect was over the moon, firstly about having been removed from Kealfadda Bridge on the night of the murder and secondly by being given a powerful incentive to nail the members of the investigation team and confirm his long-standing allegations of corrupt practices.

Buttimer wrote to her in September to express Bailey's appreciation for her being so forthcoming and that under no circumstances would he be initiating the legal proceedings against her in relation to the subject of the incidents of intimidation. A letter was then issued to Marie Farrell to that effect. In October 2005, the solicitor wrote to the Minister for Justice and the Garda Commissioner outlining his client's complaint regarding the latest development. The whole event then got widespread coverage in the media, with Buttimer giving a myriad of interviews to newspapers, radio and television.

This provided a huge publicity coup for the solicitor and his client, despite the fact that the witness was in effect admitting perjury in the court defamation proceedings in Cork in 2003, but presumably could explain that by saying that she had also been pressurised to take that course of action against her will. She had stated that she had been a reluctant witness in that case, so this development on the surface could provide corroboration of Bailey's allegations of unlawful and corrupt practices by the members of the investigation team in their efforts to "stitch him up".

In any event, on the subject of perjury by Marie Farrell, even if she admitted it in relation to the libel trial, which she would have to do in any future court proceedings, it was most unlikely that there would be legal consequences. This is simply because the outdated legislation that covers the offence in Ireland makes it almost impossible to secure a conviction, which means that witnesses in court cases can and do lie to their heart's content without the possibility of redress. The problem, according to Hugh Mohan S.C., is that the act of perjury is not properly defined in the legislation.

Which is simply unbelievable when the act of perjury itself is so simple and straightforward: To make a false statement in court, knowing it not to be true.

In contrast, in Britain, a 1911 law makes it a well-defined offence punishable by up to seven years in prison in both civil and criminal proceedings. Jeffrey Archer, the best-selling British author who lied in a libel case, served a considerable sentence for perjury, as did politician Jonathan Aitken. In Ireland, liars under oath in a court setting face no such problem.

Ian Bailey was on the cusp of a remarkable comeback on several fronts. His appeal of the libel verdict was in the legal works with the key witness of those proceedings on his side. He could confidently look at the prospect of this verdict being dismissed and the consequent reversal of damages. After all, Marie Farrell was now attesting that she had not been intimidated by the prime suspect but by key members of the investigating team who had allegedly pushed her into making statements incriminating Ian Bailey.

It had been those members, she now claimed, who had visited her shop in Schull and asked her to make the statements, and in Garda Station had given her blank witness forms to sign without completing the details beforehand. In relation to the libel trial, she alleged they had forced her to give evidence and while doing so she was scared by their presence in court.

Journalists, including myself, Ralph Riegel of the *Irish*

Independent and Mike McSweeney, the head of the Provision freelance photographic agency, who had brought her to Kealfadda Bridge a number of times including for my interviews with her, had never got the impression that she had been coerced by the officers.

She had been paid £1,500 for those interviews and I had been totally convinced of the veracity of her account of being intimidated by Bailey, with her recounting the incidents and graphically expressing her fear; in my opinion, they could not possibly have been invented. There was one incident in which Bailey had told her in the shop that he had by then filled a barrel full of sperm.

It struck me and I suppose many other observers that a woman of let us say without denigration a relatively simple background could have made up such a phrase, while it was consistent with the degenerative accounts of Bailey's behaviour in his diaries. Journalists are, of course, capable of being seduced in the pursuit of a story and subsequently given pause for thought.

Ralph Riegel hit the nail on the head by observing that after so many years since, this development was such a spectacular turnaround, which could only ensure to discredit completely any account coming from Marie Farrell in the future.

This was a prescient assessment, as future events would prove, but for the moment the backing of the witness represented a victory of some nature for Ian Bailey. In the interim, the future of Bailey's campaign looked promising, as he could now take legal action against the State with more than a reasonable prospect of succeeding, and that was exactly the journey he would embark upon.

The possibilities gained by the addition of a star witness to his side in any future court case were enormous, with the potential of sinking without trace any future criminal action – even if new evidence came to light – compromising the French investigation if there was reliance on the Garda file and winning substantial damages from the State. The prime suspect could, if successful, walk into the West Cork sunset – his reputation vindicated – a rich man, and the murder of Sophie Toscan du Plantier would be consigned to the list of unsolved murders of women in Ireland.

Frank Buttimer and his client should have been hugely upbeat, with a newly won confidence that they could take on the might of the State in the legal arena and punish the alleged wrongdoing by and corruption and conspiracy on behalf of members of the Gardai involved in the murder investigation.

Any such jubilation was of course understandable. Here was a pathway for the redemption of the man who had been exposed in the Cork Circuit Court as a violent animal and a degenerate, flayed by the media, allegedly persecuted by the Gardai and treated like a pariah by the community of West Cork. He could now be the central character in a case about an innocent man who was stitched up and framed for a murder he did not commit, a classic example of a miscarriage of justice which had ruined his reputation and his life.

For the prime suspect, Marie Farrell was now playing a blinder herself, and he was in total agreement on this point as they communicated to the media. However, the euphoria, when it faded, if it would, might lay bare some misgivings. That would not happen for one reason or another, up to and including when it would be too late. But there was plenty of previous evidence to support such misgivings.

Marie Farrell was an enigma from the first time she entered unsolicited into the murder investigation from anonymous phone calls to the Gardai and adopting the name of Fiona as an informant, in advance of her identity later being established by the Gardai.

Before and after her arrival in Schull in 1995 with her husband Chris and five children, there were what can be described as chaotic events in their lives which were centred around financial matters with a negative hue. They had come from Longford and moved back to Ireland after a period living in London. An event there had prompted the return, the details of which had profound effects then and into the future, which will be returned to later. In

January 1995, she had decided to settle in West Cork with Chris and the family.

They initially ran a stall at the Coal Quay market in Cork city, selling clothes, before opening a gift shop in Schull, where they had settled. There is nothing to suggest that Marie and her husband were concentrated on anything but getting a new start to their lives and providing a living for themselves and their family, and more than likely they could have succeeded if a catastrophic event had not intervened with the murder of Sophie Toscan du Plantier just short of a year after they had arrived.

This was of course a tragedy that impacted on many people in the community, as time would tell, but arguably in a different manner than on the Farrell family. Murders in any community have unintended effects on many members; there are always more victims than the crime itself causes in an immediate sense. The impact can be magnified not just by the crime but also any confusion or ambivalence that might arise in the course of the investigation that follows.

For confusion, the involvement of Marie Farrell would be hard to match. There are reasons for everything but I had thought that my interview with her was based on the truth she told me, and I was convinced that it was nothing else; I had been talking to a woman in fear of her life and for her family as a result of threats from Ian Bailey. Had I been turned over by her? Which would not be the first time that a journalist had been seduced by a subject. Had I been so naïve?

I was haunted by that possibility, which was maybe confirmed by her switching her allegiance to the man I believed was responsible for the crime. I had been sympathetic towards her as a result of the misfortunes she had told me that had been visited upon her and her family when she was only trying to tell the truth. So how had that truth been changed so much from the one I had accepted?

I went back to one of the newspaper interviews published on March 7, 2004. Marie Farrell was photographed by Mike

McSweeney by arrangement with her at Kealfadda Bridge, where she previously attested that she saw the prime suspect and gave an account of the most recent intimidation by him.

"Last Monday at about 4 p.m. I was just walking down the road coming down from the site of our new home. I saw this car coming and I knew it was Jules Thomas. It was Ian Bailey driving. He stopped abruptly and pulled down the window. He said: 'Next time I'll be defending myself and I will cross-examine you.' Then he laughed like a madman and drove off."

She said that she immediately reported the incident to Gardai. But by the time that they had taken a statement, Bailey had come back:

"On Friday morning, he turned up outside the house at half past seven. He drove off up the road and came back down a couple of minutes later. It's exactly what he used to do when Sophie was murdered. He was there for 15 minutes in all. Myself and my family are getting so frustrated by it all. It's just an endless nightmare.

"I gave a statement to a local officer on Friday evening and asked what he could do about it. I was told that there was little that could be done."

Recalling Bailey's campaign of intimidation in the wake of her making statements of seeing him at Kealfadda Bridge on the night of the murder, she said:

"Everywhere I went, he seemed to be close. I began to think that he had found out that I had made a statement. He was following me around. I was getting increasingly worried for myself and the kids."

She had previously given and repeated to me an account of a bizarre incident when Bailey came into her shop and read to her an extract from his diary saying:

"I was a great stud and over years I filled several barrels with sperm."

She told me that her whole life had been changed by the act of contacting the investigation about what she had seen on Keal-fadda Bridge, from settling in Schull with a degree of positive hope and expectation to an existence of fear and loathing. She blamed Bailey's toxic attentions for that and the consequent financial loss suffered when her business was neglected as a result and ultimately her shop closed, leaving her and her husband with debts.

At the time she related this tale of woe, there was no incentive for her to lie. But it was clear from our conversation that her resentment in relation to the origin of her troubles was not con-fined to Ian Bailey. She felt that the Gardai had not done enough to protect her from the attentions of the prime suspect, who had put her under intolerable pressure to retract her statements.

There was no doubt in my mind that I had interviewed a woman who had been in fear of her life from the attentions of Ian Bailey. Everything she said had the ring of truth and I corroborated the fact with confirmation of the history of her complaints and by talking to another major witness who had also been intimidated by Bailey.

The Gardai had visited Bailey about Farrell's complaints and had confronted him about his intimidation of her during his second detention in February 1998, but no legal constraints were pursued to keep him in his place. Farrell, as I discovered at the time of the interviews with her, was not the only witness that he had threatened. I spoke to another important witness, also female, who received several visits from Bailey for the same reason of withdrawing her statement. She was so frightened and fearful after the last one that she could not keep food down for three days afterwards.

Naturally, she did not want to be named at that time. It was in fact Rosie Shelley. I also spoke to other locals and a neighbour of Bailey's who had also been subjected to threats and aggressive behaviour, and all had been frightened by this unwarranted and illegal attention. It appeared and was confirmed by the locals I talked to that Bailey could do anything he liked and get away with it.

The chaos that the key witness had been thrown into had resulted in a number of warrants against her name in relation to road traffic offences. These were as a result of the financial difficulties that she and her family were experiencing. So perhaps she felt that she was being abandoned, with a lack of support from the Gardai in both matters, which demanded decisive action. The members of the force could never interfere in such an obvious manner just to placate an important witness.

Memos of a Garda sergeant in Schull Garda Station acquired by national radio station RTE revealed that he had written to Bantry Garda Station in relation to the warrants and he was told not to execute them immediately but in time. There was nothing sinister in that and it happens all the time, as any person would be given reasonable time to settle a debt.

When eventually efforts were made to secure payment for an outstanding warrant, Marie Farrell threatened to "blow the Bailey case out of the water", in one line that appeared to explain at least one of the reasons why she subsequently retracted her statements about Bailey. Even if not, it certainly displayed an animus towards the Gardai of sufficient intensity to make good her threat. The signs then were that she was about to jump ship.

Her 2005 story was radically different from the one in her original statements, with the prime suspect in the narrative being substituted by the Gardai. The man she said she had seen at Kealfadda Bridge on the night of the murder was not Ian Bailey but a man of sallow complexion, thin frame and average height.

She had, instead of by the prime suspect, been harassed and intimidated by members of the investigation team. They had continually visited her shop and contacted her by phone.

Whatever the credibility of the new story, Marie Farrell displayed at an early stage of her newly adopted role both a faulty and selective memory. There had been no less than seventeen complaints registered by her with local Gardai about the intimidation that she had suffered at the hands of Bailey, which included stalking, threats by phone and in person, frightening gestures by him drawing his hand across his throat and pointing his finger to his temple in imitation of a gun, and intimidation by blackmail.

At least one of the incidents had been witnessed by her shop assistant Geraldine O'Brien, with whom she had also communicated fear and distress she was suffering as a result of this campaign.

Now she alleged that she had been pressurised to add to her statements and sign blank witness forms. Gardai had insisted she give evidence in the 2003 libel trial and allegedly said that if she did not agree, she would be brought to court in handcuffs to give that evidence and when doing so was scared of their presence at the proceedings. If this new version was true, then it would have staggering implications for members of the investigation team and provide solid corroboration of Bailey's long-held allegations of corruption and malpractice by those members and confirm his and his partner's claim that they had been unlawfully arrested.

Nonetheless, the truth had not been established and would only be found in a court setting in which Marie Farrell's credibility as a witness could be severely tested given the fact that she in effect had lied under oath in a previous court action, the reasons for which would also have to be proven. Thus, Bailey and his solicitor Frank Buttimer should have considered some caution about the addition of a new witness to their cause on that basis. As events would show, they did not.

The first test of Marie Farrell's new role would happen when Bailey's appeal against the libel verdict of 2004 opened in the High Court on February 13, 2007, and during which Bailey repeated his allegations of unlawful behaviour on the part of the murder investigation team members, but the action suddenly ground to a halt and on the day that his star witness Marie Farrell was due to give evidence, the case was withdrawn by the plaintiff.

His solicitor Frank Buttimer attempted to portray this as a victory, as there had been a contribution towards his defence costs, but the newspapers disagreed, portraying the result as another defeat and a total capitulation by the plaintiff. Marie Farrell would have to wait some more years to give her new version of events in court.

There was a further setback when in May of the same year, the 375-page McAndrew Report found after review and made it clear to the DPP that there was a lack of evidence to support complaints made by Ian Bailey and others in their allegations against members of the Gardai. However, there was a recommendation that consideration be given to prosecuting one witness in relation to false statements and allegations.

The McAndrew Report would never be published but it would not require Sherlock Holmes to establish the identity of the witness. In any event, in advance of any release of the findings of the inquiry, Frank Buttimer had stated that irrespective of the findings, his client would be suing the State, the Gardai and other parties for unlawful arrest among a host of other charges.

The prime suspect had been defeated in his attempt to silence the media about the case, and his allegations of misconduct by members of the murder investigation team were rejected by the McAndrew Report. In boxing parlance, he had suffered two knockouts in rapid succession. There was much speculation that he would have great difficulty in getting up from the canvas, not to mind going back into the ring again.

But from another viewpoint for Bailey, it could be seen as a mere temporary setback. He and his legal team had a much bigger agenda. Later in the same year, Bailey lodged proceedings in the High Court against the Garda Commissioner, Minister for Justice and the Attorney General, for unlawful arrest and many other serious counts. The pleadings included wrongful arrest, false imprisonment, intentional infliction of emotional and psychological harm, harassment and intimidation, terrorising and oppressive behaviour, and breach of his constitutional rights.

Despite the fact that Ian Bailey clearly had a Jekyll and Hyde personality, as exposed in the defamation case, he was an intelligent man – albeit with limited resources – with plenty of legal support, and was determined not just to prove his innocence in the crime that he was suspected to have commissioned but to also wreak revenge on those who had put him in that position.

CHAPTER 14
SOPHIE'S FAMILY'S
JUSTICE CAMPAIGN

Paris/Dublin – 2007-2011

In November of the same year, 2007, there was an important development in Paris when on the last day of the month – and as the tenth anniversary of the murder approached – ASSOPH, the Association for the Truth about the Murder of Sophie Toscan du Plantier, was officially founded.

Marguerite Bouniol's brother and uncle of Sophie, Jean-Pierre Gazeau, was president. Journalist Lara Marlowe, *The Irish Times* correspondent in Paris, had taken a close interest in the case and had provided excellent coverage from the French side, and when meeting with Mr Gazeau passed on names of people who had also shown a consistent interest in the case over the years.

Maitre Éric Dupond-Moretti had represented the mother of Trevor O'Keefe, a young Irishman who had been abducted and murdered in France by an army warrant officer, Pierre Chanal, a suspected serial killer who had committed suicide in his cell just before he was due to go on trial for the killing of the Irishman. There had been a poorly conducted criminal investigation of the crime, with the wheels of justice falling off, which Dupond-Moretti had to deal with for Mrs O'Keefe. The whole process had distinct echoes of the murder of Sophie and he saw in the case an opportunity to redress another injustice.

Marguerite and Georges met him in Lille, and he agreed to represent them, and a powerful advocate was added to the team. Marguerite and Georges Bouniol were now proactively involved, as well as her brother Jean-Pierre Gazeau and family friend Jean-Antoine Bloc. They later contacted lawyer Alain Spilliaert, who would represent both the family and the association. ASSOPH would not only channel the Bouniols' frustration with the iniquities of the Irish judicial system, but also act as a powerful lobbying instrument to prompt action by the French judicial authorities and create press interest in the case.

The family and members of the association were under no illusions about the task ahead but were keenly aware of the personal effects of the DPP's decision not to bring Ian Bailey to trial.

They would have grieved in private had some elementary form of justice been done instead of being denied. Their frustration at not seeing a case come to trial in either Ireland or France was compounded by outrage at the mistakes, negligence and indifference they had encountered over the years and the petty bureaucracy, all of which had little or nothing to do with the search for truth about the murder of their beloved Sophie.

It was not as if there was any mystery about the case. There was a thorough though not perfect murder investigation, a 2,000-page Garda file, a burgeoning French police file, a prime and only suspect and a paltry forty-four-page report from the office of the DPP. Then nothing but bad news from Ireland. The nearest thing to an Irish trial which was conducted like a murder case had a profound impact on everyone when the vicious and brutally violent character of the prime suspect was exposed, as well as his mendacity on the witness stand. The family's hopes were raised and then dashed by the inaction of the DPP.

Now the main witness Marie Farrell had retracted her statements and joined the prime suspect's team, which was now suing the Irish State and judicial authorities for unlawful arrest. Salt in the wounds would hardly describe the effect, and I often wondered how those lovely people – the parents now becoming elderly and frail by the day – could get out of bed in the morning. But they did and the establishment of ASSOPH would provide both hope and comfort.

On March 9, 2008, Jean-Pierre Gazeau wrote a letter to President Nicolas Sarkozy about the case and on April 1, Dupond-Moretti, the Bouniol parents and Jean-Pierre Gazeau had a meeting with the then Head of European Affairs in the French Ministry for Justice, Elisabeth Pelsez. Marguerite and Georges also contacted lawyer Alain Spilliaert, who had worked with Maitre Haenning during the formation of the *parties civiles*. He agreed to become their lawyer and a member of ASSOPH, which he would also represent. Within a relatively short period of time, the organisation had legal counsel, a network of important contacts and the ear of the French and eventually the Irish press.

On April 9, there was a transmission by coroner Frank O'Connell of a copy of the post-mortem report on Sophie, which represented the first official document on the case brought to the attention of the Bouniol family.

On June 30, 2008, two examining magistrates, Patrick Gachon and Nathalie Dutarte – who headed up the French investigation – ordered the body of Sophie to be exhumed and examined for forensic analysis. On July 2, the body was exhumed from the Combret cemetery and a post-mortem was performed by Dr Taccoen under the supervision of Professor Lecompte. Their report dated July 24, 2008 found severe head injuries, one on the right front caused by a blunt and sharped-edged object; the skull fractures could have come from one or two blows depending on the kind of blunt object used, and further cranial injuries as an indirect consequence of the head lying on a hard surface when the frontal blows were administered.

The blows were of such force they dislocated the thick frontal bone fragment in this region of the skull. There were defensive wounds, specifically crushed bones in the fingers of the hands.

This was an encouraging development whatever the outcome, as it signalled that the French judicial authorities intended to make their own inquiries without total reliance on the results of the Irish investigation. This had a concomitant effect on the Gardai efforts and on July 8 they announced their intention to work with the French judicial authorities by sending them a copy of the case file. In August, the DPP informed Marguerite and Georges that his decision not to prosecute in the case of the murder of their daughter would stand in the absence of fresh evidence. But the case file would remain open.

But ASSOPH was not likely to lie down and the *parties civiles* filed a complaint relating to interfering with witnesses to the French judicial authorities, implicating Ian Bailey in relation to Marie Farrell. The complaint was registered and declared admissible in any future criminal court case in Paris. Whether Bailey or his legal team were even aware of this significant development, it probably did not bother them in the least, as they were convinced that they had much bigger legal fish to fry. One way or another, the French investigation had gained an impetus and had begun to act in a serious and focused fashion.

The copy of the Garda case file took a long time to be delivered and not until December 4 was it submitted to the French Embassy in Dublin. Dozens of boxes containing hundreds of folders and thousands of pages were sent to the Palais de Justice in central Paris. It would take months of work on the part of the examining magistrate and his staff. There were important pieces missing, for example Ian Bailey's diaries, which played such an important part in the 2003 trial but would only be sent three years later.

There were other missing parts of the puzzle, including Sophie's datebooks, personal papers and computer records, which had not been entered in evidence because Gardai had not considered them relevant at the time. They had been collected but not registered in the investigation file. The French were not too happy about this but were still getting appropriate co-operation and just had to get on with the job.

The sorting of the voluminous Irish case file was completed in April 2009, and in June examining magistrate Patrick Gachon, accompanied by magistrate Nathalie Dutarte, travelled to Ireland and – assisted by Gardai – visited the scene of the crime and the surrounding area, and met with senior officers who had led the initial investigation. In October 2009, the magistrate interviewed two Garda inspectors and Garda officers subsequently travelled to France to give statements to their French equivalents.

A European Arrest Warrant (EAW) was issued by the French judicial authorities in Paris on February 19, 2010, for the purposes of prosecuting Ian Bailey for the murder. The warrant was transmitted to the Irish judicial Central Authority and on April 23, 2010, endorsed by the High Court in Dublin for execution, and Bailey was on the same day arrested at his home and brought to the High Court, and granted bail until a hearing date.

This took place over two days, starting on December 10. The Minister for Justice was the applicant, Ian Bailey the respondent, and Mr Justice Michael Peart the presiding judge who adjourned the proceedings until he delivered his findings on March 18, 2011.

Bailey's legal team had pleaded a case for refusing his surrender under five headings, the fourth and fifth basically tied together. In the introduction to his judgement, Mr Justice Michael Peart, who was well practised in the handling of extradition proceedings, noted the unusual features of this case, which included the fact that the victim was French, and although the crime had been committed in Ireland, the accused was amenable to prosecution by French judicial authorities under a section of the penal code where an accused can be tried in France when the victim is a national of that State at the time the offence took place.

The first objection related to Section 44 of the Act of 2003 and Martin Giblin S.C. for Bailey submitted that because the murder took place outside France and Irish law does not allow for the prosecution of a murder committed outside the State except by an Irish citizen, so the surrender is prohibited by the provisions of Section 44. He further argued that under the principle of reciprocity, which requires that one State should not be required to extradite a person for an offence if it could not request extradition for the same offence were the roles reversed, this principle was not met in this case.

Mr Barron, for the applicant among other submissions, argued that if the interpretation of Section 44 contended by the respondent were to be correct, then it would lead to an absurd anomaly on the facts of the present case, whereby the happenstance of the respondent being a British citizen would result in his surrender being prohibited and that could never have been the intention of the legislatures of the Member States when they adopted the Framework Decision.

Mr Justice Peart said that the provisions of Section 44 could not be relied on in isolation, but in the context of the relevant sections of the Act of 2003 and in the light of the aims and objectives of the Framework Decision, and concluded that the surrender was not prohibited by the provisions of Section 44 or Article 4.7 of the Framework Decision.

The second objection in relation to Section 10 and 21A – no decision by the issuing judicial authority to try the respondent for the offence, and Section 21A, presumption rebutted, was then considered. Section 10 states that the issuing judicial authority, in this instance France, must intend to bring proceedings for the offence for which the person is sought.

Bailey's counsel argued that he was not being sought for conducting a criminal prosecution and it was clear that no decision had been made to "try" him for the offence and that the purpose of seeking surrender was to interrogate him for further investigation. On that basis, the court had no jurisdiction to surrender him. While Mr Barron S.C. for the applicant disagreed, the judge referred to the wording of the warrant, which opened with the statement that it had been issued "for the purpose of conducting a criminal prosecution".

He related that Bailey had appointed a French lawyer, Dominique Tricaud, to represent him during the proceedings, and after talking to the respondent's solicitor, Frank Buttimer, it was his impression that the French investigating magistrate Patrick Gachon was relying on information sent by Irish police only. But he admitted that not having access to the French investigation file, it was only an impression. Mr Barron for the applicant submitted that as it was only an impression and not a fact, it meant that Mr Tricaud simply did not know.

Mr Munro for Bailey submitted that he was only sought for further investigation by the French authorities based on information supplied by the Garda authorities and that there was not enough to charge his client, backed by the DPP's consistent view that the evidence was insufficient for this purpose.

Mr Justice Peart in his conclusive assessment put it thus: "This is not a case where, as submitted by the respondent [Bailey] the decision to prosecute is dependent on any further investigation producing sufficient evidence to put him on trial. The judge has already formed the opinion, as it made clear in the warrant, that there is sufficient evidence for that purpose, but is not permitted to make the decision to put him on trial until the respondent has been afforded his right to respond under Article 80.1 of the Code of Procedure. The fact that the DPP here took a different view of the available evidence is immaterial to this point of objection."

There was, the judge concluded, no reason to refuse surrender on this ground of objection. The third ground of objection related to Section 42 (c) of the Act as originally enacted in the context of the DPP's decision not to prosecute Bailey. The provision included a bar to surrender if the DPP or the Attorney General decided not to bring a prosecution of the offence specified in the EAW.

Mr Giblin for Bailey submitted that the decision of the DPP in 1997 not to prosecute the respondent amounted to a right from that date not to be surrendered on foot of any EAW issued after January 2004 and the new Section 42 could not be applied to him. Mr Barron argued that no such right or privilege was accrued to Bailey from the DPP's decision.

Mr Justice Peart observed that it would not have made any sense to have removed paragraph (c) of Section 42 but to have done so in a way that means that the amendment did not apply to warrants endorsed after March 5, 2005, which would have been an absurd result and this ground of objection must fail.

The fourth ground referred to Section 37 and unfair procedure in light of the DPP's decision not to prosecute. It was submitted that any surrender of Bailey would constitute a violation of his constitutional right to fair procedures and a breach of the '*ne bis in idem*' principle. The translation of that principle is "not twice the same thing", a legal tenet that no legal action can be pursued twice for the same cause of action. It is the equivalent of double jeopardy, which prevents a person from being tried again on the same or similar charges following a valid acquittal or prosecution.

This was contended by reason of the fact that the DPP had made the decision after several reviews of the file not to prosecute Bailey. In such circumstances the principle of double jeopardy would have prevented any further prosecution in either Ireland or France. If he was surrendered, he would lose the benefit of the decision and would face prosecution in France for the same offence – more so insofar as the evidence is known based solely on the same material before the DPP and nothing more. Bailey's legal team had no access to the French investigation file so to say that he would be tried on the same evidence before the DPP was entirely speculative and weakened the argument.

For this reason, also the decision of the DPP, counsel for Bailey argued, should be given the status of an acquittal or at least final judgement in the matter (even though this was not achieved in a court of law) and that the application for surrender amounted to an abuse and unfair procedure. However, there was a fatal flaw at the centre of this argument on behalf of Bailey, which after considering case law offered in the matter that the judge went on to focus upon.

Mr Justice Peart, while recognising that the DPP had decided that Bailey was not to face prosecution for the offence in this jurisdiction, realised that the DPP was not precluded from reopening the matter if some new evidence were to become available and whatever the possibility of that happening, the power to that remained. He said that the case had not been "finally disposed of" by any laws under which a prosecution was barred. "I am not satisfied that the letter from the DPP or the respondent's awareness that he is not to be prosecuted confers any right as such not to be surrendered, or any sufficient expectation that he would never be prosecuted here."

There was further speculation on behalf of Bailey's counsel about what might happen if he was put on trial in France, informed by Mr Tricaud's affidavit, and on the back of that information that he was at risk of not receiving a fair trial and this would be an abuse of process, and in addition that he was only being sought for the purpose of being questioned and not for prosecution. As he had already dealt with that last objection, the judge ruled that no abuse of process would arise.

With regard to the submission that Bailey, in the unusual circumstances of the case, faced a real risk of an unfair trial in France, the judge said that this court would require compelling and cogent evidence that this was the case and that there was no such evidence to back up that contention. "Bearing in mind the fact that this court must and does accord full respect to the prosecution procedures in France and to the system of trials generally in that jurisdiction, it must be presumed that procedures exist where fundamental rights of accused persons are protected. Indeed, one can easily read Mr Tricaud's affidavit as confirming this to be the case."

Mr Justice Peart then concluded that he was satisfied that there was no reason under the relevant sections that surrender should be refused and made the order that Bailey should be surrendered to the French authorities.

What was most pertinent about the decision was the reliance by Bailey's legal team on the DPP's failure to prosecute, which had failed for the second time in a court setting, the first being in the libel trial of 2003. There had been clearly undue significance given to that decision and it would be tested in the future on the same grounds. On April 13, 2011, Bailey was allowed by the High Court to appeal on a matter of public importance to the Supreme Court and instructed to lodge the appeal two days later, which his defence team did.

At a pre-trial hearing of the Supreme Court appeal on Friday, November 11, 2011, Bailey's legal team told the five-judge court that new material had come into their possession from State sources which would prove that Mr Bailey was deliberately and wrongly targeted by the murder investigation team. His counsel Martin Giblin went as far as telling the court that the material showed "significant Garda behaviour" which was "breath-taking even by the lowest standards encountered by the court".

Giblin claimed that had Bailey's lawyers been given the material for his High Court hearing, they would have been able to present a much stronger case concerning allegations of Garda misbehaviour in the murder investigation. The situation, he added, was unprecedented because the DPP, on the advice of the Attorney General, had made available material to Mr Bailey from some normally inaccessible files. It had also been sent to the French authorities.

The source of this development was former DPP Eamon Barnes, retired since 1999, who while on holiday in France read an article in *The Irish Times* about the decision to surrender Bailey to France and subsequently contacted the office of the DPP expressing concern at the possibility of an innocent man being convicted of the murder in France. It was somewhat of a strange reaction as not once in his tenure during the case did he ever make contact, pass on an opinion or register a complaint to the senior Gardai handling the investigation file.

He further said that the murder investigation was flawed and prejudiced, and an improper approach had been made by senior members of the murder investigation team to the State solicitor for West Cork, Malachi Boohig, to intervene with the Minister for Justice to have Bailey charged at a meeting at Bandon Garda Station in 1998.

Why Mr Barnes did not, given his attack on the Garda investigation, bring his concerns to the relevant authorities back in 1998 about the alleged improper approach but instead waited thirteen years after a High Court order to surrender the prime suspect is astounding. Furthermore, at the time he occupied the seat of the DPP and if he was convinced that Gardai made such an approach, he never made a note or memo about it and did not inform the Garda authorities or the Department of Justice to look into what was not just a serious matter but interference with the course of justice, which is an illegal act.

His motive for this unprecedented attempt to influence a court process in which the DPP was not a party was probably a lot more to do with the fact that the report he had stood over but never signed before his retirement in 1999, and had already discredited by the libel trial outcome and adverse media comment afterwards, would be exposed by a prosecution in France, which indeed it would be many years later.

Nothing else could explain his belated action, because if he believed the facts he quoted, including a prejudiced and flawed murder investigation and an improper approach by three senior Gardai, he would have dealt with the matter a long time before. But he certainly did nothing of the sort, instead leaving it in limbo until awoken many years later while on the way home from a holiday in Spain.

In the interim, the details of the DPP report were protected by the long-standing practice of keeping them out of the public domain. But now that changed after Barnes contacted the DDP's office, resulting in it being sent to the Attorney General and thence to Bailey's defence team. Communications from the Central Authority for mutual assistance revealed that the document had been forwarded there on October 25, 2011 by the office of the DPP and that this was unprecedented for the reasons contained principally those not to prosecute a suspect to be forwarded to any agency other than the Gardai.

But given the circumstances where another country was planning to prosecute the suspect, the DPP consented to have the document available as necessary. The minister had been advised by Attorney General Máire Whelan to make it available to the French authorities and to Bailey's defence team. But the document impacted on the good name and reputation of a significant number of individuals and there had not been an opportunity to put in place a mechanism to allow those adversely affected by details being in the public domain. A codicil that should have been observed by all parties but was not, as events transpired.

Also, the incumbent DPP James Hamilton – as a result of the intervention – requested that Eamon Barnes; the former West Cork State solicitor, Malachi Boohig; and Robert Sheehan, the legal officer in the DPP's office who handled the report and all the communications with the Garda murder investigation, provide memos to him on the allegation by Boohig that he had been requested to intervene with the Minister for Justice. The memos were provided in October 2011, just over a month before Ian Bailey's Supreme Court appeal was due to be heard.

Mr Giblin reminded the court that it was not usual for a superior court to hear evidence not presented in a lower court, but this development was unprecedented and therefore deserved consideration by the fact of the contents and that had been sent by State agencies. As a result, he was asking for an adjournment so that his team would have enough time to examine the material and decide if motions could be brought as a result.

The State did not oppose the request, but it was Mr Barron's view that the material was irrelevant. He was right and would not have been in error to claim that this was unwarranted interference in a serious judicial process and should have been stopped on the spot. At the time, it appeared to be a perfect legal storm, but a later High Court case would prove to be more like a weak piddle in a teacup and confirm Mr Barron's entirely correct assessment of the matter.

The Chief Justice Mrs Susan Denham granted the adjournment. The appeal was due to begin a hearing listed for three days the following Monday. The importance of the material, including the DPP's report justifying reasons not to charge Bailey for the murder, would prove to be greatly exaggerated and considered by the French as polluting the extradition process. Particularly because that document had no legal status and was based merely on the opinion of the DPP, whose office had always maintained a policy of never making public reasons for decisions.

In late December, there was a further adjournment until mid-January 2012. In December 2011, Ian Bailey took another move against members of the Garda murder investigation team by making a complaint to the Garda Ombudsman Commission (GSOC) based in Dublin, claiming that members of that team had conducted a corrupt investigation in relation to him and that he and his partner Jules Thomas were unlawfully arrested in February 1997 for the murder of Mme Du Plantier. Along with his High Court action, which was in the legal works, it was in effect a pincer movement.

French gendarmes had travelled to West Cork to interview witnesses between October 4 and 13, 2011. In November, the *parties civiles* represented by Bouniol family lawyer Alain Spilliaert requested that Ian Bailey be interviewed. That did not happen, as the request was refused by Irish judicial authorities, but the train of French justice had moved out of the station and was coming down the tracks, and it would prove to be a long and torturous journey.

CHAPTER 15
SEX, LIES AND
VIDEOTAPES

Dublin/Longford – 2012

It appeared that Ian Bailey had got a break and the tide of fortune would turn in his favour. This indeed proved to be the case when on March 1, 2012 the Supreme Court overturned the High Court decision to surrender. It had nothing to do with the DPP report, which was not considered, but technical points of law regarding the issue of reciprocity in EAW warrants and the unclear intention of the French to charge and put Bailey on trial.

On March 7, 2012, Bailey's star witness joined the wider battle when Marie Farrell made a complaint to GSOC alleging intimidation by certain Gardai into making false complaints against Ian Bailey and the following month, on April 23, Jules Thomas made a complaint to the police watchdog alleging that she had been illegally arrested and detained by the Gardai on a number of occasions during the course of the Garda investigation of the murder. Following consideration by the Commission on March 15, 2012, Marie Farrell's complaint was designated for investigation, as was that of Jules Thomas on April 25.

Three days before, Bailey provided a witness statement to designated GSOC officers following meetings with him. After filling in his background, he recalled arriving at the scene of the crime on December 23 with his partner Jules Thomas around 2.20 p.m. He explained to two Gardai that he was making press enquiries and was referred to the Garda Press Office. He left and returned later to the scene with a photographer, where he saw the local superintendent with a journalist (Eddie Cassidy) who had alerted him to the incident.

In the days following, he had received a number of visits from Gardai, filled in a questionnaire and gave hair and blood samples. On January 30, he stated he had got another visit from named Gardai with a superintendent present. He then stated that he was left alone at one point with the superintendent and alleged that he had told him that he was going to place Bailey at or close to the scene of the murder, and the prime suspect then said he considered this man at the centre of his allegations of Garda misconduct and conspiracy against him.

In regard to his first arrest in February 1997, he made further damning allegations while he was being driven to Bandon Station, describing the atmosphere as aggressive and accusatory, and one Garda being hostile, proceeding to jab his finger into his side and arm, saying: "You did it, just admit it, everyone knows you did it, you better get your act together. Even if we don't pin this on you, you're finished in Ireland and you will be found dead in a ditch with a bullet in the back of your head."

Such dialogue sounds both crude and suspiciously invented but the GSOC investigators were there to merely record but not challenge until the report was finished. Bailey went on complaining that the large media presence at his arrival at Bandon Station had been orchestrated by the Gardai. He went on to give his version of what had happened during his detention and questioning. He alleged that he had been bombarded with the claim he was the murderer by numerous different Gardai.

He signed statements during the interviews that did not reflect the events but signed them just to make the whole experience end. He alleged that he was told by the superintendent that Jules Thomas had accepted his guilt and never wanted to see him again, and if Bailey returned to his home there would be a lynch mob waiting for him. He alleged that subsequently he learnt that Jules Thomas had been told by two detectives that he had confessed to the crime.

Bailey had complained about an anti-English sentiment, cleverly perhaps, but his version of events was beginning to sound more like the arrest of an innocent black man in Southern Alabama in the 1960s for a murder he did not commit, redolent of a film like *In the Heat of the Night* as opposed to an arrest in West Cork in the relatively advanced 1990s by a police force well aware of historical corrupt Garda investigations that had come to grief and been properly and legally exposed.

But Bailey went on to claim that following his arrest and throughout 1997, different stories appeared about him as "the self-confessed prime suspect". He alleged that Gardai visited his home on numerous occasions and said that he was trying to interfere with and influence Marie Farrell, a witness in the case. He stated that following a chance meeting with her in a bar in Schull in the summer of 1997, he spoke with her and arranged to meet her in an ice-cream parlour run by her a week later.

During this meeting, it was suggested by Marie Farrell that two Gardai were putting pressure on her to implicate Bailey in the murder. He went on to allege that one of two men at his friend's home in Skibbereen had been recruited by Gardai and been paid in the form of cash, hash and clothes, and that the man had been offered a substantial sum of money if he could provide information that would lead to Bailey being convicted of the murder.

He alleged that during his second arrest in January 1998, when interviewed by members of the National Bureau of Criminal Investigation, that he was accused of the murder in the same aggressive and intimidating manner as his first arrest, and that the media were once again alerted of his detention and were present at Bandon Garda Station when he arrived.

He then returned to Detective Superintendent Dermot Dwyer, who he was casting as the villain responsible for his woes, alleging that he had made many erroneous allegations against him during his arrest regarding the interference with Marie Farrell. This included telling him that there was a small basement cell waiting for him in Mountjoy Prison. This of course was never said. Bailey bore a grudge against the superintendent because during the former's interrogation of the prime suspect during his first detention, his clever line of questioning had led to Bailey admitting for the first time that he had left the house on the night of the murder and thereby leaving him without an alibi.

On April 25, 2012, Jules Thomas made her witness statement to GSOC officers. She provided them with two witness statements, one made on February 9, 2006, to a detective superintendent and detective inspector. The other witness statement was an undated typed account not originating from the Gardai and became part of her witness statement to the officers. Her complaints were similar, with allegations of corruption as well as aggressive and hostile behaviour towards her by members of the investigation team.

During her detention in Bandon Station, she alleged that Garda officers told her that Bailey was the killer and had confessed to the murder. She said that they continually informed her that Bailey was the killer and would target her next. After her release, she got an anonymous phone call from a man she believed was a detective from the investigation team, who sounded drunk and yelled down the phone: "Get the fuck out! Get the fuck out!" When she asked who was speaking, he said: "You know bloody well who I am! Get the fuck out!"

She then repeated Bailey's allegation about the man from Skibbereen who had been paid by members of the investigation team in cash, hash and clothes, and had been offered a considerable sum of money – in the region of £5,000 – to provide a witness statement saying Bailey had admitted the crime. She said that the intimidation that she and Bailey had subjected Marie Farrell to were false allegations.

She had by comparison relatively little to say concerning her second arrest in September 2000, except that a Garda had been aggressive in his manner during questioning her and had commented that she had a poor taste in relationships.

The day before, April 24, Marie Farrell met with GSOC

officers in Longford, her native town where she had returned in 2006 after leaving Schull, for the first of three interview sessions, a lengthy process justified by the fact that she was considered by the Commission to be "a significant witness". This was an accurate assessment. The reliability, consistency and credibility of her testimony to the GSOC Commission would be vital not only to the outcome of this inquiry but also to the much higher stakes involved in Bailey's High Court action.

Crucially, she agreed to the interview sessions being videotaped, which the first two were but not the third as the equipment was not available. During the first interview, she began by filling in her background and the family moves from Longford to London and then to West Cork in 1995.

She referred to having been originally from Longford and had moved back to Ireland after a period of living in London. She decided to settle in West Cork with her husband Chris and their children in January 1995. She originally ran market stalls, selling clothes in Cork city, before opening a shop in Schull. On December 21, 1996, she recalled that Madame Toscan du Plantier had entered her shop on the main street in Schull around 3 p.m. At the same time, she saw a male standing on the path across from her shop.

The narrative of the early part of her account was generally in line with her statements to the investigation. But the detail naturally had to change to conform to her new role as witness for as opposed to against Ian Bailey. The man she saw outside her shop on the afternoon of Saturday, December 21, 1996 as Sophie was browsing on the premises she described as thin with sallow skin of Mediterranean looks, and of average height which she put at 5ft 8in, aged around in his late thirties to early forties. This description, except for the height, was not radically different from that of the prime suspect. This had been altered to suit her new story.

She added that it was not Ian Bailey, who she did not know at the time. She said he was wearing a long black coat (which just happened to be one of Bailey's favourite items of clothing). After Madame Du Plantier left the shop, the male walked off in the same direction as her. On December 22, she stated that she saw the same man looking for a lift around 6 a.m. outside Schull when she was driving in the opposite direction.

Later the same day, she met a man in Cork while working at the market stall and arranged to meet him later that night in Schull. She was not prepared to identify him and said that he had since died. GSOC officers noted that she had maintained her silence throughout various stages of the Garda investigation. Little wonder, as that man could have provided vital corroborative evidence of the sighting of the man at Kealfadda Bridge. But she was not budging.

It was also a fact that GSOC was aware the Gardai did not seek to bring any charges against Marie Farrell for the withholding of information, hardly surprising but still part of the ambivalent attitude towards and handling of the principal witness, who was now in the process of embarking on a course of action fraught with danger.

On the night of December 22, 1996, she stated she had left her home at about 10.30 p.m. and met the man with whom she had arranged the assignation in Schull. She then drove to Goleen, followed by the man in his car. She then got into his car and they drove around for a while and then stopped for a chat. It was most likely, as the officers no doubt realised, for sex, as anything else would not have involved the elaborate meeting arrangements and of course the long-maintained secrecy about the identity of the man and the length of time she had spent with him that night, which amounted to between five and six hours.

The most likely explanation that would come to mind for a listener to this tale of a clandestine meeting in a remote area in the depths of winter was a reigniting of an old passion by two former lovers, with the identity of the mystery male possibly known to the husband of the female participant. Marie Farrell might well in the early development of the case been attempting to spare her husband Chris some pain and herself some bother, but it could hardly have justified the silence so many years on, as he had for a long time been aware of the activity of his wife on that night.

Marie Farrell continued the narrative as the video recording rolled on. As she and her companion continued their journey after the stop, while driving towards Schull and passing Kealfadda Bridge, the headlights of the car picked up a man who was staggering along the road, the same man she had seen outside her shop the previous Saturday and the next morning looking for a lift outside Schull. This was, she said, at around 2.30 a.m. and the man was wearing a long black coat and his movement was half-running and stumbling.

Later, she and her male friend drove past Kealfadda Bridge twice more but there was no sign of the man or anybody else in the vicinity. She stated that she returned home about 4.30 a.m. She had by this account been in the company of the man for approximately six hours, a long enough time to renew an old acquaintance and stoke the fire of a stilled passion.

As she had been in a compromising position, she did not know what to do about her knowledge of the man she had seen, as she did not want her husband to find out who she was with. The man who she said was not Ian Bailey by her description was close enough. The long black coat was a signature item in his apparel. The problem for Marie Farrell, as a result of her tryst, was that as long as she wanted to keep the identity of her companion a secret, she would at the least have to be selective with the truth or lie, a process that would have begun at home before she left and after the assignation.

Marie Farrell told the GSOC officers that she became aware of the death of the victim later on, December 23, 1996, and assumed that it must have been the result of a hit and run. How without any information she would make that assumption is anyone's guess. Later that day, it was confirmed to be a murder and she realised that the woman who had been murdered was the same one who had been to her shop previously. She was still in a domestic bind concerning her knowledge of seeing the man the night of the murder.

On Christmas Day 1996, she rang Bandon Garda and told an officer about seeing a man outside the shop and looking for a lift the next morning but made no reference to the sighting at Kealfadda Bridge. Two days later, a detective called to her shop and she completed a statement or a questionnaire. The detective, she alleged, insisted on putting down the height of the man as 5' 10" as opposed to 5' 8" because the street level was lower on the side of the road where the man had been.

This was a reasonable adjustment and was still short of Bailey's height. Nothing in terms of identification turned on that because eyewitness evidence about height is generally poor in terms of accuracy.

She said another Garda came to her shop on December 28 and gave her a video to see if she recognised anyone in it. She watched it at home with her husband. It showed Ian Bailey reciting poetry at the annual swim in Schull that Christmas Day. Her husband Chris recognised him as someone who had been in the shop, but she did not and told the interviewers that he was not the same man she had seen on the Saturday or on the Monday night at Kealfadda Bridge. She returned the videotape to Schull Garda Station.

Two weeks later, she made an anonymous phone call from a telephone kiosk in Cork city using the name of "Fiona" to pass on the information about the man she had seen at Kealfadda Bridge. A few days later, she saw Ian Bailey on Schull main street. She was going to Brosnan's Spar shop and there she met two Gardai and told them that she had seen the man from the Christmas swim video and pointed out Ian Bailey, who was at the time outside the post office.

The next section of the interview with GSOC officers demonstrated the familial danger of her tryst with the mystery companion and how it weighed heavily on her. Had she been alone on the night, there would have been no reason to disguise her real identity.

She admitted making a second anonymous phone call to Gardai from the small village of Leap near Skibbereen, followed by a third from her own home, telling them that she would not be coming forward and had told them everything she knew. In the first week of February 1997, she was approached by a Garda at her shop, who asked her to come to his home outside Schull. She did so and was shown the same videotape of Ian Bailey at the Christmas swim and he told her he believed that she was "Fiona" and was the person who had made the anonymous phone calls.

Shortly, she alleged, two other detectives arrived at the Garda's home and one of them described the details of the murder, including those of the nature of the injuries, and stated that Ian Bailey had been responsible. She stated that she named Ian Bailey as the man she had seen at Kealfadda Bridge only because this detective insisted that Ian Bailey had murdered Sophie Toscan du Plantier and had convinced her that this was true. Marie Farrell then said that she now regretted making this statement naming Ian Bailey.

The narrative in this first interview was true in relation to some events but obviously as a result of the witness's newly adopted position there were details which were open to dispute from the investigation officers' point of view. For example, her version of watching the video in the presence of several Gardai was different than theirs. They were treading carefully with this witness and had no reason to force a particular angle of events. She was saying that pressure was being put on her to finger Bailey, but it had to fit her new role, which meant she had to juxtapose vital details, a juggling exercise that had obvious pitfalls.

The second interview by GSOC officers took place on May 15, 2012 and naturally would move into a territory of more contentious issues as a result of the changing of her narrative. She claimed that when Ian Bailey was arrested for the murder, she did not know him prior to his arrest and had only seen him on the street in Schull and on the videotape provided by the Gardai.

She said that on February 14, 1997 she went to Ballydehob

Garda Station after a detective called her about her statements. She alleged that she signed a number of blank witness statements amounting to three or four pages and was only there for a few minutes. A detective wanted her to state that Ian Bailey had been threatening her, parking outside her shop and making threatening gestures towards her. She alleged that the detective told her he would fill in the witness statements to say that Bailey had threatened her. She said Bailey had not threatened her and she willingly signed the blank statements because she wanted to help the Gardai and she had not been subjected to undue pressure.

This was an absurd allegation and a crude invention to explain the radical difference between the statements she had given to the Gardai, which she had stood over for eight years, and the ones she was now giving to GSOC officers. No experienced murder investigator would produce blank statement papers to any witness and then fill them in without the presence of the witness.

The contradiction was abundantly obvious, so where lay the truths and where lay the lies? The GSOC officers would have plenty of time to assess all. Far longer than they might have imagined, but the videotape recordings would tell all down the road of time. The amount of time and space given to Marie Farrell's statements would dwarf the main protagonist Ian Bailey's and his partner Jules Thomas's by the proverbial mile, which by any manner or means gave the impression that she was the most important witness.

Marie Farrell further alleged that after the meeting at Ballydehob Garda Station, the detective was repeatedly in touch with her by phone, and that she often used different public phone booths as the calls aroused suspicion on the part of her husband Chris. She was provided with a mobile phone by the Gardai as a result of the intimidation by Bailey (which she now denied happened) and the detective (who was clearly her designated handler), she alleged, called to her house, regularly drank whiskey with Chris and often drove back drunk to Bandon in an unmarked Garda car. There were rumours around Schull that she was having an affair with the officer, which she denied and claimed that he did not want his colleagues to know about the calls.

She referred to the man in the house in Skibbereen, who the detective told her that he planned to use to provide cannabis and poitín (an illegally distilled drink) to Ian Bailey to influence him to confess the murder. She alleged that the drugs and drink had been seized in Garda raids. In May 1997, the detective rang her and met her outside the church in Schull; he was upset and told her that the Skibbereen witness had double-crossed him and told Bailey about being given the cannabis and poitín.

She said that Ian Bailey had contacted the *Sunday World* and someone had taken photographs of the detective Garda handing over drugs to the Skibbereen witness, but the Garda told her that the newspaper was not running the story and she alleged he said that he had threatened the witness, who had left the country. There had of course been no drugs handed over to anybody.

She narrated the incident in which she had been given a tape recorder by the detective and was given instructions to record Bailey when he came into the shop to get information from him. Her previously explained reason was that the tape recorder had been given to her to record the threats and intimidation from Bailey.

That narrative had to change now she was on the prime suspect's side, which would not be so easy. She now said the purpose was to get information from Bailey, which was a weak explanation, and so she would have to tread carefully with her newly developing interpretation of the next event.

In June 1997, she recounted Bailey had come into her ice-cream parlour and had said to her that he knew she had been under pressure to make statements about him. She cashed a cheque for him he got for a story about the murder from *The Examiner* and he told her about the arrest and how he had been treated. It was naturally a far cry from the version of this encounter she had given before. She then told GSOC officers a truthful story about a part of the meeting which would have huge implications in a future event. Bailey told her that he was an investigative journalist and that he knew about her old address in London, and also knew the reason why she and her family had left London.

She told GSOC officers that she had been involved in a fraudulent claim for income support and housing benefits amounting to a sum in the region of £27,000. Following a dispute over money with Chris Farrell's sister and her husband, who had been working with Chris in a double-glazing firm in London, Marie Farrell had been reported to the social welfare authorities concerning the fraudulent claims she had made. After being contacted by the social welfare authorities and ordered to pay back the money, the family left London in a hurry and returned to Ireland.

Ironically, the tape recorder in the shop had failed but had it not, it would have revealed the true tone in Ian Bailey's voice when he brought up the matter of the Farrells leaving London in a hurry and the reason for it, as opposed to the flat reference in Marie Farrell's witness statement. Both were abundantly aware that this London episode amounted to a serious criminal offence. Bailey was obviously looking for a quid quo pro – his silence on the subject in return for Farrell withdrawing her statement.

The GSOC videotape was in perfect working order and recorded a crucial piece of evidence, the value of which would not be realised until over two years later in the most explosive manner.

All provided insight into the chaotic existence of Marie Farrell, one that was beset by constant financial problems, and the escape to Schull that should have but did not provide a solution. In her witness statement, she said that sometime in 1997, her husband Chris was due to appear in court in relation to an appeal against driving without car insurance but due to the intervention of her detective handler her husband did not have to appear in court. She understood that the Gardai at the detective's urging had offered no evidence about the matter and that her husband was not penalised for the offence.

She claimed that in the autumn of the same year the detective assisted her in getting a new council house through intervention with a now-deceased politician with whom he was friendly, and two meetings were arranged by the detective with the politician. During one of the meetings in Bandon, the politician allegedly told Marie and Chris Farrell they would get one of the new houses in Schull as he was owed a favour by someone in the Housing Department in County Hall in Cork city. A few months later, they got the house.

What was remarkable about this statement was the clear implication of corruption on the part of the detective and the politician in helping her and her family in securing much-needed housing with no acknowledgement of participation in a corrupt act on behalf of herself. Mean-minded could not come close to describing this accusation, which had been investigated and found to be untrue.

The McAndrew Report had dealt with this matter and found that there was no interference by members of the Garda Síochána with the politician on behalf of Marie Farrell. The politician stated that he had been contacted directly by Marie Farrell and merely mentioned the detective's name. There was no evidence of any undue influence or control in the matter. This finding meant that Marie Farrell had lied to GSOC officers about the detective's role in the matter and also the one played by the politician.

Marie Farrell said that the detective had told her everything about the murder investigation, and after, she had to return the mobile phone and buy her own. Daily contact continued with the detective, who urged her to report any intimidation by Bailey and to say that he had made threatening gestures to her. She told the officers that Ian Bailey did not threaten her or intimidate her at any time. After Bailey was arrested in early 1998, the detective told her that this was due to him persuading his bosses of the threats and intimidation to her.

To what extent Marie Farrell was skirting the line between fact and fiction would be determined by the GSOC investigation sometime in the future, but the entirely objective and independent officers must have been given pause for thought about what they would hear and record next.

The plank of her witness statements so far was built on the relatively straightforward allegations that Bailey had not intimidated or threatened her, that she had been forced in a clearly unlawful way to make false complaints against him, and that he was not the man she had seen outside her shop or at Kealfadda Bridge.

However shaky the foundations of her new narrative, it appeared they were about to be rocked by allegations of a bizarre character, as if what she had already said about members of the murder investigation team was not sufficiently damaging.

In summer 1998, she stated that she was working as restaurant manager at Coosheen Golf Club in Schull. One evening at closing time, a detective sergeant involved in the murder investigation was present in the restaurant with his wife. She alleged that she went to the ladies' toilets to check and clean them when this detective entered the toilets and pushed her against the wall, whereupon he opened his trousers and said, "Would you like some of this?"

She replied something like, "For feck sake, Chris and your wife are out there, or they could see." It was over in a few seconds and the detective sergeant went to the men's toilets. She stated that the detective sergeant apologised to her a few weeks later at the golf club. In 1999, she had been summonsed as a witness in a court case and was staying in Dublin, and alleged that the detective sergeant (who was then stationed in Dublin) called to her hotel and took her out for a drink.

In 2002, she said she had been served with a subpoena in relation to a court case taken by Ian Bailey against several newspapers. She stated that she did not want to go to court. The reason, which she did not want to go into, was obvious – she was facing her activities on the night of December 23, 1996, being subjected to examination in a case which would receive huge media coverage.

Before the commencement of the court case, she had been contacted by the detective Garda and other Gardai who told her how important it was for her to attend the court. She omitted to record that she had also been given the same message by newspaper lawyers at a meeting in Schull.

On one occasion, she attended Bandon Garda Station, where she met a detective superintendent prior to his retirement. He allegedly referred to outstanding fines which she had and advised her to pay them in instalments to the detective sergeant, saying that if "it was discovered that fines were quashed for making statements in relation to Ian Bailey, we would all be in the shit."

In 2003, she stated that the detective Garda advised her to go to the newspapers and tell her story about the intimidation and threats received from Bailey. According to her GSOC statement, she had contacted the *Sunday World* newspaper, who offered her £2,500 for the story, but as they wanted a lot of detail, she went with the *Star on Sunday* newspaper, who gave her £1,500 for the story as they wanted less detail than the former publication. This statement was on timescale inaccurate, as in that year newspapers were constrained from doing this as the Bailey libel action was ongoing and would not be held until December 2003.

It happened but not in the manner she alleged – in 2004, not 2003 as she had said – and after the verdict of the libel trial. Marie Farrell had not contacted the newspapers at all. The *Sunday World* had doorstepped her in Schull and made an offer, but I as the journalist working for the *Star on Sunday* rang her and she agreed to the interview for the £1,500 fee on the basis that I would give her a fair hearing. Clearly, she had not been prompted to do that by a detective, as it was not possible in the time frame she described. She delivered during the interview, and as published, a comprehensive account of her intimidation by Bailey and was rewarded for it.

Now apart from the obvious fabrication about the Garda and newspaper interaction, what was alarming was the paucity of her memory. The libel case was conducted in December 2003 and the verdict delivered in January 2004. The interview followed and all should have been easy to recall. If she could get such a simple fact wrong on a peripheral matter, it appeared she would have difficulty on the major issues.

Marie Farrell recounted receiving a letter from Frank Buttimer (as a result of her account of Bailey's intimidation in the newspaper interview) telling her to stop making false accusations against his client or they would take legal action against her. In 2005, the detective sergeant was in contact with her saying that the parents of Sophie Toscan du Plantier were taking a civil action against Bailey and there would be another court case. She told him she would not go back to court and she would go and see Frank Buttimer and tell him exactly what went on.

She alleged that the detective sergeant said, "Who wants to hear anything about that?" She replied, "Maybe Ian Bailey would want to hear it," to which he responded, "Who cares about that long black English bastard?" and "Do you want to turn the whole thing into another Donegal?" She told him, "Never again, I'm telling no more lies for the guards." Marie Farrell then alleged that the detective said that if she did see Frank Buttimer, that she would never have a day's peace for as long as she lived in Schull.

Again, the timeline was not accurate. The Bouniol family had lodged papers in the High Court relating to the civil action in December 2002 which received considerable media coverage afterwards, so members of the investigation team were well aware of the action, particularly when the summons was delivered to Bailey in Liscaha the next year, 2003.

There was no reason why the Garda should bring the action up such a long time later and when Marie Farrell had just told GSOC officers that contact between them had ceased in 2004. In any event, on April 22, 2005, the Bouniol family decided to abandon the action due to the financial risks involved. But it had served its purpose well in the libel action defeat of Bailey.

She told the GSOC officers of events involving Gardai and her family. In an altercation with a man, her husband had been assaulted with a shotgun, but the man was not arrested or prosecuted. Her sons were allegedly being harassed by a Garda and despite making a complaint to the Garda Complaints Board, she was told her complaint was vexatious.

Again, these matters were investigated and addressed by

the McAndrew Report. Complaints were made and the Gardai denied any improper conduct in respect of this. It was found that summonses against a son of Marie Farrell were properly processed by Garda Finn and that these summonses were issued and proceeded through the courts in the normal way.

Marie Farrell had attempted to give those events a significance of further examples of a negative attitude towards and harassment of members of her family, which might have fitted nicely into her main themes of complaint if they had any veracity, which the McAndrew Report demonstrated that they did not.

She said that she contacted Frank Buttimer in April 2005 and had meetings with him over a period of four to six months at his office in Cork city. She said that she told him the truth about her involvement in the Ian Bailey case. Marie Farrell, as the GSOC officers recorded, principally alleged that she felt intimidated by the Gardai and that she had been put under pressure to make statements in order to implicate Bailey in the murder.

Thus, in spite of much recorded evidence to the contrary both in her statements to the Gardai and in a court setting, in the press and her complaints to the investigators, she had swapped the matter of intimidation by the prime suspect to members of the investigation team. It was a position replete not just with contradiction but inherent danger to her credibility as a witness on behalf of the new side she had chosen.

In early 2006, Marie Farrell and Chris sold their home in Schull. She told the GSOC officers that she met the detective Garda by chance at Cork University Hospital and a conversation ensued during which he said that according to her account, if he had been around, he could have talked her out of going to Frank Buttimer, and he wanted to keep his name out of it all as much as she could.

Ian Bailey and Frank Buttimer might have been pleased with the substance of the statements given by Marie Farrell to GSOC, and she was a witness who they would be heavily relying upon to deliver the right result in their High Court action. But they operated at the disadvantage of not knowing the precise detail of the interviews, but perhaps a summary delivered by Marie Farrell of her recollections – and as those who have gone through such a process will know, this would be severely limited in terms of accurate memory.

On the evidence of her witness statements to GSOC, she was weaving a tangled web in terms of shifting and inaccurate narrative which was capable in many parts of being unravelled under tough cross-examination by a skilled adversary in a court setting. Also, her memory of timelines was defective and her accounts of alleged incidents wrong in factual detail. Whatever vulnerability she might have had in that context would be sure to be explored in depth in the setting of the High Court, where there was so much at stake – not least the reputations of all involved, but also costs of enormous proportions.

Ian Bailey, of all people, should have known all the possibilities after his experience under the ferocious cross-examination of Paul Gallagher in the libel trial. There was little doubt that Marie Farrell would be exposed to similar scrutiny in the High Court hearing and that all statements she had made over the years in relation to her part in the murder investigation would be obtained by the State defence team in the discovery process.

However, Bailey and his team appeared to be immune to the inherent danger of having on their side a significant witness who had developed such a casual disregard for the truth long in advance of the GSOC interviews. Perhaps their attention had been diverted by a dramatic development which could compensate for any potential deficit in the evidence of their star witness Marie Farrell.

PART THREE

CHAPTER 16
THE BANDON TAPES

Dublin/Cork/West Cork – 2013–14

In late 1995, recording of multiple telephone lines into Digital Audio Tapes (DAT) commenced with the approval of the Garda Telecommunications section at about twenty divisional Garda stations outside the Dublin Metropolitan area. It was the first time the Garda force had operated systems for the recording of non-999 emergency number lines, in particular the main station line.

On an unknown date in 1996, the telecommunications technician at Bandon Garda Station mistakenly connected the recording system to several lines outside what had been generally approved the previous year. From early 1997, a large part of the Garda investigation of the murder of Sophie Toscan du Plantier was operated from Bandon Station and number of lines used by members of the investigation were recording their conversations without the knowledge of the Gardai using them.

Most of the retained tapes, as well as a large amount of documentation in Bandon Station, had been destroyed by flooding in the town in December of 2009. The technician had stored them under lock and key in his desk, but the majority were destroyed beyond repair. A number of recorded calls on DAT tapes had escaped the destruction.

Ian Bailey had been twice arrested and questioned at the station and in 2013 his legal team for his High Court action against the State sought and secured a discovery order of documents from Bandon Station in relation to the murder investigation. The tapes would now be included as material relevant to the terms of the discovery order.

In June 2013, the telecommunications technician at Bandon Garda Station found six DAT tapes which, according to their labels, dated back to 1997 and 1998.

These tapes were recorded on the DAT recording system. In the belief that because of the dates they could have recordings related to the murder investigation, the technician handed them over to the incident room team. On June 20, he handed over a further three tapes to the officers.

The reach of the recording within Bandon Station was staggering in breadth. It covered the main station telephone line; a telephone line used by the detective sergeant responsible for preparing the murder investigation report and who was unaware of being recorded; and a line set up in the telecommunications equipment room for the detective to communicate and record with his knowledge communication with a civilian who had offered to help with the investigation of Ian Bailey as a suspect.

Also, a line in a room known as "Interview Room No. 2", which was close to the Detective Branch office and sometimes used by detectives, none of whom were aware of being recorded. Finally, one line in the technician's office – the other one unaccountably was not being recorded.

There were ten DAT tapes in total with nine of those covering various periods between March 24, 1997 up to July 21, 1998 and one December 19, 2002 to January 20, 2003. The largest number of calls on any one tape relevant to the murder investigation was 134 calls on the DAT tape that spanned the period from May 24, 1997 to June 25, 1997. The total period amounted to thirty-two weeks and four days.

The overall responsibility for co-ordinating the Garda response to the request for documentation arising from the Bailey case was held by Chief Superintendent Tom Hayes, Cork West

Division, with the assistance of Detective Inspector Joe Moore, also based in West Cork, and they assembled a small team of officers at an incident room in Anglesea Street Garda Station, Cork city. The team were assigned the considerable task of identifying and collating all documentation that fell within the terms of the discovery order.

Three of the team had already been working full-time since September 2011 at Anglesea Street on mutual assistance requests from the French authorities in relation to the Sophie Toscan du Plantier murder investigation, a big advantage as they already had a good working knowledge of the investigation. In the summer of 2013, they were joined by two more officers. They got to work on over 40,000 pages of documentation, made up of Garda correspondence, reports, statements, newspaper articles, exhibits, photographs, Garda registers and occurrence books.

Detective Inspector Moore gave an oral briefing to the officers who were assigned to the listening exercise to satisfy all concerned that the criteria used to evaluate information on the tapes were as wide-ranging as possible. They were also urged to be fully aware of all the parties involved and specifically aware of persons identified in the categories of discovery. The listening officers were told that recordings containing any mention of the case, the area involved, or any of the parties involved should be fully downloaded to be assessed for discovery.

A further four members were added to the team reviewing the calls in the first week of February 2014, following concerns that the mammoth task would not be completed within the timeframe allotted by the High Court order. The four new members were assigned to listen to Channel 1 of the tapes as that had the greatest amount of traffic, and Channel 2 was the radio channel. Other channels which had been found to contain the most significant calls relating to the murder investigation were handled by the main team, who had more detailed experience and knowledge of the case.

There was a strict culture of confidentiality among the members of the reviewing team and the subject matter of what was being discovered was not discussed among them, including any material which related to the murder investigation. It was a complex and incredibly labour-intensive operation which began in January and was completed at the end of April, by which time the team – which consisted of ten officers – had listened to just over 45,000 calls over a period of fifteen weeks.

From this total, the team had judged that 282 calls were related, a tiny percentage but more than enough depending on the content to make an impact on the High Court case which was due to open in or around nine months later. The recording of them was sent to the Garda Office of Legal Affairs and counsel decided that 123 were relevant to the murder investigation and the terms of the discovery order.

These were sent to Gwen Malone, a stenographer, to be transcribed, and when the completed transcription was returned, the team at Anglesea Street Station found a number of inaccuracies which were due to a combination of poor recording on tapes that were twenty years old, and the speakers' accents and use of colloquial phrases and language unfamiliar to the transcribing team. It was decided that the incident room officers would compare the calls to the transcripts and make the appropriate corrections.

What would those calls reveal? If there was a lack of caution on the part of the murder investigation Gardai and, worse, attempts to promote false evidence – or as Marie Farrell alleged, intimidation of a witness to make false statements – such wrongdoing or any other such unlawful or improper conduct revealed could effectively scupper the State's defence in the High Court action. It would be later made clear that the incident room members would not be reluctant to identify calls that might discredit other members of the force.

But the irony of their task must have struck them   the possibility of the provision to a prime suspect of a murder with ammunition to wreak serious damage on their colleagues, who had sweated as much on the murder investigation as they had done on the tapes, and a suspect who had continually made slanderous and unfounded allegations about their conduct during the investigation.

During the compliance process, the surviving DAT tapes were brought to the attention of the Garda discovery team by the station telecommunications technician. A sample of recorded calls, some of which were private conversations between members of the investigation team, were on review considered to contain material capable of being damaging to the force. Clearly this discovery and the sifting and transcription of the calls had not only a direct bearing on Bailey's case but could contain material which had the potential of corroborating his allegations of corruption and unlawful practices by Garda members of the murder investigation team.

The existence of the mistakenly recorded calls at Bandon, as well as the normal recordings in the other stations, was a matter which soon occupied the attention of the top brass of the force, including then Garda Commissioner Martin Callinan, Deputy Commissioner Noirin O'Sullivan and also the Attorney General Maire Whelan's office, as well as the Data Protection Commissioner Billy Hawkes. The legal situation, in the view of the Attorney General's counsel, would later conclude that there had been for decades wholesale and extensive recording of telephone calls the length and breadth of the country in Garda stations without any apparent authorisation under any of the legislation necessary to implement such an operation.

Deputy Garda Commissioner Noirin O'Sullivan became aware of the recordings in Bandon on the evening of October 17, 2013 following a discussion with Chief Superintendent Tom Hayes, who oversaw collating documents for the High Court order for discovery in the Bailey case. She directed that enquires be made as to how these calls in Bandon came to be recorded and whether similar recordings other than 999 calls existed in other Garda stations. A rake of interdepartmental communications began at the highest level of the Gardai and would eventually make their way to the highest levels of Government.

No matter what was concluded, the High Court discovery order in the Bailey case would have to be complied with, even though the recording of conversations of the officers in Bandon Station without their knowledge was not just a violation of the privacy of the callers but technically speaking the recording of the conversations was illegally obtained and raised questions of if and how they could be used as evidence in a court setting.

All participants were beginning to realise the potential negative consequences of the matter involving the integrity of and public trust in the Garda Síochána from the bottom to the top. There were, however, several other issues within the top brass of the force that would prove to have more lethal impacts than the tapes problem.

An incredible backstory was emerging to the whole issue in the corridors of power in Leinster House, the seat of the Government, as the discovery team in Cork worked day and night to meet the deadline laid down by the High Court order. Ian Bailey's case would have unintended consequences that both he and his legal team could never have imagined. It had the potential along with another emerging major scandal (a whistle blower's controversy) within the Garda force of heads rolling both at the top of the force but also at the top of the Justice Department and the Government.

Ruth Fitzgerald, Advisory Counsel at the Attorney General Maire Whelan's office, emailed a letter to Ken Ruane, Head of Legal Affairs of Garda Síochána on November 14, 2013, noting first that "this was a difficult issue on which to advise". She went on to state that the issues were complex and further that because the issue would be controversial once the information in the Bailey case came to light, that what must be done about the recordings must be considered carefully and thoroughly, and so she would seek the advice of counsel.

Superintendent Michael Flynn of the Telecommunications section was brought into the equation and in a report provided an explanation to Noirin O'Sullivan about the rationale behind the installation of the recording system which originated in the 1980s, the purpose of which was "the recordings of 999 calls and the gathering of evidence around calls regarding bomb threats and other coded word messages". The original recorders were replaced by Dictaphone recorders during the 1990s which were then replaced by NICE recorders about five years later.

When the Garda Commissioner Martin Callinan was informed of the developments at Bandon and other stations, he ordered that all recordings of non-999 calls should cease and by November 13, 2013, this was enacted. A further report by Superintendent Flynn was forwarded to Ken Ruane, Head of Legal Affairs of the Gardai, which he in turn forwarded to Ruth Fitzgerald at the Attorney General's office on February 28, 2014.

Superintendent Flynn's report provided the basis for the Garda Commissioner Martin Callinan's letter dated March 10, 2014 to Brian Purcell, Secretary General at the Department of Justice. The Commissioner was fulfilling his duty to comply with the legislative requirement to keep the Department of Justice and the Minister for Justice informed of important developments.

This letter would have at the time unforeseen and devastating consequences for the Commissioner, so it is worth quoting in part to demonstrate just what impact the High Court case taken by Ian Bailey and his partner Jules Thomas in relation to the Bandon tapes would have.

"Dear Secretary General,

I wish to bring the following to the Minister's attention in accordance with Section 41(d) of the Garda Síochána Act 2005.

"During the discovery process in the current civil proceedings being taken by Mr Ian Bailey and his partner Ms Catherine Jules Thomas for wrongful arrest under other headings, further material has come to light that is relevant in discovery in those proceedings. This material related to telephone recordings of conversations that took place on various dates during 1997 between members of An Garda Síochána at Bandon Garda Station and other members of An Garda Síochána

and also with Ms Marie Farrell and in other cases with journalists who were contacting An Garda Síochána seeking information. These tapes are currently being reviewed as part of the Discovery process and will be listed in an Affidavit of Discovery which must be sworn by An Garda Síochána before March 25, 2014."

The Commissioner then dealt with the matter raised by the report of Superintendent Flynn in relation to the general subject of the recordings in general and then in the last two paragraphs returned to the substantive matter.

"I have no doubt that when the Discovery process is completed and if copies of the tape recordings are disclosed to the plaintiff in the Ian Bailey civil proceedings that this issue will very much come into the public domain and I am anxious to resolve any data protection issues as quickly as possible. You will note however that as soon as this issue came to my attention, I took immediate steps to regularise the position and continue to do so."

The Commissioner finished by saying that a meeting had been arranged for Monday, March 10, 2014, between counsel, the Attorney General's office and An Garda Síochána, and which Assistant Commissioner Michael Flahive would attend, where the matter and other issues would be discussed. He signed his name and the date, March 10, 2014. It would not be near the end of the matter but just the beginning.

This scenario was becoming akin to some Nordic noir television series like *The Bridge*, *Borgen* or a Jo Nesbo novel where a murder in a small community in an isolated area would have reverberations that would echo right into the highest levels of Government and have the potential to compromise all of the participants on the journey but reward the perpetrator and leave the victim and the case in limbo.

The writers of a fictional series could not have invented the facts. The complicated drama continued. On March 13, 2014, Ms Fitzgerald wrote to Mr Ruane and advised that the views of the Data Protection Commissioner should be established. Six days later, the Garda Commissioner wrote to the Data Commissioner Billy Hawkes repeating the same facts as he had communicated to the Secretary General and seeking to establish whether the tape recordings other than those in the discovery order should be destroyed.

The Data Commissioner, given the time pressure involved, replied by phone and said that the tapes other than those covered by the discovery order should be destroyed. The Garda Commissioner had this advice sent to Ms Fitzgerald. She could not agree with this recommended course of action and said she found the advice "quite startling".

It was an opinion that was hard to disagree with, as the public perception not to mind the Government opposition and the media would immediately, if the tapes were destroyed, conclude that a massive cover-up was being exercised by the Gardai with the approval of the Government. In or out of the discovery order, no tapes could be destroyed.

One way or another, there was a massive black cloud gathering over Government buildings in central Dublin and Garda headquarters in the Phoenix Park. Meanwhile, the letter sent by the Garda Commissioner on March 10 to Justice Secretary General Brian Purcell had disappeared down some bureaucratic black hole and the Attorney General Maire Whelan became highly alarmed by the latest information she had received about the tape recordings.

What obviously worried her was that no one knew for sure the genesis of their implementation and the precise reason even as expressed by the Garda Commissioner in his letter of March 19 to Billy Hawkes was far too vague. She had of course not yet had available to her the earlier letter of March 10.

She realised that there had been for a time period going back to the 1980s extensive recording of calls at numerous Garda stations all over the country, except for the Dublin Metropolitan Area (DMA). But she thought the suggested rationale contained in the March 19 letter was hypothetical and she simply had not enough solid fact to issue advice on the legal issues. It would have been akin to building a house without first laying the foundations.

More alarming was the fact that what she did not know at this time was that the letter or its contents of March 10 sent to Brian Purcell and the one to Billy Hawkes on March 19 were not known to the Minister for Justice Alan Shatter, the Government or Taoiseach (Prime Minister) Enda Kenny. At a meeting on Sunday, March 23, the Attorney General Maire Whelan briefed the Taoiseach Enda Kenny and the Secretary General to the Government Martin Fraser about the telephone recording saga, the details of which Enda Kenny reacted to with shock, instantly recognising the explosive political implications.

The Taoiseach directed the Attorney General to verify the facts of the whole issue and another meeting was convened the following day, Monday, March 24 at 6 p.m., to be attended by the same parties, and after a short time the Minister for Justice Alan Shatter was summoned to attend and then Brian Purcell was also brought in to the meeting, which was thick with the atmosphere of an impending crisis.

Assistant Secretary in the Department of Justice Michael Flahive was also present at the meeting. The Taoiseach's shock was compounded by the fact that he and his Minister for Justice were being made aware for the first time about the discovery order in the Bailey case and that the whole subject of the countrywide telephone recording of calls in Garda stations had only been revealed as a result of the High Court order of Mr Justice Hedigan.

Ian Bailey's case was rattling the cages, not just of the Garda members of the murder investigation and the top Garda brass, but he was now unwittingly causing a crisis at the top echelons of Government. It would later emerge that six Garda Commissioners and three Ministers for Justice in office over the period from when the recordings began were left in total ignorance as to their existence. Without the discovery order in relation to material in Bandon Station, their existence may well have never become known.

It was the Taoiseach's view that members of the public, who would have been contacting Garda stations over a long period of time, were in a position where their messages or calls had been recorded illegally. This would give rise to great public controversy, pointing to a lack of integrity and credibility in the Garda force and causing public outrage. Given the gravity of the matter, it was vital that trust had to be restored in the Gardai, and public disquiet and anxiety allayed, and the only way to achieve the aim was to set up a Commission of Investigation into the whole matter.

The Secretary General, Brian Purcell, was instructed to go to the home of the Garda Commissioner Martin Callinan and tell him of the seriousness with which the Taoiseach viewed the developments both in the Bailey case and the general recordings issue.

He was also to be informed by Mr Purcell that a Commission of Investigation was to be set up to establish the facts of both issues. It was certainly an extraordinary decision to send the messenger bearing news of such negative import to the head of the Garda force at his private residence, when it might have been more appropriate to summon him to Leinster House.

The Garda Commissioner justifiably interpreted the action by the Taoiseach as a vote of no confidence in him and the following morning, after what could be described as a stellar career in the force, Martin Callinan announced his retirement from the Gardai. His retirement was accepted by Enda Kenny, who announced the establishment of a Commission of Investigation to look into the matters raised by the Attorney General in the preceding two days.

Over the next three weeks, the terms of reference for the Commission were drafted and Mr Justice Nial Fennelly was appointed as sole member on April 30, 2014. The terms of reference reflected the serious concern in Government circles regarding the widespread recording of telephone calls in Garda stations and the possible implications these recordings had for Gardai involved in the investigation of the murder of Sophie Toscan du Plantier in West Cork in December 1996. Approximately eighty pages of the investigation report would be devoted to the possibility of improper conduct by members of the murder investigation team who were based in Bandon Station and whose conversations were generally recorded (with one exception) without their knowledge.

The Commission was required to establish whether the recorded calls combined with other acts or events during the Garda investigation of the murder to disclose evidence of unlawful or improper conduct on the part of members of the team in connection with the investigation into the crime.

It was a focused and hugely important part of the Commission of Investigation and combined with the High Court action and the GSOC inquiry provided the prime and only suspect of the murder, Ian Bailey, with three avenues if successful in any of the cases to bring down the murder investigation and effectively halt any further action against him in the jurisdictions of Ireland and France.

In a letter dated October 8, 2014, Bailey and Thomas were invited by the Commission to submit statements relevant to the terms of reference of the investigation.

Six days later, both replied with statements alleging unlawful and improper conduct by members of the Garda murder investigation team. Both literally threw the kitchen sink at the Gardai, accusing them of unlawfully arresting them on two occasions; physical and verbal abuse of Bailey, including death threats during his first arrest; manufacturing false evidence against him in relation to Marie Farrell; conspiracy on the part of Garda officers to cast Bailey as the killer and Ms Thomas as his accomplice, telling neighbours and locals that he was the murderer and that Ms Thomas was shielding him.

Bailey also alleged that certain members of the Garda team recruited Martin Graham as a police informant and paid him in the form of cash, clothes, alcohol and cannabis. They say that if enough mud is thrown then some of it must stick. For years he had been doing just that, and to say there was a lorryload of it would be a gross understatement. But none of that would matter if the Fennelly Commission or the High Court and/or the GSOC inquiry found evidence of improper conduct or modification of or interference with evidence on the part of the members of the murder investigation team.

If that happened, then Ian Bailey would be catapulted back into the role he had created and most cherished, that of the innocent man wronged by the corrupt practices of murder detectives, the hero figure that he most fantasised about being and not the role of the villain that all his perceived enemies had cast upon him. Bailey, when fortune did not favour him, was a whinger and a crier, but when the tide was with him, he was a formidable opponent that the enemies as he perceived them would be foolish to underestimate.

The Commission decided that as the High Court proceedings were ongoing, that the members of the murder investigation involved in any of the tape recordings relevant to its inquiries would be given pseudonyms. Meanwhile, the Garda team worked on the tapes and sent them for transcription.

CHAPTER 17

THE CURIOUS INCIDENT IN THE NIGHT AND THE MISSING UNDERWEAR

Cork – 2014

A first matter of concern was identified as a statement given by Detective Garda Gamma, who was involved in interviewing Jules Thomas during her detention on February 10, 1997. In his opinion, she was trying to recollect to the best of her knowledge her movements and Bailey's over the weekend of the murder. On the morning of June 23, 1997, Detective Sergeant Alpha telephoned another member of the investigation team, Detective Sergeant Delta. They discussed the difficulties of the writing of the report.

Detective Sergeant Alpha raised the subject of the statement made by Detective Garda Gamma regarding Jules Thomas in February 1997.

Det Sgt Alpha: Okay, yeah. I need to talk to you about, erm, your colleague's statement of evidence. I need him to … but I'll talk to you first … I just want …

Det Gda Delta: Yeah.

Det Sgt Alpha: I need to talk about it anyway.

Det Gda Delta: The most honest man.

Det Sgt Alpha: Yeah.

Det Gda Delta: [Laughs.]

Det Sgt Alpha: [Laughs.] He has comments in it like, "I knew she was making every effort to tell me the truth. Do you follow?"

Det Gda Delta: Yes.

Det Sgt Alpha: I don't need them for starters.

Det Gda Delta: [Laughs.]

Det Sgt Alpha: Fuck it, she wasn't anyway.

Later, during a further conversation between the same officers:

Det Sgt Alpha: Ah, fuck it, it's awful. When I see your friend then. Like writing them fucking stupid statements, like I mean … what man … "I believe," he says, "that she was doing her best to recall the night in question and being truthful. Yes, that statement has to get fucking chopped up anyway."

There were other unrelated matters discussed and then:

Det Sgt Alpha: And you can start building up your co-partner. If you're able to do that, or maybe I'll do it myself to …

Det Gda Delta: Well the thing about it is this … it will have to be explained to him like, that is the way … I mean, surely, he can see it in hindsight now that Jules is very devious.

Det Sgt Alpha: That statement is very damaging to have in there … I mean it's not … it's not … it doesn't do himself any good anyway.

Det Gda Delta: No.

Later that evening, at around 10.30 p.m., Detective Sergeant Alpha made a telephone call asking to speak to Detective Sergeant Gamma about the statements and was told he was not there.

In a recorded conversation on June 25, 1997, with an unidentified member of the force, Detective Sergeant Alpha again referred to the problem he was having with the positive opinion of Jules Thomas's statement in custody and recorded as such by Detective Garda Gamma in his statement of the following day, February 11, 1997.

Det Sgt Alpha: But you see, there are statements here that I have to go to fill in. I have to talk to them, one man put in here: "I believe she was attempting to tell me the truth and trying to recall" – you know your man interviewing her, like. When the evidence clearly shows and everything we were doing she is anything but, she has been out there working, conniving, twisting.

The other person in the conversation pointed out that it was not evidence and Detective Sergeant Alpha replied that it was in the statement and it had to be taken out.

It appeared that Detective Sergeant Alpha, who was involved in preparing the investigation file for the DPP, was over-concerned by the detail that a member of the team had stated that Jules Thomas was attempting to truthfully recall the events in question. This from the evidence of the transcript of the interview that was true.

But to suggest that a statement be "chopped up" or in other words edited would amount, if it happened, to improper conduct with appropriate serious consequences for the investigation as a whole. The detective sergeant told colleagues at the time the chances of the case proceeding to a charge were "50/50". But these odds provided no reason to either contemplate or implement methods to improve them.

The recording of a telephone call on May 30, 1997 seemed to provide an example of a willingness to suppress relevant evidence. The participants were Detective Sergeant Alpha and Sergeant Beta, who was assisting him in preparing the file for the DPP. They were discussing two statements made by a witness.

In his second statement, he recalled encountering Ian Bailey in a pub four or five times over the evening of December 22, 1997. This differed from his initial statement he remembered "from talking to [named person] that Bailey and Thomas were in the pub that night."

In the conversation, Sergeant Beta was annoyed, saying, "That [this difference] undermines the whole thing." He asked if he would take that out. He continued, "The only thing is the opening line of the statement is 'Further to my previous statement' … What can we do? I'll leave it there for the moment and we can talk about it later maybe." He then mentions taking another statement but thought it would look a bit funny.

Again, this indicates a thought at least to remove a statement from a witness that compromises a subsequent one which is stronger and to remove a contradiction before submitting the file to the DPP. If the thought is acted upon then it will amount to the suppression of relevant evidence.

The most apparent and dangerous threat to the integrity of the investigation was the relationship that had developed between the witness Martin Graham, who had offered to help in regard to getting a confession from Ian Bailey, and his two handlers, Detective Garda Delta and Detective Garda Gamma, who had the majority of the contact with Graham. This relationship had commenced in February 1997, when the witness contacted a local Garda station.

From that time until April 1997, the Gardai believed the

witness was genuinely committed in helping them. From time to time, he requested small amounts of money as expenses; clothes and cigarettes were also granted. But in April, Detective Garda Delta became suspicious of Graham's motives. At a meeting late that month, the witness said that he was confident that he could persuade Bailey to made admissions in relation to the murder but added that if he was successful, he wanted IR £4,000 before he would make a statement.

He was told such a payment would not happen and, acting on his suspicions, Detective Garda Delta in early May asked the telecommunications technician at Bandon Garda Station to provide him with a facility to record telephone conversations between himself and Graham. The fact that the latter was willing to continue to try and get admissions from Bailey indicated to Detective Garda Delta that Graham was in fact working on Bailey's behalf, most likely to compromise the investigation in some way by means of a sting operation.

The recording of their conversations would protect the investigator in the event that if his suspicions were accurate, Graham would give his own prejudicial version of the conversations and discredit Detective Garda Delta. So, most of the significant conversations between the two were recorded on a line in the telecommunications room from May 20, 1997 to June 4, 1997.

Graham was indeed working on behalf of the prime suspect and around the end of May gave an interview to Bailey, who recorded it, in which he said that the Gardai had given him a vast amount of cannabis "as payment for helping them". He also said that a sum of IR £4,000 would be made available to him if he made a statement saying that Bailey "owned up to me to have committed the murder of Sophie du Plantier".

There were also a number of recorded calls in which Detective Garda Delta discussed Graham with other members of the investigation team and of which he was not aware they were being recorded, and they were logged as part of the discovery operation in 2014. While the investigator would naturally have exercised caution during calls he knew were being recorded, it might have been different during calls he was not aware of being recorded as he would have assumed no trace of those could ever exist.

In the course of a recorded conversation on May 20, 1997 at 8.10 p.m. between Detective Garda Delta and Graham, the word "stuff" was mentioned, and the question arose as to what exactly the word meant – drugs, clothes or money for alcohol. Obviously, the Garda and Graham would have different views of the meaning of the word.

Det Gda Delta: Did he [Bailey] mention anything to you about it, any specifics?

Mr Graham: No, he didn't say anything on the phone really. He said it would be good if you could sort of like bring some other stuff up as well, you know.

Det Gda Delta: Yes.

Mr Graham: That's all, you know, he didn't sorta like go into details or anything, you know.

Det Gda Delta: Is that right, yeah.

Mr Graham: He sounded like he wanted to sit down.

Det Gda Delta: Right.

Mr Graham: Have a chat, have a smoke or whatever, you know.

Det Gda Delta: Right, right, right.

It was a conversation that revealed little of incriminating value against the investigator, who was acting carefully as indeed was the informant, and the latter's use of the word "stuff" could have meant anything. But anyone, including Detective Garda Delta, could have read the subtext of Graham's words clearly; he was not trying to set Bailey up, quite the opposite, and the next conversation demonstrated his motive explicitly.

This happened two days later, when Detective Garda Delta was driving Graham to Bailey's house in Liscaha. They were accompanied in the car by the telecommunications technician from Bandon Station who had been instructed to record the conversation with a concealed hand-held tape recorder, which of course picked up the background sound of the car engine.

Det Gda Delta: In case you go to the pub tonight … I have a bit of money there, you know, a little bit of stuff, you know. I've a bit … I've got a few smokes as well for you.

Mr Graham: Have you got some hash?

Det Gda Delta: I have cash and I have something in a—and I have a few smokes in the—you know, you said you were starved, were you?

So, it appeared from this recorded conversation, which of course Graham was not aware of, that he was attempting by the request for hash to lead the investigator into a compromising position on behalf of his real mentor Ian Bailey, revealing the manipulative character of the prime suspect, not knowing of course that his invidious motivation had already been sussed out by the Gardai.

Or perhaps never imagining that anyone in the force – who he had previously attacked for incompetence and corruption – might have been capable of not just hitting back but could be just a mite cleverer than him, or indeed not reliant on a simply indigent man who was a well-known drug user and whose motive would be far more self-serving. For example, asking Gardai to supply him with drugs during a journey in a car in the presence of one member who he had never met before. Graham made a poor job of acting as a double agent.

But even if it was a ruse, which it obviously was planned to be by Bailey, to entrap Detective Garda Delta into improper conduct to be used against him in the future, it was both crude and incompetent, as it relied on the participation of a drug user who like all drug users could not be relied upon in any of his actions or his version of events. In Graham's case, he was desperate for money as well as drugs.

The following day, Detective Garda Delta spoke to the telecommunications technician on an internal line at Bandon Station, which unknown to him (and everyone else) recorded the conversation. It was highly ironic that the detective, having gone to the trouble of organising the recording of conversations with Graham with the latter's knowledge, was also using another line which was recording him with the potential to cancel out the advantage he had on the other line.

He told the technician that he suspected Graham had not visited Bailey the previous night as planned and as he had not managed to get him on the telephone, Graham was avoiding him, and this seemed to confirm further his suspicions about the witness's collaboration with Bailey.

> **Det Gda Delta:** All he wanted was to get me to give him a slab of you know fucking what ... go to the fucking paper ... and he would collect his few grand and he'd collect and fuck off.

It was hash, of course, that Graham was referring to as "stuff" during the previous conversation before he changed it, and it was glaringly obvious that in the highly unlikely event that he was given it, exactly how he and Bailey would have exploited this imagined opportunity by first of all tipping off a tabloid newspaper. But he was in too much of a hurry and knew that "stuff" was ambiguous.

The prime suspect was operating under the delusion that the police were not just corrupt but also stupid, and that he was the smart one. Here was an example among many others down the line of just how badly he could get it wrong.

There was a final meeting with Graham on June 7, 1997, after which Detective Garda Delta severed all contact. The cat and mouse game was over, and the ex-British Army soldier and the ex-British journalist had proved inept in the matter of an underhand conspiracy, during which their native cunning had been as transparent as the sun in a clear summer sky.

All of course was now on the radar of the investigation of the Fennelly Commission, as were some other events of potential improper conduct by members of the murder investigation team, and would feature no doubt in the High Court action taken by Bailey and Thomas against the Garda Commissioner and others. There was one other incident or scenario involving not surprisingly the former principal witness in the murder investigation, but now playing the opposite role as star witness for Ian Bailey.

It provided one more example of the difficult life of Marie Farrell that both preceded and followed her involvement in the investigation into the murder of Sophie Toscan du Plantier, and the resulting problems that involvement would present to the officers investigating the crime and add to the already complex nature of the case.

A number of recorded calls from April 1997 in Bandon Garda Station and written records from Bantry Garda Station, where there were no calls recorded, related to an occurrence which appeared somewhat peripheral to the murder investigation but raised issues in relation to the reaction of Garda members of the team and other officers outside the remit of the event.

In the early hours of April 13, 1997, a member of the Gardai in Bantry Station got two calls in quick succession relating to an alleged assault which took place at Crewe Bay in Schull. The calls were not recorded but the details entered into the Occurrence Book which recorded in writing activity at the station on a day-to-day basis. At 1.30 a.m., the caller said that a neighbour had come to his house, had been assaulted and needed a doctor. The neighbour was a "Mr C".

At 1.40 a.m., Marie Farrell rang Bantry Station and stated as recorded in the book: "When she and her husband had returned after a night out, they found a prowler around their house. They also reported the occurrence to Gardai at Schull and Bandon stations. When her husband found the prowler coming out their driveway, she said that he lost the head and beat him up. Over the previous few weeks underwear had gone missing from the clothes-line and Mr C had threatened her."

Two Garda members were dispatched from Bantry Station to the scene of the assault. As the patrol car was passing through Ballydehob, they encountered Garda Epsilon, who was on duty in foot patrol. They informed him about the incident and asked for directions to Crewe Bay. He offered to accompany them to the scene. On arrival, Garda Epsilon – being a local and the senior member of the team – took responsibility for investigating the incident.

On arrival, he spoke to Marie Farrell and her husband Chris. They told him that on arriving home earlier than expected, they found their neighbour Mr C walking away from their house to his own. Chris Farrell then chased and assaulted him. They told the officer that on a previous occasion underwear had gone missing from the clothesline and they suspected that Mr C was the culprit. The officer recalled later that the couple wanted to make a complaint against Mr C about the missing underwear and his prowling, as it was frightening to them and their children.

The investigating officer took no notes on the spot, as it was his policy that when there were disputes between neighbours that he would allow it to settle and then later after a few days talk formally to the people involved. This was an entirely reasonable course of action, as such disputes are commonly ridden with contradictions and prejudice on one side and the other. In the old adage, there are three sides to such disputes. One person's story, the other person's story and the truth.

Mr C had been taken to hospital in Bantry by Gardai that night and then returned to his home, and no written statement had been taken from him, which was in accordance presumably with the intention of later returning to the incident as per the policy of the Garda to leave the dust to settle.

So, on the face of it from the Farrells' allegation, the neighbour Mr C was not just a prowler but also some kind of oddball who also stole women's underwear, the objective of which could be anything, including possibly wearing the items. These were allegations and not proven, and based on nothing but a suspicion. Not an ideal but somewhat of a harmless neighbour if it was true, certainly not deserving of the beating which resulted in hospital treatment.

Some legal retribution should have happened in the wake of the incident, but it did not. Worse still, in a recorded conversation of April 18, 1997, discussing the possibility that Mr C might make a formal complaint of assault against Chris Farrell, Detective Garda Delta asked Garda Epsilon, "There would be no point in Mr Farrell making an old statement first, I suppose?" The response was, "We can always predate it if it comes to it, like, you know." The reply was, "Exactly, yeah." Garda Epsilon said, "No problem at all."

This exchange was of course changing the normal order of proper investigation procedure, which decrees that the complainant is interviewed first about the circumstances of what has allegedly occurred and then those details are put to the alleged suspect. Presumably, the old statement would be in relation to the alleged prowling and garment-stealing. But nonetheless the problem was the use of the word pre-dating. That indicated an action of possible improper conduct, which would be up to the Commission investigation to decide if it amounted to an intention to falsify the record.

Towards the end of the same conversation, the officers discussed the actions that were open to the Farrells in the event that Mr C might make a complaint.

Det Gda Delta: And you can always say that sure he drew a punch and missed, as you drew back, you know what I mean.

Gda Epsilon: Yeah.

Det Gda Delta: He's a man of the world, he knows what to say and do.

Gda Epsilon: Oh, yeah.

Det Gda Delta: What?

Gda Epsilon: Oh, we'll cover him all right.

The suggestion here was that Mr C threw the first punch, which was entirely at odds with the account of the incident given by Marie Farrell, who said that her husband had chased the prowler and beat him up. It was never the case that Chris Farrell was acting in self-defence.

Mr C's activities obviously in regard to prowling and the alleged stealing of underwear had been brought to the attention of Detective Garda Delta in advance of the assault on April 13, 1997. Ten days earlier, a recorded conversation between the detective (who had been assigned by his superiors to liaise with her) and Marie Farrell occurred. Although the detective had no function in relation to the later assault, he disclosed to her damaging personal and confidential information about Mr C.

He told her:

Det Gda Delta: "There is another side to him, he is telling lies to everybody about his profession, he goes around from address to address, there are warrants for him all over the country. There is a warrant for debt in Dublin for failing to pay up to yer wan [wife] he left, he is acting peculiar in many ways."

The remarks by the detective on the character of Mr C as expressed to Marie Farrell were unwarranted and with hindsight could explain the future assault incident in the context of provocation. It was information that should not have been communicated. It was redolent of a village gossip and an animus towards Mr C on behalf of the officer.

As Detective Garda Delta was in effect a handler of the witness Marie Farrell, it might be understandable how he would protect her interests and legitimately if she was being threatened, as she had been by the prime suspect Ian Bailey, but in an altercation as it happened he should have adopted a more neutral role and allowed it to be investigated by the officers responsible, and not allowed himself to be put in a position to be interfering in any way. Even allowing that the evidence suggested that the neighbour Mr C was some sort of an oddball, which is not a crime.

It was also an obvious fact that the detective was leaving himself in an invidious position as subject to the whims of a witness whose chaotic and pressurised life outside the murder investigation and directly connected to it by the circumstances she had involved herself in on the night of the murder by cheating on her husband with a man she had refused to name.

In spite of the apparent peripheral nature of the incident, there were factors involved that had the potential of not just reaching to the heart of the murder investigation and possibly compromising some aspects of it but asking further and attendant questions about the behaviour of at least one of the officers investigating the crime. The factors that would be under consideration and provide issues of potential concern to the Commission investigation were five in number.

Firstly, members of the Gardai appeared to have put Mr C under pressure not to make a formal complaint in relation to the assault; secondly, some of the recorded conversations appeared that this was done to ensure Marie Farrell's continued co-operation as a witness in the murder investigation; thirdly, members of the Gardai seemed to have adopted a hostile and prejudiced attitude towards Mr C both before and after the assault; fourthly, members of the Gardai appeared to have considered advising

Chris Farrell to give false evidence in relation to the assault; lastly, confidential information in the possession of the Gardai concerning Mr C's personal history was shared by a member with Marie Farrell.

There were four recorded calls in Bandon Station that mentioned Mr C. A call from Detective Garda Delta to Marie Farrell on April 3, 1997, ten days prior to the assault; a call from Detective Garda Delta to Garda Epsilon on April 18, five days after the assault; a call from Detective Garda Delta to Garda Epsilon on April 22, 1997, following a meeting between Mr C and Garda Epsilon at Schull Garda Station; and a call from Detective Garda Delta to Marie Farrell on April 22, made shortly after the previous call to Garda Epsilon.

The last-named Garda, though not a member of the murder investigation team, knew Marie and Chris Farrell, as he had been involved previously in the successful recovery of property that had been stolen from them. He had not met Mr C prior to the alleged assault. He had, however, known in general terms of Marie Farrell's statement about the sighting of Ian Bailey near Kealfadda Bridge in the early hours of December 23, 1996.

Apparently, Mr C, it emerged, had been questioned in a routine fashion in January 1997 by members of the investigation team to account for his movements on the night of the murder and had been quickly eliminated as a suspect, as of course had many others also questioned.

Ian Bailey had long maintained during his campaign accusations that the Garda investigation team were guilty of alleged corruption in their methods of improper practices, including disclosure of information by members to the media and others in relation to his arrests, and connection with the crime, and these allegations would also be looked at by the Commission, confined to the terms of reference to any evidence that might arise during the recordings of telephone calls in Bandon Garda Station.

It would transpire from those recorded calls quite a lot. During one week in June 1997, there were calls recorded of conversations between Detective Sergeant Alpha and a number of people, all of them being civilians, during which he discussed various aspects of the murder investigation.

On June 18, 1997, at 9.23 p.m., he spoke with an unidentified female civilian. When asked if he was any closer to a conclusion in the murder investigation, he said, "It's a very tricky one, a complicated one to try and put together and bring it together." Later he added, "Yeah, it's really cryptic and then we're up against it; he didn't leave us much to go on." He replied to a suggestion that if Bailey was not caught, then he would kill again: "Ah, it's frightening. Well, I don't want to give him that opportunity if I can help it, but the people he is living with, certainly shielding him, I think so."

The last part of the conversation was an allegation not proven. There was no evidence that any member of the Thomas family was shielding Bailey.

On June 19, 1997, at 11 a.m., Detective Garda Sergeant Alpha had a long conversation with a journalist who called him on behalf of a British newspaper. He told the reporter that as the investigation was ongoing, he could not discuss any details of it. But speaking off the record, he talked of Ian Bailey's reaction with the press and said that in his opinion, that due to negative press publicity, Bailey was attempting to create an argument for himself that as a result he would never get a fair trial.

In other words, he was like as he said another notorious criminal who tried to manipulate the press in a similar fashion. The detective was not far off the mark and this was a typical interaction between a police officer and a journalist, as of course the latter would honour the off-the-record limitation of the communication. Not all journalists do that but there was no evidence that this one did anything of that sort. However, neither of the participants in the conversation had any idea that it was being recorded.

During another call on June 24, 1997, at 12.43 p.m., Detective Garda Alpha spoke with another civilian, an employee of the

Revenue Commissioners. After discussing unrelated matters, the detective was asked about the murder case and said that there had not been much progress but, "He's [Bailey's] fucking playing some game at the minute. Oh, I'm telling you, he's some steps ahead of us at this stage. I would think that he's cute."

He then remarked that, "He has a temper threshold. He'd snap like that and beat the one he lived with. He has beaten her to a pulp a few times. In England, we reckon he did it as well." He also disclosed that "sex was the fucking motive" and that, "She did a runner if he got near her, you see, and that was it and he caught her."

That, of course, was an entirely accurate summation and based on fact, but whether the officer should be divulging that was another matter.

On the same day at 12.07 p.m., the detective phoned a T.D. in West Cork to discuss a letter of complaint that he had received from Bailey and Thomas in relation to their treatment by the Gardai during the murder investigation. He informed the politician that, "Hopefully his re-arrest is imminent, but it is not as imminent as he thinks it is."

Detective Garda Alpha spoke to a family member that day in two calls at 4.59 p.m. and 9.32 p.m. Apart from personal matters, he discussed the investigation in a small way in the first call but in more substance in the course of the second.

Det Gda Delta: Your man [Bailey] is playing an unbelievable game. He has now got to witnesses before we have got to them, believe it or not. He has copped on how we are asking anyone that he had any discussion with, and we now have discovered that there are at least two witnesses approached that shut up and wouldn't talk to us because he had been to them. There's a frightening game going on here. He's making all kinds of allegations against us to T.D.s and things like that … looking for inquiries into it – making out that we are making him to be the killer.

As such, that last statement was confirmation of Bailey's campaign of intimidation of witnesses; whether it was in some way divulging information that might have been improper in the conversation would be up to the Commission of investigation to decide. It came across much more like fair comment, as that was exactly what the prime suspect was doing.

But in the interim, the substance and the implications of the Bandon tapes would be tested as a result of the discovery order of Mr Justice John Hedigan in the upcoming High Court case taken by Bailey in the Four Courts in Dublin. This was now a situation in which the prime and only suspect for a brutal murder was not just suing the State but also had in addition active and serious complaints simultaneously under investigation by the Fennelly Commission and GSOC.

CHAPTER 18
THE STAR WITNESS
IMPLODES

Dublin – 2014–15

Ian Bailey and his legal team were now concentrating on the High Court action against the Garda Commissioner, the Minister for Justice and the State, buoyed by the 2012 decision of the Supreme Court appeal overturning the High Court decision to have the plaintiff extradited to France and the provision of the Bandon tapes, which on the face of it should have strengthened their case.

To assess the seriousness of the charges, the list is sufficient. Bailey was suing for wrongful arrest; false imprisonment; intentional infliction of emotional and psychological harm; harassment and intimidation; terrorising and oppressive behaviour; and breach of his constitutional rights. If proved, the damages would be astronomical, legal experts reckoning £1 million upwards, as the plaintiff was claiming that his life both personal and professional had been ruined and that he and his partner Jules Thomas had endured eighteen years of hell.

In 2003, Marie Farrell had faced Bailey across the courtroom in the Cork Circuit Court in the libel action and gave evidence against him which had been accepted as true by Mr Justice Patrick Moran. Now, at the historic Four Courts in Dublin, she would be giving evidence for his side against the State in front of a jury of eight men and four women, and Mr Justice John Hedigan, and would play the role of a star witness as she did in Cork but in a far bigger forum.

Sometime in advance of the action, I had been contacted by

the State solicitor's office to provide an affidavit to State counsels Paul O'Higgins and Luán O'Braonáin regarding my interview with the star witness in the articles published in 2004, which gave her account of the harassment and intimidation that she had suffered at the hands of the plaintiff during the course of the murder investigation, which she was now denying ever happened.

I told counsel that I believed that she had been telling me the truth at the time and had accepted money from the newspaper for her story, and had accompanied photographer Michael McSweeney to Kealfadda Bridge, where she said she had seen Ian Bailey on the night of the murder, and had been photographed at the site. Journalists through long experience can tell if an interviewee is telling the truth or lying. Over the next forty minutes, I delivered a lengthy affidavit on the subject, bolstered by the fact that in the aftermath of the publication of the articles Marie Farrell never expressed having an issue with the content.

The person I had interviewed, I recounted in early 2004, was an upset and frightened woman fraught and worried for her and her family's safety from the constant threats and harassment by Ian Bailey to get her to change her statement about seeing him in the early hours of the night of the murder. He had been responsible, she said, for ruining her business and leaving her in debt.

She hated and loathed him, and was in a constant state of anxiety about when and where he would appear to confront her one more time. No woman could either make this up or fake such an intense reaction unless she had been pursued and persecuted in the manner she so graphically described.

Everything she expressed to me at that time had the ring of truth. Her new version of events was in my view and in the opinion of other journalists who had covered the case just simply unbelievable. None of us could imagine how she could retain one ounce of credibility in a court setting or indeed outside it.

I left the office after giving my statement with the impression I had been in the presence of two powerful advocates, and as the plaintiff had also assembled an experienced team, that this would prove to be a battle royal in front of a highly accomplished High Court judge and of course an impartial jury. Even the most experienced observers could not possibly predict the outcome of a case that all acknowledged was of the most serious nature and the highest of stakes and cost to either side.

Twenty-one witnesses would be called on Bailey's side and seventy for the State, with some affidavits of those – including mine – being read to the jury.

Victory for Ian Bailey would have the effect of ensuring the impossibility of any future criminal action in the Irish State and as a result fatally undermine the prospects of the French investigation, which could no longer rely on vital witness statements taken by the Gardai. The murder of Sophie Toscan du Plantier would be consigned to a legal limbo and remain unsolved forever. In addition, there would be the distinct possibility of another inquiry into the conduct of the Gardai and severe political repercussions.

The allegations made against the principal Gardai were as the judge said of the gravest nature imaginable. One of the gravest amongst others was the allegation by the State solicitor for West Cork, Malachi Boohig, that after a meeting with senior Gardai and members of the murder investigation at Bandon Garda Station in the early stages of the investigation he had been approached to intervene with the Minister for Justice to put pressure on the DPP to have Ian Bailey charged with the murder.

Already, this action even before it got to court had racked up huge costs, and when the Garda operation to fulfil the discovery order of Mr Justice Hedigan was included, there would be little change out of millions of euros. The grim reality known to all parties involved was that no matter what the outcome, the bill was going to be picked up by the taxpayer, as the plaintiff was living off social welfare benefits and possessed no assets or property.

At the higher echelons of the defendants during an earlier pre-trial period, there was some informal discussion about the possibility of a settlement. This, of course, quite apart from the financial implications, was extremely risky in terms of political, legal and public perception, in a murder case which had dragged on for eighteen years.

In a lot of such cases, there are exploratory moves to see if a settlement is possible. In this case, it provided its own problems because sometime in the future, as the murder case itself was still open, if the plaintiff as a result of the emergence of new evidence was charged, put on trial for the offence and found guilty, then the State, the Garda Commissioner and Attorney General would have been responsible for rewarding a murderer by default.

In any event, a State official during a fishing expedition had casually sought a ball-park settlement figure and was given the sum of multiple lottery-winning figures which drove him out the door never to return.

There was another extraordinary element to this trial. Three retired officials of the office of the DPP had been subpoenaed by the plaintiff's side to give evidence, including former directors Eamon Barnes and James Hamilton and legal officer Robert Sheehan. Bailey's side also unsuccessfully attempted to have the forty-four-page DPP report justifying not charging the plaintiff for the murder entered into evidence.

All observers and interested parties could predict was high drama in the case, which opened on November 5, 2014 with a strong opening submission by Tom Creed S.C. for Bailey. The packed No. 3 court heard from counsel that the Gardai had targeted his client as early as four days after the murder. Information had been fed to the press on a constant basis, creating an atmosphere of fear and paranoia in the local community. His client had been threatened with death by an officer bringing him to Bandon Garda Station during his first arrest on February 10, 1997.

One sensational and serious allegation followed another; interference with a State solicitor in order to get Bailey charged by the DPP; he was being tracked by a Garda monitor as recently as two years ago. All has been on "Mr Bailey's life for the past eighteen years. It is worse than a life sentence." Marie Farrell, claimed counsel, had been coerced into making false statements against his client by members of the investigation team.

Summing up, Mr Creed said, "We are talking about deliberate behaviour, deliberate corrupt behaviour." His client's life had been ruined and he was looking for compensation for the eighteen lost years caused by this corruption based on what counsel described as "bogus evidence".

To say that his counsel was pushing out the boat would be a gross understatement, and there is little doubt that Ian Bailey was being represented by powerful advocates on a pro bono basis given the fact that he had lived most of the time in West Cork on state benefits. But he and they had to face an opposition legal team of the highest order in a contest in which no quarter would be given and last, including pre-trial hearings, sixty-four days over five months.

However, his side suffered an early setback when the DPP's forty-four-page report was ruled inadmissible and the contents could not be referred to, particularly in evidence being given by the former officials of the office. Those officials would also be precluded from giving their opinions about the core issues of the investigation under the rules of evidence but would be able to give testimony on the facts.

This ruling established without a shadow of a doubt that the DPP report was worthless in a legal context or any legal inquiry which would be confirmed in later events in both inquiry and trial findings. One of the reasons was that the contents and opinions expressed were extremely prejudicial to the Garda murder investigation. An attitude that should never have been the remit of such a report, which is supposed to be objective and dispassionate in assessment. That objectivity and dispassion would be required of the ex-officials when giving evidence to the court.

Ian Bailey had from the early days attempted to profit from the murder by his reporting of the crime, later by his suit against the newspapers and now by the High Court action. Would he at last get a huge payday? Would the Bandon tapes and Marie Farrell's evidence merely bolster or determine the success of the plaintiff's case? All questions that occupy the minds of the parties and the observers, impossible to predict in the early stages but that help to magnify the tensions that are part of the cut and thrust of a high-profile court case.

In an adversarial court context, opposing counsel will address each other as friends. My friend says this, that and the other. It is anything but friendly, more like a war in a legal context, during which every submission will be contested and attacked at every turn. To use a sporting analogy, say with rugby and scrums and mauls, the judge will act as the referee and punish one or another if they transgress the rules.

To underline and succinctly assess the implications of the case, Mr Justice Hedigan would later say that the case was one of the most serious to come before the High Court: "There are huge issues at stake here. If one side is correct, they have suffered a terrible injustice. If the other side is correct, they have suffered a terrible injustice and in the middle of it all is the interests of the State, you and I and everyone else in the rule of law in our country."

In other words, Ian Bailey was a victim of injustice or the Gardai he was suing were victims of the injustice. The plaintiff had made all kinds of allegations over the years about the improper conduct of the investigation team, many of which were presented to the media by both him and his solicitor Frank Buttimer. The latter, for this reason, stood out in the conservative world of the Irish legal community (most of whose members would avoid publicity) and adopted a strategy closer to the practice of American lawyers who often fight trials in both the media and in the courts. There was little doubt that he would be taken to task for such a strategy by the defence.

The evidence of Bailey and Jules Thomas would and did follow the old traditional pattern set in the libel trial and repeated in inquiries, in statements and to the media. It had all been heard before ad nauseam and nothing in this case would turn on the long-worn path of Bailey or his partner's version of events. The credibility of Marie Farrell's evidence would be paramount in determining the outcome.

In addition to her already publicised allegations of being put under pressure by Gardai to fabricate statements implicating Ian Bailey in the murder and being given blank statements for them to fill in, she had also made allegations of a sexual nature against two investigators, which were hugely damaging to them and by extension to their relations with their spouses and families.

In the course of my reporting on the murder, I had a lot of interaction with one Jim Fitzgerald and I could not have found a contact of better decency and integrity, and could not believe that he was capable of such a stupid act. If so, I would not believe it of the second, with whom I had no contact. This was not just ridiculous but outrageous, and for the life of me I could not understand how the plaintiff's lawyers could not have decided that this was a bridge too far in terms of presenting it as evidence.

Firstly, the allegations had nothing to do with the substance of Bailey's pleadings and were entirely irrelevant in the context of the case his legal team was putting forward. The suggestion that this Garda or any other respectable person would enter a ladies' toilet to expose themselves in a busy golf club with the risk of being witnessed and lose their livelihood was patently ludicrous.

Equally, the act of a man stripping naked as a tool of seduction made no sense, as it would most certainly have the opposite effect on the trembling damsel than the one intended. Quite apart from the fact that the house owner or key holder could have entered at any time and stumbled upon a tryst so unlikely it would not have made it into a soap opera script. There was an added problem with the stripping naked scenario, as the witness could not remember in which house it took place or the time or day or date when it allegedly occurred.

And to put it bluntly, the actors involved in this fantastic scenario would not at the time or any other time be cast as Romeo or Juliet. In addition, there was not even a scintilla of corroboration of the allegations. They should have been left where they originated in the imagination of the witness.

In the role of witness, Marie Farrell had many problems,

including two major ones. She had to justify and convince the jury that the new version of the truth was the correct one. She also had multiple versions of statements she made to remember, including to the murder investigation team, the McAndrew Report and to GSOC officers, all of which were of course available to the defence team. In relation to the transfer of the matter of intimidation to the Gardai instead of the plaintiff, she had made seventeen official complaints for intimidations and threats against Bailey which had been noted by the investigators and conveyed to the plaintiff.

In early December 2014, Marie Farrell came to the witness box and gave evidence which predictably attempted to fit the new narrative of her allegations that she had been put under pressure by the Gardai to falsely implicate Ian Bailey in the murder of Sophie Toscan du Plantier. Her mantra was that it did not matter what position she had adopted in the past – she was now telling the truth. It was of course that the new position she had taken had the potential to unravel at any time under the cosh of tough and clever cross-examination.

She had come to court as the star witness who would expose the corrupt behaviour of the Gardai and the use of bogus evidence as referred to by Bailey's counsel on the opening day. In the libel trial, admittedly over a decade ago, she was an attractive woman, but the intervening years had as with Bailey not been kind to her and her attitude had hardened. One thing was certain and not to be underestimated: she was going to be subjected to a robust cross examination by the defence.

That happened to a degree during the first week of her testimony but ramped up considerably in the second, prompting her to tell the court that it was turning into an assault on her personal life. She said that Bailey was not the man that she saw at Kealfadda Bridge and she had falsely identified him due to pressure put on her by Gardai, and consequently she had made up evidence that he had harassed and intimidated her, and signed blank statements for investigators. She admitted lying under oath at the libel trial of 2003. Any journalist that covered that case knew the opposite was true and her evidence had been accepted as that by a highly experienced judge.

Paul O'Higgins S.C. for the defence questioned the credibility of various aspects of her evidence, including lewd allegations against two senior Garda investigators and inconsistencies in statements she had made in the early stages of the murder investigation and to various internal reviews into the investigation.

She had claimed that one Garda, Maurice Walsh, had exposed himself to her in the ladies' toilet in a local golf club while his wife and her husband were in the bar. She said that Detective Garda Jim Fitzgerald had called to a house in Schull in which she was cleaning. She went upstairs and when she returned, he had stripped naked in a downstairs bedroom and was suggesting sex.

Counsel pointed out that both would strenuously deny that any such events ever happened. "How often do people parade naked in front of you?" enquired counsel. "I have had two episodes," she replied. Mr O'Higgins said these allegations would be dismissed as the "height of fantasy".

Counsel questioned her on the matter of signing blank witness statements in Ballydehob Garda Station in February 1997. Mr O'Higgins pointed out that she had told the McAndrew Report on the case in 2006 that she had never made any statement in Ballydehob, but had gone to Schull Station to sign four pages of prepared statements, as she said, "even though their contents were false". This indicated that the statements were not blank. Marie Farrell replied that she could not remember who she had told about the blank statements but "that is what happened".

What happened was that she had told the *Irish Daily Mirror* on March 7, 2012, that she had signed prepared statements. But subsequently, when Bailey told Vincent Browne on his TV show that she had signed blank statements, she changed her story a short time later to GSOC officers, telling them that she had signed blank statements and was now telling the court (and more pertinently the jury) that she had signed blank statements in

Balleydehob Station – not prepared statements in Schull Station.

Counsel suggested, "If you are really telling the truth, you don't have to remember what you said. The story does not vary." She replied, "I am telling the truth." Marie Farrell had already admitted that she had lied under oath in another court hearing and the question must have arisen in the minds of the jury that, if so, was she performing a similar act in this court hearing to suit the new narrative of her evidence?

There had been a vital matter at the heart of the murder investigation that until this point it had been impossible to resolve. That was regarding the identity of the man who was with the star witness on the night of the murder and with whom she had "romanced" on that occasion. That man could have provided corroboration of what she had seen in relation to the other man who had been at Kealfadda Bridge had she agreed to identify him at the early stages of the investigation.

Marie Farrell had consistently and resolutely refused to reveal his name. But on two occasions, one in 2002, she gave the name of a Longford musician and on another that of a former lover. She had lied about those men, who had not been with her on the night in question, in one of her statements to Gardai but later admitted in another statement that she wanted to get revenge on one who abandoned her after she had become pregnant by him.

Mr O'Higgins turned his attention to the matter. "I am asking you to inform the jury so we can get to the bottom of the truth of this. Who was the man you were with?"

"I won't tell you," she replied.

Mr Justice Hedigan then intervened. "Ms Farrell, this is the most serious case we have heard in this house for many years." He asked her to give the name.

"I'm not going to. I am not having nothing more to do with it."

Marie Farrell then grabbed her handbag and coat, left the witness box and hurried out of the court. The blood visibly drained from Ian Bailey's face and his legal team looked shell-shocked. She was followed by the plaintiff's solicitor Frank Buttimer, who scurried after her. Outside the court, the photographers and cameramen were busy taking shots of the solicitor and witness engaged in a street conference.

Saffron Thomas for the plaintiff filled the gap in the witness box until later Buttimer returned with Farrell in tow. The judge was not impressed. Mr Justice Hedigan addressed her from the bench. "The next walk out will be your last."

When recalled to the witness box, she said instead of naming the man in open court she would write it on a note for the judge. Mr Justice Hedigan was having none of that. He said that there would be no secret evidence. "So, who was it?"

"It was John Reilly; someone I knew from Longford. I knew him when I was a teenager."

Mr O'Higgins, resuming cross-examination, asked if he was an important person in her life. Not particularly, she replied, and he asked that if so, why all the secrecy, and she replied that she just wanted a quiet life at home and it just made life easier. Well, by her action she was not making her life easier, or for that matter Ian Bailey's or his legal team's. Apparently, according to her story, her mother said the man had gone to England and had since died.

The defence counsel had exposed a credibility gap in her evidence and if she thought for a moment that the cross-examination would get better, she was much mistaken. It would get worse, much worse.

Counsel then turned to another episode in her evidence, a statement made to Gardai. Mr O'Higgins suggested she was not telling the truth about the matter.

"I am telling the truth. I am gaining nothing by being here, only more personal aggravation, so I am not telling lies," she replied. In the statement to Gardai, she claimed that Ian Bailey had come into her shop, intimidated her and had personal information about her previous life in London, including her home address. She now told the court that this was not true, that she had made it up.

Mr O'Higgins begged to differ – it was true. Bailey had

obtained information on how she and her family came to be in West Cork. She had gotten into trouble with the social services in London and was effectively "on the run". Marie Farrell should have paused for thought but did not and insisted that this was not true, claiming that she had not got into any trouble. Someone had complained about her but, "It was investigated and found to be a false complaint."

Mr O'Higgins did not hesitate; he could have asked her to consider if she was telling the truth, but he did not. "Can I suggest to you that this is an outright, barefaced lie to the jury." What he knew and she had forgotten was that she had given a totally different version of that story to GSOC officers when interviewed in Longford two years previously, and now a totally contradictory version to the ladies and gentlemen of the jury. There was no problem about written records – it was on videotape.

She also must have forgotten that her shop assistant Geraldine O'Brien was present and had witnessed the incident during which Marie Farrell had become upset enough to ask her that when she was going out to a nearby shop, to contact her Garda handler for help. Any observer present with a better recall of the facts of this incident knew that a big moment was coming up, but even if not, it was like watching a play or a film and knowing exactly what was going to happen in the next scene, like when the character played by Janet Leigh in Hitchcock's *Psycho* gets into the shower in the room in the Bates Motel.

Counsel gave a signal to have the videotape played to the court. It was a section in which she told the off-camera GSOC officers that Bailey had come into her shop in Schull and told her that he was an investigative journalist and knew the reason why she and her family had left London.

She recounted that she had been involved in a fraudulent claim of income support and housing benefits claimed on the status of a sole parent. There had been a dispute over money with Chris Farrell's sister and husband, who had been working in a double-glazing business in London.

Afterwards, she had been reported to the social welfare authorities, who told her to pay back the money, amounting to £27,000. The family fled London overnight and that was how they ended up in West Cork.

The videotape paused and a flustered star witness blurted out a pathetic response: "The evidence I gave was the truth, I am getting confused with fact and fiction there." She was not getting confused about anything but had delivered to the court a perfect demonstration of the cliché that no good liar can afford to have a bad memory.

Mr Justice Hedigan addressed her. He warned, "I would like you to give very careful consideration to the manner in which you are giving evidence ... there are very serious legal sanctions for perjury."

"I am telling the truth," she replied.

"Don't say anything. Think about it overnight," the judge said.

However much the lady protested on the matter of the truth, the stark reality was that the credibility of the witness who the judge described as the central plank of Bailey's case had been undermined when she had been caught brazenly lying to the court.

It did not matter what she had said beforehand or subsequently, nothing that passed her lips could be believed. In those fifteen minutes, including the ten of the videotape being shown, Ian Bailey's case had suffered huge damage. It would remain to be seen if it would be capable of being recovered.

She had of course told other lies and would continue to do so of less telling consequence. She had complained that she need not have been in the court. "I am gaining nothing by being here ... I am not telling lies." This was yet another porky.

Geraldine O'Brien, her one-time teenage shop assistant who worked in 1997 in Farrell's shop in Schull, later testified that between November 2013 and February 2014, during a conversation with her former employer about fees for a course Geraldine had been running in Cork, Farrell had told her there was a case coming up in which Ian Bailey was involved and he would be getting, she was told, substantial money, maybe a couple of million, and Farrell said she would get some of that. Marie Farrell denied that any such conversation had taken place.

There had been little or no media speculation for legal imperatives about the reason for her dramatic volte-face before the case. Bailey had described it as "coming over to the side of good", an explanation that would have been ridiculously self-serving and laughable if it was not such a serious matter. It was also indicative of his expectations of the outcome.

Earlier in the proceedings, Farrell had continued to lie, this time about a matter in my witness affidavit which had been read into the court record. It was put to her that she received £1,500 for the interview given to me and published in the *Star on Sunday* newspaper. She replied that this was not the case, saying that she had only got £150 and had donated it to a local football club. I had been given the cheque to post to her and it was made out for £1,500. She had no good reason to lie about this fact, but she could not resist.

After she joined Ian Bailey, Marie Farrell became incapable of telling the truth about anything, as indeed was her then-new mentor, the professor of mendacity, who had just received a stiff lesson on relying on the word of a witness with such a casual and destructive disregard for veracity. He now must have realised – unless he was in total denial – that she had potentially derailed any possibility of success for his action.

The case would trundle on into the New Year, with the all-too-familiar and well-travelled details of the murder and the libel case evidence being revisited, with several witnesses from the Cork Circuit Court reappearing in the Dublin High Court almost exactly twelve years later.

It became quickly apparent that the plaintiff's legal team had a mountain to climb in the wake of the implosion of their star witness. Bailey's allegations of conspiracy and ill treatment at the hands of the Gardai had little or no credible corroboration. The dreadlocked ex-British Army man Martin Graham's accusation that his Gardai handlers had given him cannabis in exchange for framing Bailey was not supported by independent evidence even from the Bandon tapes.

He did not contact the Gardai until after Bailey's first arrest in 1997 and it became clear that he was in fact acting not for his handlers but for Bailey in an enterprise to entrap them in a corrupt act by supplying Graham with drugs. This, the witness claimed, was part of an effort to soften up Bailey to get him to admit to the crime. He then told Bailey he was "being stitched up".

Not even the Bandon tapes could support that allegation, as the Gardai had quickly neutralised the informant's role. In every sense, Graham was a weak witness with doubtful credibility. He was also in poor physical shape and during cross-examination had paused for four minutes before answering.

On January 23, 2015, the next most potentially damaging evidence on behalf of Bailey against the Gardai and the State was ventilated. This involved State solicitor for West Cork Malachi Boohig, retired officials, former DPP Eamon Barnes, senior legal officer Robert Sheehan and former DPP James Hamilton.

Boohig had alleged that after a meeting in Bandon Garda Station in 1998 with leading members of the murder investigation team, he had been approached by the late Garda Chief Superintendent Sean Camon to arrange a meeting with his former classmate, the then Minister for Justice John O'Donoghue, for the purpose of increasing pressure to get Bailey charged.

The State solicitor had not made contemporaneous notes or a memo of the meeting, nor did he make any written complaint to the DPP or the Garda Commissioner about the alleged approach which, if it did take place, he must have known was an illegal act.

The memo he did make in October of 2011 at the request of the then DPP James Hamilton was both inaccurate and contradictory, stating that the meeting took place in 1991/92 (four years before the murder), and further memos which amended the date of the meeting to March 9, 1998 gave three different versions of what went on at the meeting in Bandon. Notes and memos taken at the time of such events are the only ones that count in a court case, as ruled correctly by the judge. Otherwise, the witness must rely on their own recollection of the event.

Boohig's recollection was hazy and confusing. He remembered being called to the meeting by phone by Dermot Dwyer. When he arrived, he said he was brought upstairs to the office of the Chief Superintendent of Bandon Station where there were a number of Gardai present, including some he did not know. He was not sure if the Chief Superintendent was Sean Camon or whether his status was Assistant Commissioner. He thought that it was Detective Garda Superintendent Dermot Dwyer who chaired the meeting. Detective Sergeant Liam Hogan was also present. There was a suggestion that "a Martin McQuinn was also present, but I am not sure he was there".

He was not sure if it was McQuinn or Dwyer who was the Chief Superintendent of Bandon. There was, he added, a brief review of the murder investigation file and evidence gathered, and it was clear to him that the Gardai present were unhappy that the DPP had opted not to charge Bailey. It was suggested that certain submissions should be put to the Director to convince him that a charge of murder would be appropriate. All perfect good practice and legally correct.

He then testified that when leaving (outside the office), he was approached by Detective Chief Superintendent Camon and he believed that Detective Superintendent Dwyer was also there, and the former said he understood that he (Boohig) was in college with the Minister for Justice John O'Donoghue and would he contact him to approach the Director (of the DPP) to get him to prefer a charge. He replied that this was completely inappropriate, as the Director was autonomous and made decisions without any interference, and he had then left. Detective Chief Superintendent Camon was now deceased and Dermot Dwyer would in evidence deny any such suggestion as made by Boohig about an approach.

The following morning, Boohig said he rang the then Director Eamon Barnes and informed him of the approach, and also told the same to Robert Sheehan, the then legal officer in charge of dealing with the investigation file at the DPP's office.

Some months later, not specified by date, Boohig said he had travelled to Dublin and met with Robert Sheehan and Mr Barnes in the DPP offices. There was a longer meeting with the former and one lasting about five minutes with the latter. During those two meetings there was, he said, no mention of the highly controversial approach made to him at the Bandon meeting with the murder investigators.

The extraordinary fact was that there had been no record taken in either meeting by the State solicitor or by the then DPP or the chief legal officer in relation to the second one in Dublin. Regarding the phone calls made by Boohig the day after the Bandon meeting, Sheehan had written a note of his call, had it typed up and then passed it on to the DPP. It was not suggested that what Boohig had alleged did not happen but his recollection in evidence would have to give a credible and accurate version to an evidential standard that would be accepted by the court.

Retrospective memos taken so many years later, in 2011 or beyond, could or would not carry any weight in a court trial, as Mr Justice Hedigan pointed out: "Contemporaneous notes are set at gold standard as they tend to be of a high probative assistance in recording events accurately. Notes taken years afterwards are regarded as not acceptable."

Further, what was considered all these years later as such a serious matter did not prompt the then DPP to notify the Attorney General at the time to have it investigated.

This cast doubt over the whole matter, quite apart from the poor recollection of the witness being entered into evidence, and begged the question of whether anyone in the chain from the DPP's office to the Attorney General's and thence to the Bailey defence team in the Supreme Court appeal had read those 2011 memos properly in regard to their legal efficacy and contradictory versions?

There had been much made of the matter in the media by Bailey's legal team at the time of the Supreme Court hearing of it being a scandal and proof of improper conduct by three senior Gardai. The real scandal was that those Gardai had never been given a chance or a channel by which they could defend themselves from a serious accusation and had to live with having no right of reply until this case three years or so on.

Eamon Barnes, now sixteen years in retirement from the position of DPP, testified that he had been on holiday in Spain when he read a news item in *The Irish Times* about the extradition hearing in the High Court which had ordered the surrender of Ian Bailey to France for the murder but stayed pending a Supreme Court appeal. In Paris on the way home, he rang the DPP's office and spoke to an official. His worry was that the French file was based on information from the Garda investigation. Even if it had been, this opinion did not take account of a French investigation which had commenced in 2008.

In that event, he thought that the whole story of the Bailey case had not been made known to the French authorities. He contacted his successor James Hamilton later and said the matter should be brought to the attention of the Attorney General for consideration in advance of the Supreme Court appeal proceedings. Hamilton asked him to put his concerns in writing. He conveyed them by email to the Director in October 2011.

While he admitted to the court that he could not be sure of the accuracy of some of his recollections, he felt clear about the central facts. Nonetheless, he needed to refer to and read out the contents of the email, a copy of which he had brought with him to court. Reading from the document, he recounted that Malachi Boohig had contacted him about a matter he did not want to discuss over the phone. "He said he would come to Dublin to meet me and he did."

He continued, "I expressed my gratitude and praise to Mr Boohig for his actions in coming to me, which I assumed was because he wanted me to be aware that the Garda investigation was lacking in objectivity and was indeed heavily prejudiced, and to forewarn me of the possibility of further pressure being brought to bear on the office."

The narrative by Barnes of this meeting totally contradicted Boohig's earlier evidence, which was that he had communicated details of the event by phone, and when he later met the DPP for five minutes it was not discussed.

Even if the second version of the meeting was correct, again it was difficult to comprehend why the State solicitor for West Cork and the Director of Public Prosecutions did not take one note or memo regarding the substance of that conversation or any other on the subject but instead waited twelve years to do so at the request of James Hamilton. There might have been some excuse with a five-minute meeting, but the evidence of Barnes in relation to his version indicated a much longer meeting of which there could be no excuse for not having a written record or even a simple memo.

He also testified that he could not remember if there was anyone else present at the meeting. It was his usual practice, he said, to have another member of staff present at such meetings. Well, if the former Director could not, then the State solicitor for West Cork surely could. But Boohig had remembered a completely different version of a meeting with Barnes, in which the alleged Bandon incident had never been mentioned. Confusing would be inadequate to describe it – an evidential mess would be closer.

CHAPTER 19
THE TURNING OF THE
DEFENCE SCREW

Dublin – 2015

Barnes had included criticism of the Garda investigation in his reading of the mail, which halted the proceedings after an objection by Luán O'Braonáin, defence counsel.

In the absence of the jury, Mr Justice Hedigan said that the opinion expressed went to the core issue of the trial and so was up to the jury to decide, not Mr Barnes. Having read the mail, "It leapt out of the page at me of being a highly prejudicial opinion … expressed on a matter which I referred to earlier as the core issue before the court, the ultimate issue."

The last paragraph of the email, which was in effect a further attack on the Garda murder investigation, displaying an animus totally inappropriate for any DPP, was ruled inadmissible.

The highly prejudicial opinion of Mr Barnes that struck the judge followed his other line, also not evidence but the opinion that: "There is now apparently a real possibility that Bailey may be charged in France and perhaps receive a lengthy prison sentence."

This is what was ruled out: "Presumably on the basis, inter alia of 'evidence' and conclusions provided what I regarded of having been a thoroughly flawed and prejudiced Garda investigation culminating in a grossly improper attempt to achieve or even enforce a prosecutorial decision which accorded with that prejudice. I felt accordingly that as a matter of ordinary justice I was obliged to bring the matter to appropriate attention."

From this statement, the prejudice as noted by the judge was on the part of the former DPP and clearly against the Garda murder investigation. That prejudice was even more emphasised by the witness's assessment of the Bandon event, the language of which had leapt out at the judge. If Barnes had really thought that, then why had he buried it for such a long time and left a paperless trail?

Also, such a statement was not just highly prejudicial to a murder investigation, which had produced a file amounting to 2,000 pages, but couched in language utterly and entirely inappropriate for any public servant holding such an important office.

The problem in the High Court hearing was as with the report and evidence of the retired DPP, and this would rear its head with the evidence following of Robert Sheehan that they could not refrain from opinion, bias and speculation, instead of sticking to the facts, even in a court setting. All raised troubling questions about the content of the DPP report in which prejudice or bias of any kind has no right to reside.

In advance, Mr Justice Hedigan made it clear to the plaintiff's counsel Tom Creed about the problem of biased opinion. There was to be no reference to the Sheehan report, no more than the French assessment of the case contained in the EAW warrant that might be relied upon by the defence. Both were inadmissible. Regarding Sheehan's evidence, he was to stick to the facts and was not to express an opinion as to issues that were for the jury to decide.

The judge could not have put it more simply: "It is misleading to a jury to refer to something which is inadmissible and which they cannot be allowed to see."

Well, to state the obvious, any legal official in any grade – not to mind a high one in the office of the DPP – ought to have a firm grasp of such a basic rule of evidence and should not have to be reminded of it in a High Court setting, or any other court for that matter.

After being called to the stand, it did not take long for Robert Sheehan to get into trouble by referring to notes that were not contemporaneous and wandering into the territory of opinion which had just a short while before been the subject of the court's attention. Tom Creed complained that his witness was completely hamstrung. Understandably, Mr Justice Hedigan was tiring of having to remind the counsel and witness of simple rules of evidence.

"He is not hamstrung. There is no difficulty at all. He is here to give evidence of a specific nature. He is trying to go too far and too wide in ways that are no help to the case whatsoever. He is not hamstrung you just keep trying to get back at a ruling that has been made. Nobody else's opinion of whether he thinks the Gardai have made a mess of it or whether they got themselves into a conspiracy, none of that is admissible. None of it. His opinion is of no relevance."

The counsel's frustration might have been understandable even if he was wrong. A plank of his client's case which must have appeared strong in advance was being splintered by witnesses who given their status and background in criminal law, familiarity with the rules of evidence, say the least of it, ought to have known better. In several instances with Sheehan, the judge acknowledged it was not as a result of a leading question by counsel but blurted out by the witness.

That Robert Sheehan was an opinionated witness was evidenced when he suggested to Mr Justice Hedigan that the notes he had were an accurate reflection of material submitted to the office from the Gardai and therefore different than contemporaneous notes or later taken notes – "apples and oranges" – Luán O'Braonáin was quick to make an objection..

"The court made a ruling that the witness is trying to make a legal submission to the court. That is inappropriate."

Mr Sheehan, it appeared from his inappropriate submission to the judge using the phrase "apples and oranges", was fond of fruit analogies.

In his report ruled inadmissible on page twelve in relation to the arrests in February 1997, he opined:

"It should be noted that anything said by Bailey during the course of his detention may be inadmissible on the basis that much that was put to him was gleaned from Jules Thomas during the course of her unlawful detention and the fruit of the poison tree rule might well apply."

Apart from the analogy, this opinion would be proved wrong even without being discussed later in the proceedings.

The way Robert Sheehan was giving evidence was causing continued problems for both the judge – despite his rulings – and the defence protests. Luán O'Braonáin requested an adjournment in the absence of the jury members, who were about to leave for the weekend. This was granted and the jury left the courtroom. Mr O'Braonáin began his submission by pointing out that the ruling was to be respected while the jury was present, and not to be subverted or treated with contempt. "The witness who is a lawyer knows what the position is, as does Mr Creed."

He said that Sheehan was going through the matters contained in the report which the court had ruled out. "As far as the statements are concerned, this witness actually knows nothing about what happened in Schull, in Skibbereen other than going through materials that went to him. Those materials have been ventilated before the jury and are going to be further addressed by witnesses who were actually there and it is (the jury's) function to deal with the matters in that way rather than the function of the witness on the basis of hearsay."

The witness, counsel continued, had been asked about February 1997: was there a discussion of matters other than Marie Farrell? "He said there was and that included that Mr Bailey would kill again imminently and that they were concerned about that." Then the witness goes on to say, "I don't know if I am allowed to express an opinion on that." Well now, suggested counsel, firstly he knew well that he was not allowed to express an opinion on that.

"Saying in front of the jury, I don't know if I am allowed to express an opinion, does nothing but to convey to the jury that he has an opinion on it and that is clear in the context in which he is giving his evidence; the witness's opinion is one that is at variance with the position that is adopted by the Gardai and he is doing it in a different way, the thing that the court has ruled should not be done."

The witness, counsel said, was making references to the forty-four-page report in relation to the matters when the court had made abundantly clear that was not to be done. The defence counsel was taking the transgression of the court ruling so seriously as to have the jury sent away and the case stopped.

Luán O'Braonáin continued, stating that were it not for the amount of time and resources that had been put into the trial, this was a case in which an application to the court could be made for the discharge of the jury with costs at this juncture. This demonstrated the seriousness of the transgression of the court ruling by the retired legal officer, recognised by the court as the chief author of the report, to justify not charging Bailey with the murder.

Mr O'Braonáin was blunt about his view of the way the witness had approached giving evidence. "It is simply not acceptable for the court's rulings to be treated with the contempt they are being treated and it is being done in a way that is absolutely bound to prejudice the jury. I wonder I have to say whether Mr Sheehan's evidence should be heard in the absence of the jury to see whether or not there is actually anything in what Mr Sheehan has to say that is relevant and therefore admissible before the jury."

The problem seemed to be, according to what the defence counsel was submitting, that Sheehan's notes in preparation for giving evidence were indelibly linked to the report that he had written and he could not appear to be able to avoid reference to a report that was nothing more than opinion by adding further opinion in his replies to plaintiff's counsel. In doing so, the witness was contravening the court's ruling not once but twice.

Mr Creed said that he could not respond immediately and would need time, and the judge said he had until Tuesday morning. Mr O'Braonáin said that the rulings of the court should be strictly adhered to and there were ways which he illustrated in which the witness could give evidence of facts without straying into the territory of opinion.

The judge said that he had overlooked some matters in this respect just to attempt to keep the trial going without too much interruption, but if continued he would seriously consider discharging the jury.

Mr Justice Hedigan expressed himself most unimpressed with some of the phrases used by Sheehan, like "lo and behold", and regarded it as melodramatic language, completely inappropriate for somebody who had worked in the DPP's office. He wanted Mr Creed to make sure that the witness was controlled. Mr Creed suggested that it was Mr O'Braonáin who said that and not the witness.

The judge rejected that out of hand. "The witness did say that, he certainly did say it, and I must say my eyebrows rose very high when I saw that language completely inappropriate for a public servant to be giving, somebody who worked in the DPP's office. Dispassionate evidence is what is to be given by this witness and any other witness."

He said that Mr Barnes had given evidence in this manner and he wanted this witness to be controlled. Mr Justice Hedigan then unequivocally stated the seriousness of the matter. "I am not making an idle threat. If I do form the impression and I have already had concerns about this that there is a level of unfairness developing in relation to this matter, I will discharge the jury. I don't want to do that but I will do so because unless I can get a decision from this jury that is entirely fair and made in accordance with the evidence then I don't think they should be allowed to continue to a verdict at all."

The evidence continually wandering into prejudice of the former DPP legal officer, who had handled the murder file from the beginning, had in effect almost brought the trial to a halt. The defence counsel Luán O'Braonáin had pointed out that he was a lawyer and should have known better.

Mr Justice Hedigan had gone much further in his assessment

of using language totally inappropriate for his previous position. Interestingly, Sheehan later was further cross-examined, as follows, by Luán O'Braonáin:

Mr O'Braonáin: You had a conversation with Malachi Boohig, who gave evidence, I think, on Friday in relation to a meeting that he attended in Bandon Garda Station, about which he spoke to the ladies and gentlemen of the jury?

Mr Sheehan: I did indeed.

Mr O'Braonáin: I think in the course of your discussion with him he indicated to you at the conclusion of the meeting that he was followed out by I think Assistant Commissioner McQuinn, who said to him that he knew that Mr Boohig was a classmate of Minister O'Donoghue and could he exercise influence?

Mr Sheehan: That's correct.

Mr O'Braonáin: You subsequently, I think, made a note of that indication to you?

Mr Sheehan: Yes, I did. I received a phone call on March 9, 1998; I dictated into a Dictaphone on the same date I got. The typed record was returned to me the following day, March 10.

Mr O'Braonáin: Which is dated March 10?

Mr Sheehan: And I signed it March 10.

Mr O'Braonáin: Thank you, Mr Sheehan.

In fairness to Robert Sheehan, he was the only one who made a note of anything at the time. But it exposed a further contradiction in Boohig's evidence to the court, in which he stated that it was

Detective Chief Superintendent Camon who made the approach and not Assistant Commissioner McQuinn, of whom he said he was not sure was even there.

In his original memo Boohig incorrectly stated that the Bandon meeting took place four years before the murder. That memo read:

"Having walked out into the hallway I was followed out by Detective Superintendent Camon and Detective Superintendent Dwyer. Both stated in very strong terms that I would have to persuade the Director to direct a prosecution. Detective Superintendent Dwyer stated he was aware that I had attended college and studied with John O'Donoghue, the Minister for Justice, and I should use that connection to see if something could be done."

After that meeting, according to Boohig and confirmed by Robert Sheehan, the State solicitor rang the DPP office, spoke to him about the meeting and said that it was Assistant Commissioner Martin McQuinn who had made the approach. Sheehan's memo read:

"On leaving the room, Malachi was followed by Martin McQuinn, who said to him he knew Malachi was a classmate of John O'Donoghue and could he use his influence to assist in getting Bailey charged."

Boohig had nominated three different people for the role of making the approach. This was a man who had made a complaint to the DPP about senior Gardai with unblemished careers which could have been ruined if proven, but because of the inexplicable contradictions in his versions of the alleged incident, his evidence was shorn of credibility. Sean Camon was deceased, and Martin McQuinn was at the time terminally ill. Dermot Dwyer was alive and sitting in the court. The reputations of all three had been at stake and much maligned by publicity in the media. Thus far, based on what had been presented to the court on the matter, Dermot Dwyer had little to worry about.

The third ex-DPP witness, the former Director James Hamilton, was next in the box. For a good length of his evidence, he admirably stuck to the facts. In relation to the Bandon meeting, he said he had been aware it had taken place two years before he became DPP but not in any great detail.

He said that he had no direct knowledge of it other than that which he knew from the files, but when it was brought to his attention by Mr Barnes, he had to draw it to the attention of the Attorney General. He told her about his concern about the possibility of a miscarriage of justice. This was all factual evidence but inevitably he strayed into the area of opinion.

When telling the court about his communication with the AG, he said he was concerned because, "I believed there had been a lot of shortcomings in the investigation which I had made known my view in the memorandum of analysis which was sent to the Gardai."

The AG's advice was to send it to the Central Authority for transmission to the French authorities and to Mr Bailey's solicitor, which is what he did. He also testified that the decision not to prosecute Bailey was not a final decision, meaning the case had not been finally disposed of by his office. This was a hugely important statement, as the opposite had been argued by Bailey's defence in extradition proceedings.

Before cross-examination, Mr O'Braonáin objected to the witness remarking about shortcomings in the investigation, which statement was inadmissible, and it was a reference to the forty-four-page report also ruled inadmissible. Counsel also pointed out that the Central Authority and the Attorney General were not responsible for either mutual assistance or execution of EAWs. This was the responsibility of the Minister for Justice. Mr Justice Hedigan agreed and suggested that media reports that were alleged to be based on information from the Gardai were unfair.

Mr Hamilton said that the report had gone out as his and it had analysed what the office saw as shortcomings in the evidence and he did not know to what extent he could say anything about the evidence as distinct from criticising the investigation. This was the core of the issue; the report indeed focused on the alleged shortcomings of the investigation and the evidence based on an opinionated critique which the court had adjudged as prejudicial to the defendants.

The judge pointed out that it was still possible for Hamilton to say he had read the whole file from beginning to end and concluded that there was insufficient evidence to warrant a prosecution, which is fact. But bringing in shortcomings is opinion and therefore a problem. As Mr O'Braonáin observed, the judge agreed there should be no reference to a document that was ruled out.

There was further argument about various issues in the absence of the jury and at the finish the judge summed up by saying that the reference to shortcomings in the investigation should be dropped and also media reports relating to the matter. There should be no reference to the analysis document which had become a bête noire of the testimony of the ex-DPP officials and subject of incessant objections by the defence.

Otherwise, the judge said the evidence was fine, and so it transpired. Mr Hamilton had performed far better than his former colleague Sheehan and ex-DPP Barnes.

He had made clear in his evidence of his desire to have the report forwarded to the French authorities at the time, obviously after discussion with Mr Barnes, on the basis that it was somehow invidious and unfair that the French authorities should act without the rationale behind the DPP's decision not to prosecute. As defence counsel pointed out, the DPP was not a party to that process by law, no more than the Attorney General. Mr Hamilton, counsel said simply, did not know what information was in the hands of the French side.

The reality outside the court proceedings was that by 2011, the

French had been conducting their own inquiries for three years and apart from receiving assistance from the Garda investigation file, had interviewed witnesses and received mutual assistance all in conformity with European legislation covering the area and from the designated agencies. The DPP's office had absolutely no role to play in this and no reason whatsoever to assume that the much-disputed report would have been of any benefit, which it could not possibly have been considering its prejudiced content.

The releasing of the report and the details of the Bandon meeting to the Attorney General would end up at the Justice Department and ultimately with Bailey's defence team in the Supreme Court appeal, and possibly assist a refusal of surrender by that court. If that had been the motivation of Eamon Barnes and certainly not James Hamilton's, who simply did his duty, it had succeeded in a limited way. As Mr Barron, the State counsel, in the appeal noted, it was irrelevant to the issues involved, which was certainly correct.

As for the allegations of Malachi Boohig, Mr Hamilton was perfectly correct to inform the Attorney General, as should have been done by his predecessor in 1998. He would also be reliant on the advice of the AG on how to proceed and could never have envisaged what would transpire from thereon.

But the memos he had received at his own invitation from Malachi Boohig, Eamon Barnes and Robert Sheehan and had passed on contained the contradictions and prejudice mentioned above, which would have provided a formidable obstacle to an inquiry by whatever relevant legal agency. The other problem was that not one of the senior Gardai had been contacted by any agency at any time to defend themselves or even offer some explanation about what had happened at the meeting, which was their legal and constitutional right.

There was nothing wrong with Sheehan's memo; it was helpful and exposed one further contradiction, the fact that it was the only record in a paperless trail.

Frank Buttimer, Bailey's solicitor, took the stand at the end of January 2015 and told the plaintiff's counsel Jim Duggan that he had begun to represent Ian Bailey in 2004, after his previous solicitor Con Murphy was elevated to the Circuit Court as a judge. He recalled issuing a letter to Marie Farrell stating that if she did not retract her claims of being threatened and harassed by his client, proceedings would be taken against her and an application for costs.

Her solicitor Ernest Cantillon replied by letter stating that his client had been engaging in threatening and abusive behaviour towards Marie Farrell and there would be no retraction, no undertaking and, if Bailey continued his behaviour, a counter-suit and injunction would be issued on behalf of his client. Mr Duggan then brought him to the time in April 2005 when he had been contacted by phone by Marie Farrell.

Buttimer told the court that at first, he was reluctant to engage with her due to the notice of proceedings he had issued and he did not want to engage in any questionable conduct, but he decided to meet her; in total, there had been three meetings and numerous phone calls between them over the next few months. The first meeting occurred on May 10, the next on June 7 – both in his office in Cork – and a third on July 27 in a car park in Clonakilty.

He organised to have independent legal advice for Marie Farrell from the solicitor Donal Daly. He wrote a letter to her in September 2005 to express his client Ian Bailey's appreciation for her being so forthcoming and that he would not be initiating the proceedings mentioned in the letter in March 2004. As a result of his client's concerns about what Marie Farrell had said at the meetings in October 2005, Buttimer said he wrote a letter to the Minister for Justice and the Garda Commissioner outlining Bailey's complaint concerning the matter.

While the withdrawal of the proceedings would naturally be in order for any proposed co-operation by Marie Farrell with Ian Bailey in the future in the normal course of events, they had little chance of succeeding as she had registered seventeen official complaints to the Gardai about Bailey's threatening behaviour with witnesses such as Geraldine O'Brien and Garda officers to corroborate the fact. On foot of those complaints, Gardai visited Bailey and requested him to desist, a request he ignored.

After some discussion about the extradition proceedings involving Bailey, the solicitor said he told his client that he could not depart the country even to his native England: "If he sets foot outside the Republic of Ireland into any country where the EAW systems operate [he is liable to] immediate arrest, which include more than twenty countries ... I don't claim to have the greatest expertise in relation to the matter, but Mr Bailey cannot risk, he cannot depart this country."

He was then cross-examined by defence counsel Luán O'Braonáin, who would first concentrate on the whole matter of the meetings with Marie Farrell to somewhat establish what went on at those meetings and during the numerous phone calls and the documentation concerning all.

> **Luán O'Braonáin:** "So the documentation that was discovered by the defendants had redactions in it and bore a documents identification number. Do you see that?"

> **Frank Buttimer:** "If you say so. I can't comment."

> **Luán O'Braonáin:** "I am sorry, surely you can comment. Isn't the position that you had in your possession statements that had been made by Marie Farrell long before the process of discovery had been entered into in these proceedings?"

> **Frank Buttimer:** "Statements at that time were given to us on foot of a discovery order made with the consent of the DPP."

> **Luán O'Braonáin:** "You see what the affidavit does, Mr Buttimer, I think you may recognise this, it conveys the impression that you did not have any of Marie Farrell's statements to the Gardai, for instance, during the time that you were meeting her in 2005?"

Frank Buttimer: "I did not."

Luán O'Braonáin: "You did not have any statement?"

Frank Buttimer: "Absolutely."

Luán O'Braonáin: "So you did not have any of the statements [to the Gardai] that were made by Marie Farrell?"

Frank Buttimer: "No."

This was a clear and forthright position on behalf of the plaintiff's solicitor that he did not have any of her statements to the Gardai during their meetings in 2005 and that he was absolutely certain of the fact.

Counsel referred to Buttimer's own affidavit of discovery:

Luán O'Braonáin: "'All documentation in relation to and regarding contact between Marie Farrell and the defendants between the dates in question.' And then: 'All contact by and on behalf of the plaintiff.' Do you see that?"

Mr Buttimer replied that the affidavit had been made after the commencement of the trial. Counsel then referred to another section of the discovery affidavit:

Luán O'Braonáin: "I reviewed various statements given by Marie Farrell in the course of her visit on the 7th. Okay?"

Frank Buttimer: "Um hmm."

Luán O'Braonáin: "It is clear that she did not make a statement on the day she was door-stepped by Garda Kelleher when he brought her to his house. There is, however, a memorandum committed to writing which is not signed by Marie Farrell but is witnessed by a member of the Garda Síochána."

Frank Buttimer: "Yes."

Luán O'Braonáin: "You have at this stage Marie Farrell's statements."

Frank Buttimer: "Yes, I must have had."

Luán O'Braonáin: "And a memo of the interview."

Frank Buttimer: "I must have had."

Luán O'Braonáin: "You indicated to the ladies and gentlemen of the jury about ten minutes ago that you did not."

Frank Buttimer: "Yes."

Luán O'Braonáin: "Whereas in fact the position is that you did."

Frank Buttimer: "If you say so, I accept that is the case."

Luán O'Braonáin: "I am sorry, that is what you say in your own attendance."

Frank Buttimer: "Okay, fine."

After another short exchange, counsel came to the nub of the matter in relation to both Bailey and his solicitor's affidavits:

Luán O'Braonáin: "What they conveyed to the defendants, to the court or whoever read them, is the only way you got those documents was in discovery in November 2013, whereas in fact you had all those materials throughout 2005, if not earlier?"

Frank Buttimer: "I can't say."

The defence counsel was having none of the vague answers like "I can't say" when the witness could say when confronted with the evidence of his own affidavit of discovery. It was abundantly clear, counsel proposed from the witness's attendance notes, that he did have the statements. Buttimer said that he had got discovery from the DPP in 2006 and this when he got the statements which were the creation of the Garda Síochána.

Whatever he said, he was not going to best the defence counsel, who was at the very top of his game and obviously had done a great deal of homework:

> **Luán O'Braonáin:** "With respect, Mr Buttimer, that cannot be right because if you only got them in 2006, how are you making notes in 2005 about going through the statements with Marie Farrell?"

The witness could not say; it may be something she said to him, he just did not know, he added. Counsel pointed out that this was not what he had said in his notes but that he had reviewed various statements given by Marie Farrell to the Gardai. Counsel responded by saying if he had said that he had reviewed various statements given to the Gardai, then he must have had them. Buttimer replied that he just could not say:

> **Luán O'Braonáin:** "Now can I suggest to you, Mr Buttimer, whenever you refer to copies of the statements made by Marie Farrell that those were statements made to the Gardai?"

> **Frank Buttimer:** "Yes, they could well …"

> **Luán O'Braonáin:** "Okay, you had them in 2005 to send to Mr Daly?"

> **Frank Buttimer:** "Sounds like it, I just don't recall. I accept it."

Luán O'Braonáin: "Okay. You see this is important, Mr Buttimer, because Marie Farrell says she didn't have the statements during that process. Do you understand that?"

Frank Buttimer: "I …"

Luán O'Braonáin: "Where did you get the statements?"

Frank Buttimer: "I don't know."

Luán O'Braonáin: "Did Mr Bailey give you the statements?"

Frank Buttimer: "No."

Luán O'Braonáin: "Did Ms Farrell give you the …"

Frank Buttimer: "I believe not."

Luán O'Braonáin: "But he may have?"

Frank Buttimer: "He may have."

Counsel may have been forgiven for feeling that this matter of the statements was much akin to pulling teeth, but he was on a roll and was not hesitating. The witness later asked for forgiveness of his oversight or lack of memory on the subject. He had them (the statements), no doubt, but he just could not recall it earlier. Counsel was not in the mood for forgiveness:

Luán O'Braonáin: "Yes. The difficulty is, Mr Buttimer, that things get said to the ladies and gentlemen of the jury with absolute certainty?"

Frank Buttimer: "Yeah."

Luán O'Braonáin: "Then what was said to them transpired to be absolutely wrong?"

Frank Buttimer: "There you are."

That line was in the order of a throwaway comment hardly appropriate for a witness whose reliability had been so firmly challenged by the defence counsel, who then elicited the fact that Buttimer had not made attendance notes on numerous phone calls he had had with Marie Farrell. When asked why not, the witness said that, "I just don't."

Luán O'Braonáin: "You had on the phone, it would appear, someone who wanted to confess to being a perjurious liar. Isn't that right?"

The witness replied that was not correct, she had rung him to speak to him about matters he did not know about at the time.

CHAPTER 20
THE JURY DECIDES

Dublin – 2015

Mr O'Braonáin then moved on to the predilection of the witness to engage on a grand scale with the media, sometimes in advance of proceedings involving juries. In the present case, counsel suggested that the witness thought it a good thing to have the media publishing material in relation to the case in advance of it actually being heard by a jury. The witness replied not necessarily, and he thought this case attracted media attention.

> **Luán O'Braonáin:** "But as I understand it, Mr Buttimer, your view is that it is a good thing to try and influence the perception of the ladies and gentlemen of the jury?"

> **Frank Buttimer:** "No."

> **Luán O'Braonáin:** "Through the media?"

> **Frank Buttimer:** "No, absolutely – I don't know where you get that idea from."

Counsel pointed out that the witness had given an interview to a legal publication called the *Parchment* in which he had outlined his thoughts about the importance of the media and in one passage he said:

> "*I talk to clients to make sure that they are conscious of the potential influence the media will have, particularly from the perspective of the*

members of the public who might end up on a jury 12 or 18 months down the line. My opinion is that the media has an enormous impact on the justice system in Ireland.'"

Further on in the interview, counsel quoted another passage:

"'Whenever I do a case, particularly one which is likely to generate public interest, I am hugely conscious from the outset that the media will have a role and sometimes a very significant role in how a particular outcome will happen.'"

The witness agreed with counsel that he had said these words. After numerous exchanges, he also agreed that this case was to be tried by the jury based on evidence and not by arriving to the case with preformed ideas influenced by the media with the engagement with or interaction with legal practitioners. Defence counsel then reminded the witness that in the wake of his letter to the Garda Commissioner on October 13, 2005, he gave interviews to multiple media outlets and he had extensive engagement with the media right up to 2007.

In February of that year, he gave an interview to Barry Roche of *The Irish Times* confirming that Frank Buttimer would proceed with an action for damages against the State for what he described to the reporter as Garda misbehaviour. He said that the action would be brought irrespective of whether a review by Commissioner McAndrew finds any wrongdoing by Gardai. He expected that it would be twelve to eighteen months before the case would be held before the High Court. Furthermore, counsel said that the *Parchment* article had been published in the summer of 2014 (in the same year that the trial was scheduled to begin):

Luán O'Braonáin: "You went on to what you said to Mr Roche. Mr Buttimer told *The Irish Times*: 'These claims for damages will certainly proceed in relation to what has been done to him by the State and agents of the State with regard to why he was selected as an offender in this case and the consequences that he suffered as being falsely labelled as the offender.' That is what you were saying to *The Irish Times* and through it to the people of Ireland and through it to people on a jury panel?"

Frank Buttimer: "We had not at all at that point in time. In fact, the decision that this matter would proceed before a jury was in the past. In the past twelve months. Subject to correction."

Luán O'Braonáin: "You see, I have to suggest to you, Mr Buttimer, that there has been constant engagement with the media by you on Mr Bailey's behalf in relation to this matter. In fact, it was set down [to be tried] by a judge and jury in November 2009, which is over five years ago."

Mr Buttimer claimed that it was to redress the adverse media reaction that his client had suffered. That, counsel suggested, had been his client's evidence and tested by the jury. What he explained was not good enough and not appropriate to deal with in the manner he described by going to the media. The witness disagreed and counsel finished his cross-examination.

Retired Detective Superintendent Garda Dermot Dwyer denied in evidence that he had contacted Malachi Boohig in the manner described to come to the meeting. He had never spoken to Martin McQuinn there, nor was he present with Chief Superintendent Camon when he allegedly asked the State solicitor to intervene with the Minister, and he had never gone to college with the Minister as mentioned in the first memo, nor had he suggested anything untoward to Boohig on the matter.

Answering Tom Creed's question if he would agree that it was an improper advance to Mr Boohig to tell him to get on to Mr O'Donoghue to put pressure on the DPP, he said: "I want to say categorically this: first of all, I never knew that John O'Donoghue and Malachi Boohig went to college together, a fact. Two, I never asked Malachi Boohig to go to anybody about the case, never. Three, I was forty years in the Garda Síochána and I never approached any politician to do anything for me or the force, and I would also like to say that no politician ever came to me and asked me to do something wrong. Never. But that is a total and utter lie."

The witness further pointed out that from 1998 until May 2014, he never heard a word from Malachi Boohig, Mr Barnes, Mr Sheehan or the Garda Commissioner that he or anyone else had made an approach to anybody. This completely concurred with the earlier evidence of Boohig and Barnes; the fact that this apparently improper approach to the Minister was just left aside for twelve years and suddenly pulled out like a rabbit from a hat in the first instance before the Supreme Court extradition when Eamon Barnes went public on the matter. It was now rearing its head once again in these proceedings.

Mr Creed read a section from Malachi Boohig's evidence which recollected that Dermot Dwyer would have hosted or chaired the meeting and effectively would have been no more than that. The witness said that he outlined with Detective Chief Superintendent Camon that they felt they had a good case and went through the evidence. They had between 200 and 300 correspondences from the DPP's office but never once saw the name of the DPP on any of them. He asked the West Cork State solicitor to go to the DPP and not anyone else about the evidence and their concerns about the case:

Dermot Dwyer: "I did not ask Mr Boohig to go to John O'Donoghue. I did not know that they went to school together. At no stage did anyone put pressure on the DPP's office. I asked Mr Boohig would he go up and sit down and talk to the DPP about this because in all the years of correspondence, never once did I see the DPP's name. I said will you go and talk to the DPP. That was the end of the story as far as I was concerned."

Mr Creed brought up the matter in Boohig's evidence that officers Camon and Dwyer were present when the former suggested to him that he should go to his old classmate, the then Minister for Justice, to approach the DPP to get him to prefer a charge:

Tom Creed: "So he says that when Detective Superintendent Camon said that you were right beside him."

Dermot Dwyer: "I never heard the late Sean Camon say that. I certainly did not say it and I never heard it being said one way or another."

Tom Creed: "You were in court when you heard him say those words?"

Dermot Dwyer: "And what did you want me to do? Stand up and shout at him?"

Tom Creed: "You could have instructed your counsel to say he is not telling the truth."

Luán O'Braonáin: "Mr Creed is asking the witness to speculate why I didn't ask the question and if I might be permitted to answer the question. Mr Boohig had given by any account a number of different versions of the event, he had given one version to Mr Barnes, he had given a different version to Mr Sheehan and he had given again a different version to the ladies and gentlemen of the jury in the course of his testimony, and that much was elicited in the course of the trial and that gives rise to the possibility for counsel to appropriately comment on the reliability of Mr Boohig's account in relation to these matters."

In any event, counsel said that it was up to him not to put a question if the evidence did not require it and he was not the counsel for the witness. Mr Creed turned to the subject of Marie Farrell and many warrants for driving offences which Mr Dwyer said over several years, from 1997 onwards, amounted to £15,700, of which £15,200 was paid. The residue of warrants was the responsibility of her husband. Counsel was suggesting that because she was a witness in the murder case, she was getting special treatment in relation to the execution of the warrants. The witness rejected this, saying that it was unfair comment. Some had been held back for a while, but she paid all in the end.

When it was suggested that Marie Farrell had, in advance of the libel trial in 2003, lied a number of times in her earlier statements to the Gardai, the retired head of the murder investigation gave a generous account of a woman who had one time told the truth: "There are different ways of looking at Marie, even the biggest liar that ever walked tells the truth sometimes. The way I look at Marie even today, she was out there where she shouldn't be. She saw something, if she was bad, very bad she would have closed her eyes and said I saw nothing. There was a bit of goodness in her and she did pick up the phone and anonymously spoke as Fiona. She then was caught and made statements to the Gardai saying she saw Mr Bailey on the Saturday afternoon in Schull and it transpired three witnesses saw him also there.

"She made a statement that she saw him at Airhill in the morning around 7 a.m. and that was also true. Many of things she said in the first five or six months were true. She was then in a complicated situation when she could not tell us who she was with that night. It was difficult for her and I think things went out of control from about 2004 onwards. She did in her own way a little bit of good."

The witness also said that with her account of seeing Bailey at Kealfadda Bridge, how was she to know that it would be verified by statements given by Jules Thomas and Bailey that he had left the bed and was not seen until the next morning. And the same happened in regard to Airhill, which would also be verified (by other witnesses), so she had told the truth about those matters.

Following another suggestion by Mr Creed to Mr Dwyer about speechifying and misconstruing evidence, the judge put the plaintiff's counsel plainly in his place. He told counsel, "You can criticise him all you like, Mr Creed, but you cannot criticise him for giving a full answer. Make sure you give a full answer as you see it. You are not here to please him; you are here to inform the jury as to exactly what happened as best you can."

Otherwise, with regard to Detective Superintendent Garda Dermot Dwyer, all Bailey – whose imagination was limitless when making accusations –could come up with in his evidence was that the chief investigator and nemesis of the prime suspect had called to his house, availed of his hospitality, eaten his mince pies and left with a parting comment: "I'll place you at Kealfadda Bridge." It was denied by Dwyer.

The Bandon tapes, which had promised so much, delivered little or nothing in terms of the incriminating evidence required by Bailey to win his case. The calls with the most potential about Graham proved worthless and the ones with the next best between Detective Jim Fitzgerald and Marie Farrell might have made up some difference. A recording of a conversation which took place on October 9, 1997 was played to the court.

Immediately after a redacted section, Marie Farrell told Fitzgerald, "You are a pervert," to which he replied, "I fucking am not and if I am, I'm talking to one." Counsel for the plaintiff Mr Creed suggested that this was a conversation between two people who were having a "very close relationship". Fitzgerald said he had been in the Farrell house a number of times and had two beers with her husband on December 23, 1997, the first anniversary of the murder.

He gave them information about threatening phone calls from a public phone in the car park in Schull. He also discussed matters with Marie Farrell concerning a babysitter. He testified that he had never looked after summons for Ms Farrell and denied that he had introduced her to a senator at a hotel about assisting the Farrells with a housing issue.

He denied that it was his idea that Ms Farrell should instruct a solicitor to write to Mr Bailey's solicitor complaining that Mr Bailey was threatening her.

This was all innocuous stuff; the phone exchange was somewhat fraught but proved nothing to sustain the inference provided by counsel that it depicted a close personal relationship. Dealing with Marie Farrell as a handler could not have been an easy task given her mercurial temperament. Now to have to face the ordeal in public court of her toxic and fictitious allegations must have been galling. The longer the proceedings went on, the greater the shadow of the star witness grew, but providing little comfort for the plaintiff.

In relation to her outrageous allegation about Jim Fitzgerald stripping naked in the house in Schull, there were of course no witnesses, but based on her evidence in advance there was little doubt who was going to believed. She could not even propose a time or date for when it had allegedly occurred. Clearly her evidence on that matter was worthless.

It was quite a different matter in terms of corroboration when it came to Garda Walsh. Linda Morgan, owner with her husband of the Schull Golf Club at the time, told the court that when Farrell testified that she reported the incident "that never happened".

Bernie O'Shea, who employed Farrell at the golf club restaurant from 1997, said that she never locked up the premises on a regular basis and she knew of no reason why she should have been cleaning the toilets. Further, Marie Farrell never told her that she was attacked in the toilets and had she been, she would have informed her.

Another witness testified that she and her husband were friends with Sergeant Walsh and went to dinner with him and his wife at Schull Golf Club one summer's evening.

There had been no incident on the night in question and Sergeant Walsh was "most definitely the most upright citizen I could hope to meet".

One could only imagine the stress that these allegations could have visited on the two Gardai and their families, experienced by the most questionable evidence of the star witness not just during the proceedings but long in advance, without one ounce of corroboration. While the general trend of her testimony was obviously motivated by the possibility of financial gain and the need to justify her new narrative, these accusations against Fitzgerald and Walsh demonstrated a particularly nasty vein of malice.

Bernie Griffin told the court that she had let properties to Marie Farrell and her family in Schull, but they had failed to make payments and she had great difficulty in getting them out afterwards. That evidence aligned to numerous incidents of Farrell being charged with four offences of driving without insurance, also ventilated in court evidence, and in addition to Geraldine O'Brien's evidence provided and confirmed why exactly that Marie Farrell had been motivated to give testimony on behalf of Ian Bailey.

It was pitiful in a way if her evidence had demonstrated an absence of malice or a motivation other than to anticipate a financial reward. Once upon a time, she had told the truth and maintained that position for close to a decade. Dermot Dwyer accepted when in evidence in reply to the plaintiff's counsel that, "Even the greatest liar tells the truth sometimes." But he also gave her credit for coming forward originally to give statements that identified Bailey at Kealfadda Bridge and seeing him in Schull on the day that the victim was there. Evidence that had been corroborated by Dan Griffin, who also saw Bailey on the street around the same time.

In relation to the identification of John Reilly, Catherine Keane, executive officer in the office of the General Registrar of Births, testified that she had been given a list of seventeen men – with the name Reilly or O'Reilly from Longford – but could find no corresponding details for any of those men. Marie Farrell had testified that she had met him in her early teens, and he was a few years older.

She had left Longford when she was twenty and told Paul O'Higgins that she had never spoken to him again after the night of December 26, 1996, and when asked why replied that the "situation was bad enough". Mr O'Higgins was of the view that this man she described was an invention, which she denied.

Was the man with Marie Farrell on the fateful night really John Reilly? If so, it could not be confirmed even by post-trial intensive searches in Longford and England by the Gardai.

A Garda documents inspector told the court that he had examined statements of Garda interviews with Marie Farrell in 1996 and 1997 and could find no suspicious alterations on them.

It was the end of March 2015 and one of the longest cases in Irish High Court civil action history entered the final phase. The defence then made an application to have much of the evidence all or in part struck out on the basis of the statute of limitations, which in civil cases is six years, and a large part of the evidence predated that limit; it had been open to either party to invoke that but the defence had to hear the entirety of the evidence before making that submission.

The plaintiff's team argued that it was in the interests of justice that the jury deliver a verdict on considering the whole of the evidence. It would be up to Mr Justice Hedigan, who had this far shown patience, fairness and decisiveness to make this crucial decision, which he delivered on March 26, 2015.

He said that he would be reluctant to withdraw all or any part of the case from the jury but by law he was obliged to do so. While the application was made at the last minute, the defendants argued that the statute had been pleaded at the beginning of the case and if the plaintiff wished, he could have sought himself a preliminary hearing, but he pressed hard for the urgent hearing of the full case.

The allegations against the principal Gardai involved were of the gravest nature imaginable. The Gardai had been anxious to have the opportunity in court in public to deny those allegations, which they had vigorously done.

Mr Justice Hedigan pointed out that the proceedings had commenced on May 1, 2007. The statute runs from the time an act is committed, as any claims based on actions occurring before May 1, 2007 are barred. "The arrests in 1997 and 1998 are barred but having heard all the evidence, I think they would also have been withdrawn from the jury on the basis that no jury properly instructed could reasonably find that the Gardai did not have reasonable grounds for suspicion and that was so strong that had the Gardai not arrested Ian Bailey, they would have been derelict in their duty."

The judge noted that the arrests were grounded on numerous reasons other than the statement of Marie Farrell, each of which would give grounds for reasonable suspicion of involvement in the offence and thus reasonable grounds for arrest.

Graham's evidence was statute barred but even had it been accepted, there was no consequence for Bailey, as no confessions or prejudicial information were obtained. The alleged attempt to pressure the DPP at Bandon was also barred. The judge hardly had to remark that the evidence riddled with contradictions and prejudice would not have been helpful to the plaintiff's case.

The alleged oppression of the EAW process which brought Bailey to the High Court and Supreme Court, the judge said, was a process provided by law in accordance with Ireland's international obligations. It is a process that might involve stress, but it is a process provided by law and no Garda misdeeds could stymie such a process. The French conducted their own investigation and it was impossible to speculate what reasons there were for that investigation. No action arose from the EAW process.

Regarding Marie Farrell, the judge said that her statements remained in existence on the Garda file. The Gardai insisted that they were true statements made by her and are an accurate account of what she said. The investigation of the murder was still alive, and Ian Bailey remained a person of interest.

"If the Gardai did what the plaintiff alleges, it was an action that was an affront to all norms of law and an attack on the rule of law. It would be, if true, an attempt to pervert the course of justice and remains a live attempt if true. Thus, these statements remain lying heavily on the reputation of the plaintiff although retracted by Marie Farrell, who now says that they are false; the Gardai insist today that they wrote down exactly what Marie Farrell said at the time."

The original statements of Marie Farrell, he said, remained in the file of what was still a live investigation. The Gardai said that they were true accounts of what she had said. Ian Bailey was still a person of interest. "In my judgement, this alleged conspiracy, if it existed, is still alive today whether it happened or not. This is a matter for the decision of the jury. There were two questions for the jury which were at the core of the case from the beginning."

The first was whether Detective Garda Jim Fitzgerald, Detective Garda Jim Slattery and Detective Garda Kevin Kelleher, or any combination of them, conspired to implicate Ian Bailey in the murder of Sophie Toscan du Plantier by obtaining statements from Marie Farrell by threats, inducements or intimidation, identifying him as the man she saw at Kealfadda Bridge in the early morning of December 23, 1996 when they knew these statements to be false.

The second was whether Detective Garda Jim Fitzgerald and Detective Sergeant Maurice Walsh had conspired together to obtain from Marie Farrell by threats, inducement or intimidation statements that Ian Bailey had intimidated her.

On the following day, the closing speeches would follow and the judge's charge to the jury. The judge emphasised the focus of the speeches: "The speeches should focus; we don't want any slips betwixt cup and lip at this stage of the proceedings. They should focus exclusively on the issued that are going to the jury and I think you will be able to easily reduce to two simple questions and then a third question if the answer is blah, blah then."

It became utterly clear that the net issue in the case for the jury would be whether Marie Farrell's evidence was to be accepted, as opposed to that of the Gardai. As Barry Roche wrote in *The Irish*

Times: "The case would always rest on her credibility." And that is exactly what transpired. "Bailey's case was reduced to two aspects of Farrell's evidence – the two conspiracy questions that were put to the jury by Mr Justice Hedigan for decision," observed Roche.

In his final submission, Tom Creed S.C. on behalf of Bailey put it to the jury that the case was not about the credibility of Marie Farrell but that of the Gardai.

Mr O'Higgins for the State said that there was little independent corroboration of the matters to be decided, but that the jury should consider that Ms Farrell had given several different versions of the events, which were not consistent with a person telling the truth. She had given dishonest evidence about Bailey coming into her shop and the welfare fraud in London.

Mr Justice Hedigan told the jury they should reach a unanimous verdict on the claims of conspiracy but emphasised that they need not decide whether Bailey was responsible for the murder. This was because Bailey's counsel Tom Creed had said in his closing address that the case was taken to once and for all show that Bailey had nothing to do with the 1996 murder and had been a victim of a conspiracy going on for eighteen years. Mr Creed had also made a David and Goliath comparison. The judge said they were also not asked whether Marie Farrell's statements were true or not.

"David and Goliath comparisons are misleading. Be careful of that. Goliath has as much right to justice as little David has. Ian Bailey says Gardai tried to frame him and he put forward Marie Farrell to testify how they did that. Gardai rejected that claim. Their case is that she is an untruthful witness."

The jury retired and returned after two hours and answered NO to both questions put to them by the judge. Ian Bailey's legal attempt to slander and destroy the work of the murder investigation team had failed both spectacularly and catastrophically. It was confirmation that his "victory lap" when Marie Farrell, in the plaintiff's phrase, "came over to the side of good" was fatally misconceived.

There was one final indignity when Mr Justice Hedigan said that he was referring a transcript of her evidence to the DPP to decide if there were any other consequences for her as a result of her testimony to the High Court. The heroine of the Cork District Court, where she told the truth, was the villainess of the High Court, where she was proved to be a consummate liar.

Sometime later, I was interviewed by two detectives from Harcourt St in relation to my interviews with Marie Farrell. They were investigating as a result of the judge's order that her evidence be sent to the DPP as to whether there was a case of perjury. It was an open-and-shut case; the witness had been proved to be lying in the court under oath. The judge had warned her of the legal consequences of such a serious act but for some reason best known to the DPP, she was never charged for the act of the perjury she had so obviously committed, defence counsel Luán O'Braonáin describing her as "a perjurious liar".

In Shakespeare's *Julius Caesar*, Brutus observes that there is a tide in the affairs of men which taken at flood leads on to fortune. The reverse, he suggests, is bound in shallows and miseries. The latter state is where Ian Bailey found himself in the wake of the court verdict, when the tide inexorably turned against him and to use another of the Bard's phrases, troubles began to visit him not in singles but battalions. As he left the Four Courts, surrounded by media, he looked embattled, worn and defeated, and his ambitions of putting the murder case beyond the reach of any jurisdiction and retiring to West Cork a rich man were left in shreds on the courtroom floor like playbills scattered on the floor of a darkened theatre. In fairness, his solicitor Frank Buttimer, despite this defeat would continue to act for his client after this historic action though it would cost him personally a lot of money: evidence of his commitment to the cause of Ian Bailey.

PART FOUR

CHAPTER 21
JUSTICE IN SIGHT

Paris/Dublin – 2016–18

In Paris, the French investigation which had been stalled by the High Court action was provided with fresh impetus for both the legal authorities and ASSOPH representing the interests of the Bouniol family and associates. Bailey, the only suspect in the two jurisdictions, was in late 2016 charged with the voluntary homicide of Sophie Toscan du Plantier on December 23, 1996. The exhaustive French legal process had begun in 2008 in earnest, and continued under the direction of magistrates Gachon, Dutarte and Turquey, with the assistance prescribed by European legislation of the Irish Gardai, who not only provided the Irish investigation file but set up a mutual assistance unit based in Cork.

During July 2016, magistrate Nathalie Turquey was completing and polishing the results of the exhaustive French investigation into the murder of Sophie Toscan du Plantier and preparing the charge sheet which would conclude that Ian Bailey was the person responsible for the murder. The following summarises her reasons for coming to that conclusion. There was little doubt in the minds of her and the members of ASSOPH that he would appeal the charges in French courts, and that the Irish High Court would reject the EAW that would be issued as a result of her findings.

One way or another, Ian Bailey would be a subject of French

justice, which had been so assiduously avoided by the Irish Director of Public Prosecutions.

The post-mortem examination on the exhumed body of the victim by French experts would not apart from time and degree differ much from the original examination of the Irish pathologist Dr John Harbison. But in common with American investigators of particularly heinous murders, the French when building the case took into account the personality and psychology of the suspect which was capable of being determined by both previous history and the nature of the crime, both of which could also provide a motive for the killing.

French investigators gathered evidence and statements that provided a personality profile of Ian Bailey and in particular his attitude towards women, a hugely important element in the case, which Irish courts and investigators had taken into account but which was considered of no value by the office of the DPP.

Sarah Limbrick, his former wife, had given an insight into his personality and behaviour from 1980, their conjugal life until their separation in 1984 and divorce in 1988. She described him as charming before their marriage but that he eventually revealed his true nature to be abusive and violent, not directly towards her but punching walls, overturning tables and throwing her typewriter across the room. He indulged in extramarital relationships, she found over time, and he was selfish, mean and dishonest, addicted to alcohol and cannabis. She also said that he had forged her signature on a life insurance policy covering her death.

In addition, Bailey had told two witnesses that he had during a row with Sarah Limbrick attempted to strangle her but had pulled back at the last minute. She had given a statement to the same effect to Avon police but was too scared of him to go to court and give evidence against him.

On May 25, 2000, Peter Bielecki stated that he had been on good terms with Ian Bailey until mid-1996, when the latter gave Jules Thomas "a good beating". Before this event, they had seen each other quite often. On one occasion when they had met,

Bailey had told him that during one of the quarrels with his wife Sarah, he had tried to strangle her and caught her by the throat to finish her off before changing his mind at the last minute.

During an interview with Bielecki, a friend of the Thomas/Bailey family said that after the summer of 1995, he found Bailey troubled, drinking more and more and becoming aggressive towards Virginia Oliver, Jules's daughter. According to the witness, Bailey's capacity to control his emotions declined while his belief in dark forces (such as the influence of the moon and Earth) grew. Bailey, he said, had a strong belief in his ability to dominate the world with his intelligence and cunning.

He knew the effects of whiskey on him and used it as a force to do things he would not so when he was sober. Having learned first-hand about Bailey's aggression towards Jules Thomas in May 1996, he resided at the Thomas household in Liscaha at the request of the daughters to protect them in case Bailey returned there.

In an interview the same month, Ceri Williams, partner of Peter Bielecki, confirmed what Ian Bailey had said during a conversation about his former wife, stating that he recounted becoming angry with her, had a temper tantrum, lost all cognisance of time and after recovering, realised that he had completely lost control, grabbed her by the neck and tried to strangle her, ceasing only when he realised the gravity of his actions.

Colette Gallagher stated that while sleeping in a house on Jules Thomas's land in 1993, she had felt a hand on her leg and woke to find Ian Bailey had slipped into her bed. Jules Thomas entered the room and she and Bailey started to quarrel, so she gathered her clothes and ran to the main house to get dressed. Jules Thomas followed and apologised to her for Bailey's behaviour while he shouted and whined outside. Thomas told her that he did worse things than that and lifted her skirt and T-shirt, displaying the bruises that covered her legs and sides.

This event obviously occurred after Bailey's first savage assault on his partner in the same year, details of which were gathered as evidence for the French investigation file, as well as subsequent assaults on May 2, 1996 and August 20, 2001. There were photographs and medical certificates included. According to the Cork hospital report in relation to the assault of August 21, 1993, Jules Thomas arrived at 5.40 p.m. as a victim of an assault that took place in her home at 4.40 p.m., having received a kick in the chest and complained of pains in her right side. She refused to have an X-ray examination offered by hospital staff, signed a discharge document and then left.

She never made a complaint but subsequently filed two in relation to the 1996 and 2001 assaults before later withdrawing them.

The French file contained statements given to Irish investigators about Bailey's bizarre behaviour by local witnesses, while not providing evidence of any possible connection to the crime demonstrated an unhinged personality. Several people saw him one night when he was walking down a road shouting under the rain wearing only his undergarments and a hat; another night he was staring at the sky and howling like a wolf, and yet another saw him covered in excrement, telling the witness that it was good for the skin.

Another witness stated that she had heard Bailey on a night of a full moon in February 1997 outside her house screaming "no" and "sorry".

Unsurprisingly, there was reference to Bailey's diaries in which he chronicled his assaults on his partner, his desire to kill her and his degenerate obsession with drugs, alcohol and sex.

Based on all this, the French magistrate in charge, Patrick Gachon, ordered a psychological profile of Bailey on May 14, 2014. The experts appointed for the task were Dr Masson, a psychiatrist, and Mrs Lorenzo-Regreny, a psychologist. Clearly, as they would not have the benefit of interviewing Ian Bailey, they would have to rely on the evidence of his personality and behaviour, most particularly in advance of the crime. But they would also have the benefit of the knowledge provided by the physical details involved in the commission of the murder.

Of course, one might question the efficacy of the exercise of carrying out a psychological assessment of a suspect in the absence of the subject. Nonetheless, it has been a method carried out for a long time, first of all in the identification of a suspect before apprehension, and also in the trial of an accused in a situation where it needs to be proved whether the accused was on the evidence actually capable of committing the crime.

Ironically, the circumstances in which the accused is directly interviewed by the psychiatrist in advance of the trial, whether by the prosecution or defence, has been shown to be potentially prejudicial to the accused's case. For example, in assessing whether such evidence should be admissible in the Jeff McDonald case, Judge Dupree summed up the psychiatric report based on an interview with the accused thus: "This [assessment] tends to indicate that the defendant did indeed possess traits of character which are consistent with his commission of the crimes with which he is charged and that he possesses other traits which tend to cast serious doubt on the credibility of how the crimes occurred."

Another psychiatrist in the same case was of the opinion a person who has not been examined can be better assessed if he has a personality disorder because the subject is going to lie through his teeth. A trait that Bailey had shown during the whole progress of the case in every arena, including interviews with the media and court cases.

The French experts concluded in relation to Bailey: He had a tendency of presenting a personality constructed on narcissism, psycho-rigidity, violence, impulsiveness, egocentricity with an intolerance for frustration and a great need for recognition. Under the liberating effects of alcohol, he had the tendency to become violent. He also presented as having some kind of histrionism, meaning the pleasure of seeing one's self in some kind of theatrical performance, to resort to the imaginary, to surrender to ambiguity and provocation either as an amusement or even as an instruction, or as a way of defiance.

According to the experts, these characteristics that he possessed define a dual and contradictory behaviour of having profound impulsive tendencies and at the same time having a perfect mastery of himself. The psychological traits of such a personality are often observed in persons who are qualified as being on the "borderline" or "in the limits" without necessarily being psychotic. They added that he did not have any impairment that would have influenced him to carry out the incriminating act. If he were found guilty, one would talk about a dangerous state only in the criminal sense of the term.

The case file then acknowledges that no biological evidence was found at the scene to provide a link to the killer. Only the blood type and genetic profile of the victim were identified by the seals and samples taken from the scene and from the body, with the exception of a male genetic profile that was identified in 2011 by the INPS (National Institute of the Scientific Police) on the base of the leg over one shoe. This could not have been valid, as the seal was already opened when the specialist received it. This profile had not been found in any other medium; the victim was still wearing the shoe when found and had been subsequently removed in no confirmed circumstance.

Other samples had not been identified (blood type of the bloodstains found on the shoes, on the concrete block found near the body and on the brambles adjacent). While no explanation is offered in the file for these anomalies, they are likely due to general contamination due to weather conditions over a long period of time and in the case of the male genetic profile on the leg, probably sustained as a result of contact during the removal of the body.

General observations on the well-established post-mortem findings follow, chronicling the sustained and incredibly violent attack on the fleeing victim and the commission of the murder with the use of a light, sharp instrument, a slate-like rock, a concrete block and a Dr. Martens-type boot. Lacerations and contusions sustained by thorns and brambles were also noted, as well as no physical evidence of a hand-to-hand fight.

Lastly, the location of the small and bloodstained stone discovered between the house and pumping station, the fact that it was far from the body, that it was partly sunk into the ground and had only one drop of blood that matched the victim's on it, and that it bore no trace of contact, are elements that suggest that object was not used as a weapon and that it had only been stained with Sophie Bouniol's blood while she fled from the house, already wounded.

As a result, the examining magistrate concluded that the crime of voluntary homicide had been established, with the intention of homicide resulting from the nature, the number and the location of the blows administered to the victim, all elements revealing the extreme violence of the author of the crime, who chose to hit Sophie Bouniol particularly on the head and specifically while she was lying on the ground, as revealed by the circular stains formed by the drops of blood that fell from her head to her clothes and not by flowing from the head to the legs.

Among the persons who were interviewed after the murder, only Ian Bailey had wounds that justified further investigation. He had not contested the existence of the wounds, which were seen by Arianna Boarina (on the hands and forearms) on December 23, 1996; on December 24, around noon, by Denis O'Callaghan (on the back of the left hand); on December 27 in Schull by officers O'Leary and Kelleher (on the back of the hands, left hand and wrist); then again on the following day, December 28, in his house when investigators called to ask him to fill in a questionnaire. Witnesses thought that the wounds had been caused by brambles.

On December 25, Mark McCarthy saw a scratch on Ian Bailey's right temple, a lesion that matched the cut that Garda O'Leary observed on December 28 as being deep and clear, and localised on the right side of the former's forehead. Jules Thomas, interviewed on February 10, 1997, mentioned having seen a fresh and slightly bleeding cut on Bailey's forehead on Monday morning, December 23.

Ian Bailey explained that the lesions came from cutting the top of a tree and the killing of turkeys on December 22, 1996. This was confirmed by Jules Thomas, Saffron Thomas and indirectly by Liam O'Driscoll, who saw Bailey and one of Thomas's daughters dragging along a Christmas tree on the same day. Furthermore, Ian Bailey showed investigators a tree with the top cut off and finally it was consistent that a turkey had been delivered to Mr O'Sullivan on the morning of December 23, 1996.

No one mentioned having seen a scratch on one hand; none of those who were interviewed and who had met Ian Bailey during the evening of December 22 in the Galley pub noticed them. All witnesses, on the contrary, agreed that Ian Bailey did not have any marks on his arms, hands or face, considering they were all in a well-lit room when Bailey was in close proximity and presented himself to them to recite some poems and play some music, even rolling up his sleeves to play the bodhran.

The witnesses believed the wounds emanated from contact with brambles and/or thorns, and yet there was no such vegetation at the foot of the tree that Bailey identified as having been cut. Sophie Bouniol's body lay close to and on brambles, and bore many scratches corresponding to brambles and thorns.

The wound on Ian Bailey's face that he claimed came from killing turkeys was not of the same nature. On the other hand, the victim's hands bore incisions that in Dr Harbison's opinion could have come from a sharp weapon. Lastly, it is to be noted that the medical observations did not mention finding any haematoma that could have resulted from a bare-handed punch, and that no element justified that a hand-to-hand fight had occurred between Sophie Bouniol and her attacker, or that she could have scratched or hit him.

Consequently, it is certain that on the day of, and a few hours after the murder, Ian Bailey bore traces of the same nature as some of the lesions that were observed on the victim's body and the environment near it. The reasons he gave for them could not explain them.

Moreover, all throughout the investigation, Ian Bailey's answers and declarations concerning his time schedule from the evening of December 22 to the morning of December 23, 1996 kept changing.

First, he omitted mentioning having passed through Hunt's Hill upon coming home on the evening of December 22/23, 1996. He mentioned it during his interview on December 31 and on February 10, 1997; he added that they had parked the car to admire the full moon; on January 27, 1998, he admitted having a sense of foreboding.

On the events of the evening of the murder on February 10, 1997, he first declared that he had slept with Jules Thomas without leaving the house, got up early, made some coffee, brought some up to Jules Thomas at around 9.30 a.m., went back to bed at 10 a.m. and listened to the radio; then he remembered getting up during the night to go to the studio to write an article and going to the main house at around 11 a.m.; on January 27, 1998, he stated that he had got up during the night, wrote a little and went to the studio at 9 a.m.; then he explained he had got up at 4 a.m., went back to bed thirty to forty-five minutes later, got up at 9 a.m. and went to the studio to finish an article that he had to submit to the *Sunday Tribune* the same day before lunchtime, and also said that Richard Curran had changed the deadline of the article to Tuesday over the phone on Monday morning between 10 a.m. and 10.30 a.m.

As for the statements made by Jules Thomas in regard to the events, the file noted: She did not mention in her answers to the first questionnaire that they made a stop on the way home; she described their trip through the Arderawinney Hill in her statement of December 31, 1996; on February 10, 1997, she said that Ian Bailey parked the car at Hunt's Hill and he went out to look at the moon, saying its reflection was lovely, and that once home they went to bed at around 1 a.m. to wake up at around 9 a.m., and that Ian Bailey did not get up during the night; in another interview she said that Ian Bailey, upon entering the car after the stop at Hunt's Hill, told her that he felt a sense of foreboding and that he saw a light from Alfie's house, that he got up one hour after she went to bed to finish an article, returning at 9 a.m. and bringing her some coffee; on January 27, 1998, she said that after bringing her some coffee, he went to the studio to finish an article and make a phone call (surely to the newspaper).

The statements of Fenella Thomas were then examined about the same event and timelines. On January 27, 1998, she stated that she heard Ian Bailey snoring during the night; on September 21, 2000, she said that Ian Bailey was not the snorer and she could not determine who it was, then said it was her mother and then finally admitted that she did not know who was snoring.

The examining magistrate then concluded that three persons had concealed the fact that Ian Bailey did not remain in Jules Thomas's house the whole night and that he had the material possibility of going to Sophie Bouniol's house on the night of the murder.

In addition, statements from Tom McEneany and Richard Curran of the *Sunday Tribune* at the time proved that Ian Bailey had not submitted the article in the morning and in fact dictated it to the newspaper in the afternoon. This, the file states, shows that the article had not been finished on the morning of December 23, 1996, invalidating a part of Ian Bailey's explanations regarding his time schedule on the night of December 22 to the morning of December 23, 1996.

According to elements in the file, the route that Ian Bailey took back to the house was not the shortest. However, it offers a lovely view of the region from Hunt's Hill, especially during clear weather and under a full moon like they had on the night of the events. If the reason for this tour remains unknown, it is certain that this itinerary made it possible for Bailey to see Sophie Bouniol's house. Moreover, it was possible that the lights were turned on for the telephone call between the Toscan du Plantier couple which took place around midnight (Paris time, 11 p.m. Irish), and according to the bar owner, Ian Bailey and Jules Thomas left his establishment around 12.30 a.m. Furthermore, Marie Farrell stated that she saw Ian Bailey at around 3 a.m. in the morning on the road at 30 yards west of the Kealfadda/Dunmanus crossroad, staggering with his hands over his head.

It is certain that this testimony has also changed, that it was first received through an anonymous message under the name of a false caller, and Marie Farrell withdrew it in 2005. Nevertheless, there is reason to consider that the message that was exposed by the witness, who explained many times that she was torn between her desire to relate facts that she considered important, and her need to protect her family situation, since the man who was accompanying her on December 23, 1996 was not her husband.

Furthermore, the investigators and Geraldine O'Brien's testimonies confirmed Bailey's trip to Marie Farrell's shop on June 28, 1997 to show her some documents, and the woman's worried state. The circumstances of her reversal, almost eight years after her first interview, its written form and the contacts she had with Ian Bailey's defence, make the spontaneity of her retraction doubtful.

Moreover, if Marie Farrell attested that Ian Bailey stayed for ten minutes on the main road of Schull on December 21, 1996 while Sophie Bouniol was inside her shop, their presence were confirmed by Dan Griffin, who saw a man whose description matched that of Ian Bailey in Schull on December 20 or 21, 1996 and by Ceri Williams, who affirmed having seen the "French woman" on December 21, 1996 in Schull, just after seeing Ian Bailey on the other side of the road.

As a matter of fact, Ian Bailey admitted to being in Schull on Saturday, December 21, wearing a long black coat, but denied having seen Sophie Bouniol.

Furthermore, if Ian Bailey contested having met Sophie Bouniol, apart from seeing her once eighteen months before her death in Alfie Lyons's while working there, the investigators during the house search heard him tell Jules Thomas that he saw her in Schull on the Saturday before her death.

Marie Farrell stated that she saw Ian Bailey on the road to Airhill on December 22, 1996 at around 7.15 a.m. and yet, he claimed that he had spent the night with the Murphys, 100 metres from the place that Marie Farrell had indicated, and that Tony Doran claimed having heard someone leave the house around 7.30 a.m. This element enhances the credibility of Marie Farrell's testimony.

On the other hand, Guy Girard's testimonies – though invalidated by Mr Roget – not those of Alexandra Levy, who could not remember a particular name, could affirm that Ian Bailey had tried to contact Sophie Bouniol. The theory of an accidental meeting during a summer festival in Cape Clear could not be confirmed.

In March 1999, the film director Guy Girard came forward and stated that he had worked with Sophie on a documentary in the months before the murder. One day in November 1996, at a meeting, he spoke to her about a lecture on violence that he had given to a secondary school in the town of Besançon and Sophie mentioned that an Irishman, Eoin Bailey, in the neighbourhood of her holiday home was interested in that topic.

He was sure that at another meeting at the production office of Sophie on December 19, 1996 with her, himself and Vincent Roget present, that the name of Bailey was again mentioned, but Roget said that he did not recall that. Later in the evening, before the flight to Ireland the following day, she told him that she was taking along a book for Bailey. Roget was not present for that conversation.

So, on the testimony of Girard, both conversations with Sophie mentioning Bailey in November and on the evening of December 19 could not be invalidated by Roget, just the one on the day of December 19.

The indictment went on: In the event there is no proof of a prior link or a common interest between Ian Bailey and Sophie Bouniol, it should be remembered that the lights inside the house [in Toormore] were out when the investigators entered and that no trace of a second person had been identified. As a matter of fact, only a glass that was half-filled, with the thumb marks of the victim, had been found; the others were washed; if the two chairs were placed face to face, they were not positioned far enough [away from each other] for two persons to sit in them and this set-up corresponded to Sophie Bouniol's habit, as her mother described of placing her feet on a chair in front of her while she sat.

The telephone was on the floor beside the bed, a circumstance corresponding to what Daniel Toscan du Plantier mentioned about them having a telephone conversation earlier, and the victim was found in her night clothes. A trace of blood that matched that of the victim was found on the exterior part of the back door.

In view of these elements, it is possible that the murderer appeared at the front door and that he and Sophie Bouniol started a conversation and that it got out of hand, and that consequently the young woman, hurt, first tried to enter the house and then had to flee, crossing the field while being followed by the attacker, until he caught her at the wall which she attempted to climb because the gate was closed.

The specialists and the witnesses affirmed that Ian Bailey had a strong taste for women, a violent nature that awoke under the influence of alcohol, intellectual ambitions and a belief in super-natural powers during full moon nights, all of which match the elements of this theory. He also had been condemned (in court) for violence against his companion Jules Thomas, and his former wife complained of having similar mishaps.

Ian Bailey already knew where the victim's body was found and her nationality before it entered the public domain. In fact, he said that he had been informed of the murder at 1.40 p.m. through a phone call from Eddie Cassidy, who told him that the victim was a French woman.

Eddie Cassidy confirmed making the telephone call but denied knowing the victim's nationality. Richard and Caroline Leftwick testified that on the morning of December 23, 1996 before 2 p.m., Ian Bailey cancelled his appointment with them.

Caroline Leftwick situated the call to be between 11 a.m. and 12.30 p.m. and remembered that Ian Bailey mentioned that the victim's nationality was French.

Padraig Beirne recalled that during their telephone conversation before 2 p.m., that Ian Bailey mentioned to him that the victim was French and that she was beautiful. Dick Cross said that around 1.45 p.m., Ian Bailey proposed to him some photographs of the crime scene.

Furthermore, Bill Fuller saw Jules Thomas in her car somewhere near Kealfadda Bridge at 11 a.m., a statement that agreed with that of James Camier, who stated having seen Jules Thomas in Goleen the same day between 11 a.m. and 11.30 a.m., and to whom she talked of a murder that Ian Bailey was about to make a report on.

Moreover, Fenella Thomas on many occasions in statements to investigators remembered having seen her mother and the latter's companion leave for Goleen on the morning of December 23, 1996 at around 9 a.m. or 10 a.m.

Jules Thomas herself, on September 21, 2000, related that on the morning of December 23, 1996 at around 11 a.m., she went to the crime scene and took some photographs of the water, then headed to Goleen to talk to Mr Camier.

Furthermore, at 2 p.m. Ian Bailey and Jules Thomas went to Toormore. Shirley Foster (who met them on the way) contested pointing out any place to them.

Lastly, according to Patrick Lowney in May 2000, Ian Bailey asked him to develop a roll of photographs which presented a place that was identical to the scene of the crime and a woman who was lying near some brambles and a stone wall, details which corresponded to the location of Sophie Bouniol's body.

Ian Bailey's explanations were therefore insufficient to justify why, before anyone else, apart from investigators, he knew so much about the crime. Moreover, he had offered photographs of the crime scene when given the presence of investigators who had forbidden anyone to approach the body.

Furthermore, on many occasions and in front of different people, Ian Bailey admitted to the crime or rendered speeches in which he indirectly confessed to it. If we could employ Ian Bailey's personality and the pleasure he gets from making theatrical performances to explain the conversations with James Kenna, Helen Callanan, Martin Graham, Colin Deady and Russell Barret, it could not be the case with the scene described by Richie Shelley and Rosie Shelley, who related Ian Bailey's disarray and tears while he declared, "I did it. I did it. I went too far." And with Malachi Reed's narrative.

As a matter of fact, the words, "I went to her place with a stone one night and I bashed her fucking brain", spoken to a teenager inside the privacy of his own car and far from any act of defiance or boasting, appears to be a confession on Ian Bailey's part.

More attention should be paid to Bill Fuller's testimony. On February 20, 1997, he related having a conversation with Ian Bailey during which the latter declared, "You did it … you saw her in Spar, and she got you excited as she walked through the alleys with her tight butt. You went to her place to see what you could get, but she wasn't interested and so you attacked her. She tried to escape, and you ran after her. Then you threw something at the back of her head, and you went further than you had planned to."

Now the layout of the place, the total absence of blood or disorder inside the house, the drop of blood on the stone in the field, the location of the pumping station that was along the path between the house and the body, the fact that a block was missing from the top of the wall at the angle that faced the passageway and that another block was found beside the body and was covered in blood, present a plausible case that the aggressor, while pursuing the victim, could have grabbed a block from the wall and hit her on the back with either it or a sharp weapon that he had used earlier to administer the cut on her hand and the lesions by Dr Harbison on her back.

The consecutive reports of the investigators established that no one who was not part of their team was able to approach the body from December 23, 1996 at 10.38 a.m. until it was taken away on December 24, 1996. Regarding the lesions on the back of the victim, even if Ian Bailey had seen the corpse at the crime scene, a fact that he did not affirm, it would have been impossible for him to have known in any case that the body bore wounds on the dorsal level, for it lay on its back.

Lastly, the medical examiner's report, which described the lesions on the back as coming from oblique blows from the concrete block that was found near the body, was written on March 24, 1997. In all conditions, and before this date, only the author (perpetrator) and first-hand witnesses of the crime (at the scene) could have known that Sophie Bouniol had been hit from behind, and more, with the means of an object.

It is certain that neither the blood nor the genetic profile of the victim have been found on any of Ian Bailey's clothes that were seized on February 10, 1997. However, no house search had been conducted between December 23, 1996 and February 10, 1997. Moreover, certain objects had been destroyed in a bonfire that had been lit on December 26 and that two witnesses perceived sometime during the Christmas season. Garda Gilligan found some fabric and shoelaces in the fire's debris.

Numerous verifications and searches were conducted, as much in Ireland as in France, to make it possible to eliminate people from the inquiries who had once been doubted, like Bruno Carbonnet, and to exclude the theory of a prowler.

On the aggravating circumstance of premeditation, no element supported the theory that Sophie Bouniol's murder was planned. The fact that the victim was killed outside her house, was within reach of her neighbours and by blows with a concrete block that was taken from a nearby structure along the victim's escape route are elements that support an act that that had been accomplished without any preliminary preparation.

Hence, in view of the elements presented, despite the denials of the concerned party, we maintain that there is grave and coherent evidence against Ian Bailey that he had willingly murdered Sophie Bouniol on December 23, 1996 in Schull.

It is not necessary in the present order to proceed with the re-qualification required in the final summing up that has been carried through with the release of an arrest warrant on July 13, 2016.

In the matter of evidence tampering, an offence that would have been committed by one foreigner to another outside the Republic's territory, it must be said in the absence of elements that would allow us to determine if this offence would be punished by Irish legislation, the necessary judicial conditions to pursue the matter in France have not been met. We say, therefore, that this matter will not be pursued.

"Given that from judicial inquiry and within the time limit for court action there is sufficient evidence against Ian Bailey for having willingly murdered Sophie Bouniol married name Toscan du Plantier on December 23, 1996 in Schull, Ireland.

"We hereby order the indictment of Ian Bailey by the criminal court (cour d'assises) of Paris within the time limitation for court action, having willingly murdered Sophie Bouniol married Toscan du Plantier on December 23, 1996 in Schull, Ireland."

The inquiry evidence and indictment were signed off by the Vice President in charge of investigation, Mrs Nathalie Turquey, on July 27, 2016.

The French judicial authorities and indeed the family of the victim and ASSOPH members expected that Ian Bailey would appeal the charge and the indictment, but little did they know that his defence would be based solely on the Irish DPP's report not to charge him. Therefore, it would be a contest fought before the highest courts in France in which the DPP's analysis and conclusions would be subject to further legal scrutiny of the most exhaustive examination.

Whether it was a result of the pressure of actually being charged with the murder for the first time after such a long lapse in years, Bailey responded late in the year by calling on the DPP Claire Loftus to review the decisions of her predecessors not to have him prosecuted. It may have also been motivated by the knowledge that after all this time a position adopted not to prosecute was unlikely to be altered. If he did not want to spend long years in a French jail, all he had to do was confess to the Irish authorities.

In Dublin, the Fennelly Commission published its report in March 2017 in relation to the Bandon tapes with special reference to the recorded calls and the Garda investigation into the murder of Sophie Toscan du Plantier. Most of Bailey's allegations against the team were found to be outside the terms of reference of the inquiry. There was no evidence found by the inquiry that alteration, modification or suppression of evidence was carried out by members of the investigation team.

Neither did the Gardai offer substantial sums of money or drugs to Martin Graham, and the recorded calls to him demonstrated no evidence of improper conduct. In relation to Marie Farrell, the review of calls by and to her recorded in Bandon did not provide evidence that she had been pressurised into giving false information by members of the investigation team. Nor was there evidence of unlawful conduct by members but for one incident, that of improper behaviour.

Bailey had appealed the French murder indictment. His lawyer Dominique Tricaud used the DPP report as his plaintiff's defence. In November 2017, the three-judge Chambre d'Instruction (High Court) heard Bailey's appeal and submissions from the prosecution, defence lawyer Dominique Tricaud and lawyers representing the victim's family. The public prosecutor put forward the evidence of the incriminating scratches and wounds on the accused on December 23, 1998; his contradictory statements about his movements on December 22 and 23; his knowledge of facts about the identity of the victim and the murder in advance of coming into the public domain; and his confessions of his responsibility for the crime to various witnesses.

The court took into account the pleadings of the defence based on the translated reasons of the DPP's argument not to prosecute; a request to nullify the EAW in light of the Supreme

Court decision; the accused's rights to be defended on an equitable basis; and the risk of double jeopardy (ne bis in idem) as no prosecution had been taken against Bailey in Ireland.

The court ruled that Bailey had written to the French inquiry judge in November 2011 and stated that he would remain silent before that judge. He knew he was wanted by French justice and had tried to avoid it. In 2013, the French judge had written to the Irish authorities and requested authority to question Bailey, which was refused. On this ground, the EAW was necessary and remained valid.

Bailey's lawyers had full access to the French investigation file before the appeal. The indictment had been translated to English as well at the pleadings before the court of the prosecutor. Therefore, there was no violation of the legal rights of the defence. In relation to double jeopardy, the DPP's office had written on two occasions to the French inquiry judge to state that there would be no prosecution undertaken but the case was still open. The Irish Central Authority confirmed to the French bureau that the investigation was still ongoing and the DPP wrote to the Bouniol parents saying the case was definitely not closed.

The court ruled that the DPP report with no date and no signature could not give rise to an argument of double jeopardy and could not be admissible in a final judgement. Having considered these matters and the reasons in evidence for charging Bailey, on February 1, 2018, the appeal was dismissed.

A further appeal to the Cour de Cassation (Supreme Court) was heard by five judges and again dismissed in May 2018. Eight superior court judges had roundly rejected the interpretation of evidence, prejudice and bias contained in the DPP report and offered as a defence against the murder indictment.

CHAPTER 22
THE HAUNTING
OF GRIEF

Paris – 2018

In June 2018, I had travelled to Paris to interview Bouniol family lawyer Alain Spilliaert, who has unparalleled knowledge of the French investigation and the legal process of the country's justice department. I also went to see members of the family and Jean-Antoine Bloc, vice president of the Association for Justice for Sophie (ASSOPH). I first got my bearings in Montparnasse, where I was staying in Avenue De La Maine.

By now, I had had constant interaction over many years with Alain about every development in the case in Ireland to keep him and the family not just informed but also providing information that might be of assistance in their fight for justice. It was the least I could do given that justice would not happen in my native country.

It seemed a long time since I was last there on the case seventeen years ago, when I was based in Rue de Seine just over the river from Notre Dame Cathedral, where Sophie had made her first communion. I was farther away now but the mind has a way of minimising distance in both kilometres and time.

Maybe it was being in Paris where Sophie grew up, went to school, worked and married that jolted my memory. My mission at the time was to give Sophie an identity other than that of a murder victim and an image other than the austere passport photo reproduced in the newspapers after the murder, which gave no hint of her translucent beauty, no reflection of her equally beautiful mind or spirit.

It was sixteen years ago that month that I first met the Bouniol family in Bantry in West Cork, while I was in Schull doing research for the first book. I had asked my police contact to set up a meeting to secure their co-operation and get to know Sophie as a person so that I could translate that knowledge to the wider public.

The family, and husband Daniel, had cut off all contact with the media because of some appalling stories published in the print media, mostly by Ian Bailey, about Sophie and the circumstances surrounding the murder.

I had to convince the family that I was genuine and not going to produce such salacious nonsense. My contact warned they would be incredibly cautious about helping me. So, I approached the meeting at the hotel in the lovely seaside town of Bantry with some trepidation and a lot of jangling nerves. It all worked well and beyond my expectations, and so I embarked on the long journey with many twists and turns. One of the most enduring benefits was to get to know Sophie's wonderful family and be in a constant state of amazement and admiration at the dignity all showed in the face of a tragedy.

I was also a recipient of their social generosity on many occasions over the years and thoroughly enjoyed their company. I was able, courtesy of my late mother Patsy and sisters Grainne and Christine, to be able to return in some small way that generosity when they hosted a wonderful night at Patsy's house for Georges, Marguerite and Marie Madeleine. To say the Sheridan family were impressed with the guests would indeed be an understatement.

I was now back in Paris in 2018, spending hours in Alain's office dealing with the frustrations and complexities of the case. He leant over the desk at one stage and said, "It was Judge Gachon who ordered the exhumation of Sophie's body in 2008 and from then on, in spite of delays, the case was moving; it was Sophie's soul that got it going." I couldn't argue with that. If ever a case needed that spiritual dimension, it was this one. How could any soul rest when their family was suffering salt poured into their wounds again and again by unrelenting injustice?

I took a lengthy walk every morning, part of which took me through Montparnasse's beautiful old cemetery, which dated back to 1843. It had an untidy grandeur, and an incredibly peaceful atmosphere that is entirely appropriate for its inhabitants, which include Jean-Paul Sartre and Simone de Beauvoir, the dramatist Eugène Ionesco, our own Samuel Beckett and his wife in a plain flat grave that belies his greatness but mirrors his modest view of his place in literary history.

You can see in the simple detail of many graves of the inhabitants that you can view in a short time, that whatever the lives led, there is a pleasing anonymity in death. The American actress Jean Seberg's grave had a plenitude of mementoes. But it exuded a sense of sadness, or was that because I know that she committed suicide?

Here is also the resting place of actor Philippe Noiret and director Maurice Pialat, the latter who had worked with Daniel and become friendly with Sophie, and who had died in 2003, the same year as Daniel, and is buried in Père Lachaise. Even a cemetery as large as this is a small world.

I sat on a seat under the coolness of some trees under the sun and clear sky and thought of Sophie in her grave, and wondered how she could possibly rest after all that had challenged the search for truth and justice. I thought of Beckett, lying just around the corner, and his phrase that we are all born astride the grave.

Sophie had a life but like with all murder victims, it often gets lost in the translation of the crime. The perpetrator, as the villain, gets a lot more attention, which is true in an entirely different way in this case, where the prime suspect actively sought the spotlight.

Sophie's paternal grandparents hailed from the Lozère region in south-central France, which is primarily agricultural and sparsely populated, as many young people emigrate to the bigger cities in search of work. The terrain is rough and mountainous, not unlike parts of the Irish landscape. Her grandparents moved to Paris in 1924 and ran and lived above a coffee shop, where Sophie's father Georges was born in 1926, five minutes away from the present family home.

Sophie's mother Marguerite was the first of four children of Raymond Gazeau, a rural electrification engineer, and his wife Therese Cros. They had met in Lozère, where he was based at the time. They married in Montpellier and their other children were Marie Madeleine, Michel and Jean-Pierre. Georges and Marguerite met at a gathering of Lozèrians in Paris, married in 1954 and moved into the building and apartment in Rue Tiquetonne when Georges took over the dental practice of an older dentist.

For Lozèrians, as with Irish emigrants, family was a hugely important element in their lives. So it was with the Bouniols, and with great delight they welcomed their first-born Sophie into the world on July 28, 1957, and called their beautiful baby their cherry blossom. Two boys, Bertrand and Stephane, followed. As Sophie moved through primary and secondary school, she demonstrated great interest in literature and languages.

Images from the family album in the house at Rue Tiquetonne came flooding back to me from when I saw them in the summer of 2002, the weather then just as it was now. Marguerite, Sophie and Bertrand sat on a wall with the sea in the background on a holiday in Spain. They were framed in a golden light, and Marguerite leant protectively towards Bertrand.

Photographs tell as much of a life as any narrative. Outside Notre Dame Cathedral at the occasion of Sophie's First Holy Communion, a smiling Marie Madeleine was in a wide-brimmed white hat, white outfit and gloves, looking down at her niece Sophie, whose blonde hair was encased in a white hood, a crucifix sitting chest-high on her white robes. There was a smiling, wondrous expression on her milk-smooth face. To her right was her cousin Alexandra, luscious dark hair cascading onto the white dress, and her other cousin Patricia, left of her aunt and in between the shadowy head of brown-haired Bertrand.

A picture of Sophie, a freckle-faced teenager, bleached-blonde hair framing her round face. It spoke of innocence and expectation of a life to be lived with future achievement a given. Another picture with her lovely mother smiling on a summer's day. And later a stunningly beautiful twenty-two-year-old bride pictured against the background of a tree, her pristine white trousseau hugging her svelte figure and spreading across the grass beneath her. She held a bouquet in her hands.

It was while in college, from which she eventually would drop out, that Sophie met fellow student Pierre Baudey-Vignaud, who would become her first husband. They married on June 21, 1980 in a ceremony conducted by his mother's second husband, a mayor of their village near Orléans. She quickly became pregnant and their son Pierre Louis was born the following year. Perhaps it was the taking on of such adult responsibilities so young that led to their separation and subsequent divorce in 1983.

Sophie emanates a luminous presence in a photograph with Pierre, his handsomeness matching her beauty, and her looking the definition of a caring and loving mother as she cradles and rests her cheek on the side of the head of her gorgeous three-year-old Pierre Louis. A picture of perfect and innocent love. The positions were reversed six years later, as the freckled Pierre Louis leans into the neck and head of his smiling mother.

She was incredibly single-minded and independent, and she adapted to the life of a lone mother with the support and help of her parents. She had relationships and jobs, but none that were of any lasting value. Sophie's stubborn attitude at times led to family friction, but she was always the first to resolve it, particularly with her mother Marguerite, who was also possessed of a strong personality. Fate set her adrift; her life would take another direction after she secured a position in the press department of the French film organisation UniFrance and later married the chief executive, Daniel Toscan du Plantier.

I have observed the grief and frustration of the Bouniol family first-hand and tried my best to articulate it. I try to understand it, but could anyone really understand unless they became a living witness to the murder of a loved one and were then consigned to a living hell as justice and resolution were denied? I think not.

I realised early in the case, which mirrored others I had covered, also without resolution, that Sophie's family were decent and good people upon whom an undeserved tragedy had descended. Their reward was to be visited by pure and unadulterated evil, resulting in the savage murder of their only daughter, sister, niece. For over two decades, it seemed that evil would triumph, not only over good but also over justice.

There should be a future after bereavement but who can predict when that begins. Acceptance is assumed to be an indicator of the healing process, but that is but a beginning, not an end. It depends on the nature of the bereavement and many other variables. For example, how often has this phrase been heard: "They will never get over the death of their child." Why? Because it flies in the face of nature for a parent to bury a child, and the haunting will not just involve what has been but also what might have been. A double-edged sword of grief, a void that stretches backwards and forwards.

One can barely imagine as a parent, a brother and sister first of all viewing a daughter and sister, having to identify their beloved on the mortuary slab with their features unrecognisable and with every blow and thrust of the attack imprinted on the once beautiful, delicate and perfect body, distorting it, discolouring it. Profaning it, destroying it. Imagine the grief, the anger, the rage and the impotence in the face of this image which tells the story of the last terrifying minutes of a loved one, now robbed of identity and given the name of victim.

In the prologue to *Justice Denied*, published by ASSOPH in 2014, Sophie's mother Marguerite recorded her feelings about the case, seventeen years on, under the title "When Night Falls". The evening sun poured through the hotel window on Avenue du Maine as I read the chronicle of a mother twice wronged, first by the savage murder of her daughter and then by justice delayed and thus denied. By the time I finished, I was possessed by admiration but also extreme sadness and not a little rage.

"*I remember one day, Sophie, my sister Marie Madeleine and I were amusing ourselves by reading our palms. Pointing out the short lifeline crossing her hand, my daughter looked at me and said: 'I will die young.'*

"*It was only a harmless game, born of a moment of warmth between a child grown into a woman, her mother and her aunt. We were pretending to believe, getting into the spirit, but too sensible to see it as a sign of destiny.*

"*It was a bright, hot, happy day, but it was the kind of warmth and happiness that you don't stop to notice. We had known other days like it, just as happy, we never realised that they could be numbered. Today the memory of that day comes back to me.*

"*A few weeks later, the death of a French woman in the south of Ireland was announced on the television news. Nothing yet could confirm it, but I knew it was Sophie. As the hours went by and the telephone in her house rang out, on the TV screen, the south of Ireland narrowed to Cork, Cork gave way to the countryside surrounding it and finally the name of the village of Schull appeared. It could be no longer doubted.*

"*This is how my husband and I learnt of our daughter's death from the television. Before her name was announced, but long after it was known to the French and Irish authorities. No one in any Government department, in any chancellery had deigned to call us, to tell us Sophie had been murdered, to tell us what we should do next.*

"*A cold silence fell on us, on me. A silence that neither my family nor Sophie's friends have been able to dispel. A silence that swallows their cries and mine, that smothers our grief. The night she was murdered was a cold dark winter's night, and for me that night has never ended.*"

In the article, Marguerite, reviewing the passage of time since the murder, feels that she has been stumbling into the wilderness. Her hopes were raised when the Gardai informed the family they had a suspect, but then dashed when Bailey was arrested and released twice. She expresses the disappointment and frustration over the Supreme Court overturning the extradition order. It seems to her that the court tossed aside the country's commitments to preserve the suspect from trial in France.

"With each new development, and during the long periods when the case stagnated, I have been obliged to betray my daughter. Married to a man in the public eye, Sophie avoided journalists. For the last sixteen years I have disregarded this rule of hers. I cry out her name so that she will not be forgotten, but the silence always returns and the darkness always closes in again, on me and on her. I have betrayed my daughter's wishes so that justice might be done."

She speaks of the plethora of letters she has written to judges, elected officials and ministers, so many she cannot even number them. As much as she tries to push back the darkness surrounding her, it has become thicker, dense as a wall. While she has the condolences and the pity, the Irish authorities have become more unreachable and the French more unmovable.

"Until then, I had a good life, a comfortable, simple and peaceful life. I didn't know violence until it struck down my daughter. I didn't know hatred until it invaded me at the thought of the killer.

"The haunting thought that Sophie's last look, a look of pain and terror fell on the crazed eyes of a man bringing down a concrete block on her face. I have felt shame for this hatred, this strange passion, contrary to all I have been taught. But education has proved powerless against murder, and the shame has worn thin along with my patience. The night reigns and with it this raging fire I am able to fight, this impotent fire of hatred."

I have talked to people in West Cork whose hatred and emotions would stretch farther than Marguerite's. When as part of my early investigations into the case I learnt of the actual physical details of the murder and the subsequent machinations of the killer as he became "the expert" on it, it was hard to avoid feeling a burning hatred for a person who would commit such an act. But one is taught to be dispassionate and objective and that certainly is a less consuming reaction, but not always possible.

There are countless examples in Ireland which prove that the rights of the perpetrator are paramount in the criminal justice system and the rights of the victim and family count for little. The murder of Sophie provides a classical example. Marguerite discovered this unpalatable fact quickly.

Until this awful event, she had trusted institutions – after all, she had no reason not to – but nothing prepared her for the battles she has faced. I once asked her how the tragedy had impacted on her religious faith. She replied that she did not believe in anything anymore. She had fought for justice for her beloved daughter too many years before that fight became a fight against systemic inaction.

"In 2007, during my annual visit to Sophie's house in Ireland, I spoke with an Irish policeman of the feeling of resignation that was threatening to overwhelm me. I told him that from then on, I was going to let those close to me fight in their own way. I told him about the association and how it was created to get proceedings moving where they had stopped or been abandoned, without me having to face the authorities head on. I still remember his reaction: 'Finally!'

"It took me time to understand that neither my daughter nor the suspect were really at the heart of the story unfolding before me. Around the murder a confrontation was taking place between the Irish police and prosecutors and between the Irish justice system and our own. Where is my daughter in all of this? Where is the truth? Who will fight for it?"

Marguerite gives credit to the support of those close to her – husband, sister and brothers, Sophie's friends and strangers touched by the injustice that had absorbed their lives.

"But how can their friendship, their solidarity or even their commitment to the cause be effective when in Ireland there is no place for the families of victims in the investigation? When there is nothing

to reassure these families that society will support them, will redress the balance broken by the murder? What is the use of my friends' heart-breaking affection when I see their distress, their despair to see such an important investigation, the longest and more far-reaching in Ireland, come to nothing?"

Finally, she says, France is waking up and the local investigation is underway, and more would have been done but for the Irish Supreme Court decision on the extradition of Ian Bailey. Happily for Marguerite, the loss of Bailey's case against the State cleared the way for the final lap of the French investigation.

But the pain *"continues to isolate me. I cannot say I am alone in wandering down this dark path, but dawn is still long in coming"*. It is much closer four years on from this account, which does not take one iota away from the heartbreaking and true sentiments contained in the account. And proves the harsh fact that a murderer slays more than the victim.

During my trip, I also met with and interviewed Sophie's son Pierre Louis, brother Bertrand and Jean-Antoine Bloc, all of whose dignity, patience and perseverance, as well as Alain's, struck me as not just admirable but astounding given the trauma they had been subjected to, not just by the loss of Sophie but by the iniquities of the passage of the case. None wanted revenge but craved, as they deserved, justice.

They and Marguerite, Georges and Marie Madeleine are decent, good and law-abiding people, in total contrast to the arrogant, belligerent and degenerate Bailey, who never demonstrated the least ounce of compassion for their plight, but rather cast himself in the role of victim in a relentless campaign of bombastic self-justification. It made me sick to the stomach that my native country had failed miserably to afford the legal retribution that the devil in the hills of West Cork deserved. I was confident that France would make up for that abject and unjustified failure.

He had, in fairness to the country he hid behind, been ripped to shreds in two Irish courts, and his foul and malicious allegations against the media and the murder investigation had proven to be seen for what they were – total, abject nonsense.

I returned to Dublin with renewed confidence that this would indeed be the case.

CHAPTER 23
ANOTHER
HUMILIATING DEFEAT

Dublin – 2018

In Dublin, the GSOC investigation report into the complaints lodged by Ian Bailey, Jules Thomas and Marie Farrell of high-level corruption in the conduct of the murder investigation was published at the end of July 2018. One of the most important findings was that there was not a whit of evidence to undermine the decision to arrest Bailey and Thomas, and nothing to prove that either constituted an unlawful arrest. This was significant, as the DPP had in the report suggested that Jules Thomas had been unlawfully arrested and therefore Bailey's statements would not be admissible.

Bailey had claimed the murder case against him had been based on a false narrative and so-called "evidence" garnered by a large number of officers under the direction and command of various senior officers, including three named senior officers, that was falsified, forged and fabricated with one overriding intention to "frame" him.

GSOC considered this allegation central to its investigation and reviewed a large amount of documentation and re-interviewed witnesses. There was no evidence found that Ian Bailey was "framed" for the murder or that evidence was falsified, forged or fabricated by members of the Garda Síochána. This finding and rejection of the scurrilous attack was right in line with the conclusion about the matter by the Fennelly Commission. Once more, the persistent and unrelenting predilection for lying was exposed. Bailey was the person who was falsifying and fabricating, which he had started as far back as his reporting of the murder.

GSOC then put the DPP report into perspective, as Bailey had asserted that in the report new information had come to light, with evidence of a concerted, ongoing conspiracy by Gardai to pervert the course of justice in the murder case.

"The new information referred to by Mr Bailey in respect of this allegation concerns a lengthy critique of the Garda murder investigation which came to light during related court proceedings. GSOC has established that this critique was written by a senior solicitor of that office but in the name of the DPP Jim Hamilton. *It is noted that this critique is the opinion of the DPP and is not evidential in or of itself. There is no evidence within the critique that members of the Garda Síochána had attempted to pervert the course of justice."*

The GSOC finding confirmed that the forty-four-page memorandum in relation to the murder investigation was written by Robert Sheehan, not by the DPP, but with James Hamilton's name attached.

The accusation that senior members of the investigation team had tried to improperly influence the State solicitor Malachi Boohig to intervene with the Minister for Justice to prosecute Bailey was given short shrift: *"His recollection of the meeting was different to that of other witnesses interviewed in respect of this issue and would not support the allegation made by Mr Bailey to any evidential standard."*

So, in that regard, as a result of contradictory witness evidence, the allegation of improper conduct on the part of the Gardai by Eamon Barnes to put pressure on the DPP to charge Bailey simply did not stand up. In a curious twist on this whole saga, the report stated that a group of witnesses who had dealings with the original murder investigation gave a different impression. These were the State solicitor for West Cork (Malachi Boohig) and two former DPPs (Eamon Barnes and James Hamilton). All three met with GSOC officers between June 2012 and April 2013.

The report stated:

"On the question of pressure being brought to bear on the office of the DPP at that time, the view given to the GSOC investigators was that this was indirect pressure via the media as opposed to pressure from the Garda Síochána."

So, astoundingly if this was the view given to the GSOC inquiry, it contradicted not only what Barnes alleged around the time of the Supreme Court appeal in 2011 but also the evidence he gave to the High Court in 2015, and also the evidence given by Boohig in the same case. James Hamilton was not party to the origins of the subject, as he did not take over the reins of the office until 1999.

There was no evidence found that Marie Farrell was coerced or intimidated by Gardai to make false statements against Bailey or that Martin Graham was provided with drugs as an incentive to, in Bailey's phrase, "stitch him up". The tide had indeed turned against the prime suspect; this was another humiliating defeat and the last chance saloon for making false accusations against the investigators and trying to profit financially from those unfounded allegations.

In the report, the DPP claimed that the arrest of Jules Thomas was unlawful, therefore by the fruit of the poisonous tree, Bailey's statements in detention were inadmissible. The Circuit Court judge disagreed, saying the arrests were perfectly justified, and Mr Justice Hedigan in the High Court said that the Gardai would have been derelict in their duty not to arrest Bailey. The GSOC inquiry rejected the complaint by Jules Thomas that she was illegally arrested and concluded that she and Bailey had been lawfully detained.

Mr Hamilton told the GSOC inquiry that he had the opinion of three counsels who agreed with his assessment of evidence. But so also did GSOC engage counsel and they disagreed with their counterparts for the DPP on several points, most graphically in the opinion that Jules Thomas had been unlawfully arrested.

The DPP opines in the report that Jules Thomas was severely damaged by her detention, which she felt was biased and that she was press-ganged. This was a prejudiced assertion and not backed by any independent corroboration. All the statements, memos and documentation disproved this statement. All the appropriate regulations were strictly observed by the Gardai. The arrests were perfectly lawful and the opinion of the DPP was in serious error.

To further emphasise that incorrect opinion, there was subsequently no successful legal challenge of arrest by Jules Thomas or indeed Bailey. This pernicious and toxic individual had fought a long and dirty war against the investigation team, convinced of his omnipotence, and had wreaked damage on them along the campaign. For years, prominent members of the team with exemplary careers had to live with the vile false slanders heaped upon them with the suspicion engendered by them, however untrue. All were reported in the media. Mud sticks, as they say. I could not count the times I had to rebut these allegations by ordinary, unsuspecting people who assumed that the whole problem in not solving the case lay with the incompetence, corruption and stupidity of the Gardai.

I had of course over the duration of my coverage of the case as a journalist and author much interaction with the investigators, all of whom I had found to be men of integrity and honesty. That might not have been the view of certain journalists who had a prejudiced attitude in general towards the Gardai. There was nothing new about that in the media business. But I have to say that journalists such as Barry Roche, Ralph Riegel, Ann Mooney, Lara Marlowe, Ann Murphy, Eddie Cassidy, Senan Molony, Carol Mangez and others who had covered the case from the start acted with the balance and integrity demanded of the profession.

CHAPTER 24
THE FRENCH TRIAL

Paris – May 27–31, 2019

Just almost one year later, I was back in Paris for the trial *in absentia* of Ian Bailey for the murder of Sophie Toscan du Plantier. Bailey, in what the prosecutor would describe as an act of a coward, had refused either to travel or offer a defence. Instead, from afar he and his solicitor Frank Buttimer threw insults from at the French justice system, calling it a show trial and a farce.

One is reminded of a saying by Hippocrates:

"To know is science; merely to believe one knows is ignorance."

The only farcical element was that he did not show up. It was also an act of supreme hypocrisy, as he had already engaged extensively with the system in the course of his appeals, during which time he had never muttered a bad word about a system which afforded him a defence team, translated the indictment and pleadings, and given the time and consideration of eight superior court judges, for all of which the French taxpayer footed the bill.

Mr Buttimer is a highly experienced lawyer and his client had in some years of sobriety in fairness to him got some law degrees while studying in University College Cork. Both should have paid more attention to a much more legally qualified Irish Court Judge, Mr Justice Peart, when in his judgement to extradite Bailey he said, "Bearing in mind the fact that this court must and does accord full respect to the prosecution procedures in France and to the system of trials generally in that jurisdiction, it must be presumed that procedures exist where fundamental rights of the accused persons are protected."

Mr Buttimer had already told the Irish High Court in 2015 that his client could have been arrested by no less than twenty states in Europe under the legislation and been extradited to the issuing extradition State France to face charges for the crime. So why was he telling the media that it was a show trial when all those states would co-operate?

They both, as proved, possessed a form of arrogance that they could take on, as demonstrated in the Irish High Court, not just the State but also hugely qualified advocates both with tremendous qualifications and insight into the issues that were presented to the jury. They dared and tried unsuccessfully to challenge those and failed. Both would not bother to face the same result in a French court for the most obvious reasons.

In France in the eighteenth century, there had already been established the inquisitorial system of the examining magistrate or juge d'instruction sifting out prosecution witnesses and the criminal trial procedure involving judges, jurors and attending counsel. The presiding judge directed the proceedings and asked questions of witnesses, but the counsel could recommend further questions.

The adversarial system in England and Ireland was a relatively late development. Until well into the late eighteenth century, the judge was both examiner and cross-examiner, as is the case in France today. Later, the defence and prosecution counsel were added and began to dominate trials with opening and closing speeches and extensive examination and cross-examination of witnesses. Other facets were added, like the rules of evidence (more complicated, as a prominent barrister remarked, than the rules of cricket) and the right to silence of the accused.

Ludovic Kennedy, the legendary British broadcaster, author and great advocate against miscarriages of justice, far preferred the French inquisitorial system than the adversarial system because the former, he said, sought the truth of the matter while the latter tried to bury it chiefly by ruling certain evidence inadmissible. "In a system whose object is to find the truth, there is very little evidence, as long as it is relevant, that is not admissible."

He viewed the right to silence of the accused and the rules of evidence as instruments in the British system (inherited, of course, by the Irish system) designed to prevent the ventilation of the truth and encourage a spurious sense of drama by opposing counsel. "If there is evidence sufficient to justify taking the accused to trial, it surely follows that he is obliged to give account of himself, as he is in the inquisitorial system and if he refuses the court will be entitled to draw its own conclusions."

He adjudged the French system far superior, fairer and efficient than the British system, which had a far greater propensity to result in the jailing of the innocent and the freeing of the guilty. He pointed to statistics which proved that theory – miscarriages of justice in France were only a tiny proportion of those in Britain. The French trials were also much shorter in duration.

He quoted Nicholas Cowdery Q.C., New South Wales Director of Public Prosecutions: "The adversarial system is not directed to the ascertainment of the truth, to the contrary ... In our system a lawyer with a client works hard to avoid justice being done or, even worse, the truth being discovered."

Let us say that the cheap insults born of contempt for the French system (which both were happy to engage with in the appeals process) by Bailey and Frank Buttimer bear no comparison to the opinion of a titan like the late Ludovic Kennedy, a man who at any time they would not have been fit to lick his boots. They had also been stripped by the findings of the High Court and subsequent inquiries of their long-trumpeted accusation that the French trial was based on a flawed and corrupt Irish murder investigation.

The trial was scheduled between May 27–31, with a one-day public holiday break. I travelled three days before and booked into Hotel La Louisiane in Rue de Seine, where I had stayed on my first trip to interview the Bouniol family in 2002. It seemed like a century ago, so long this case has dragged on, but there was a resolution on the immediate horizon and a renewed hope for justice.

It is a modest and comfortable small hotel with the tremendous advantage of being in striking distance to anywhere in central Paris. On the second day after breakfast, I walked down to the Seine across the bridge towards the Palais de Justice, where the trial would be held in the Victor Hugo courtroom. To my right in the distance I could see Notre Dame Cathedral under a clear blue sky, its magnificent façade covered by scaffolding erected in the wake of the terrible fire. A sad sight to see such injurious consequences to an iconic historical building.

This is Île de la Cité, a section steeped in history and an atmosphere that is tangible and fascinating, and a feast for the eyes. Just a short distance down Boulevard du Palais, I stopped outside the entrance to the court, the Cour du Mai, and the wonderful wrought iron gate there since the time of Louis XVI in the late-eighteenth century. Just adjacent are Sainte-Chapelle, built in the sixteenth century, and the Conciergerie, a former prison and now museum where Marie Antoinette was incarcerated before her execution.

During the Reign of Terror, the Revolutionary Tribunal was set up in the former royal palace, the Palais de Justice, to dispense of heads at the rate of knots, and condemned over 2,000 prisoners to the guillotine; the Conciergerie served as the holding facility for all those facing certain death, including Danton and Robespierre.

From the courtyard, a steep set of steps lead to the three main entrance doors and into the main hall, called the Galerie Marchande, and to the Salle des Pas Perdus (the Hall of Lost Steps), a reference to time spent there by hopeful and hopeless litigants. The Victor Hugo courtroom is just a few flights of steeply ascending stone steps up from the main hall.

It is a setting in which the defendant, had he the courage to appear, might have inspired given his past craving for attention some better lines in the doggerel he wrote masquerading as poetry.

But he preferred to stay in the safety of West Cork and write more self-published rubbish, and make outlandish, self-serving statements awaiting the judgement of the Paris court.

The murder-accused 'poet' was the last thing on my mind as I walked around the streets of a city I had always loved since the first time I had visited many decades before to stay with the family of my friend Patrick Froissart and get a sense of the joys of French life in the capital. What more occupied me was the Bouniol family, who unlike me as an observer, had never experienced the inevitable and understandable iniquities of a murder trial during which the events of their much-loved-one's death would be trawled through in forensic and painful detail.

Worse still, not to have the accused in the dock, which would usually provide both a different focus and comfort, with the expectation that he would face in real time the details of the horrendous action of his crime and the possibility of legal retribution, and for them to be able to see Ian Bailey being subjected to the merciless examination he had experienced in both the libel and High Court proceedings in Ireland. One more sting to their long-standing suffering.

In France, one gets a different perspective of that suffering and the murder within both a personal and societal framework. It has been framed for a long time as an intriguing unsolved mystery, ranking just below the murder of "Le Petit Grégory" Villemin, a child deliberately drowned in a remote part of Eastern France, an act for which nobody was convicted and was a fixture in a large scale of media reports in the 1980s.

The portrayal of the Bouniol family in the French media is one of decent middle-class people who have as underdogs fought against all the odds for justice for their murdered daughter.

This is in stark contrast to the Irish/UK perception of a well-connected family with ties to the elite world of French cinema and glamour attempting to pull all the strings legally and politically to avenge the murder of their beautiful daughter. This ignores the fact that the family were far from being well connected in any sphere.

It was only partly true by default when Sophie married Daniel Toscan du Plantier, who the family did not particularly like but considered her old enough to make her own decisions. It was far from the red carpet of Cannes that both Sophie's maternal and paternal origins sprang.

The marriage to the king of French film royalty bestowed a media image on Sophie which was far from the truth, as she was a person who assiduously avoided the limelight and, according to Daniel as he told me, was most uncomfortable in the glare of publicity, a dichotomy which caused some problems for their relationship. Her need for privacy was never more evident than by the purchase of the house in the remote peninsula of West Cork.

Any reflected influence evaporated with the death of Daniel in February 2003, and the family members were on their own, but given extra weight to their position by the establishment of ASSOPH. Nonetheless, they had to endure the iniquities of bureaucracy in two jurisdictions – a denial of justice in one, much postponed in the other – and constant delay of law and disappointment, all the spurns of an epic tragedy, the slings and arrows of outrageous fortune mirrored in Hamlet's soliloquy – To be, or not to be:

> *There's the respect*
> *That makes calamity of so long life.*
> *For who would bear the whips and scorns of time,*
> *Th' oppressor's wrong, the proud man's contumely,*
> *The pangs of despised love, the law's delay,*
> *The insolence of office, and the spurns*
> *That patient merit of th' unworthy takes.*

Anyone who imagined that because he was being tried in Paris, Ian Bailey – even if he was present, as any innocent man would be – was the underdog and the Bouniol family somehow had an upper hand, was severely deluded. Their battle had been fought on scarce resources and a 115,000-euro award from the French Government. Over the same period, the indigent accused, who had barely done an honest day's work in his life, had alone with his failed High Court action cost the Irish taxpayer five million euros. It had cost the newspapers close to one million euros to defend his libel action.

When the raft of other hearings and appeals, the Fennelly and GSOC inquiries and Garda reviews in Ireland, the French legal proceedings and appeals up to this point are all taken into account, the failed journalist, poet, gardener, bodhran player, assaulter and persecutor of women, alcoholic, sick psycho diarist had figuratively speaking been afforded over two decades a war chest which would not have left much change out of eight million euros. And he was bleating about some ill-perceived injustice. Beggaring belief would not vaguely come into the equation.

His lone success up to this point was to get away with murder and not be extradited to face justice. The trial in the Palais de Justice would establish if that would remain the status quo. The signs were not good. He and his legal team's efforts to confirm years and years of allegations of corrupt practices and illegal conduct on the part of the Irish murder investigation and dub the efforts flawed and prejudiced had failed.

This meant that the public prosecutor and first advocate general Jean-Pierre Bonthoux could properly rely on Garda-gathered witness statements as well as those conducted by French investigators, which were considerable. The defence that Bailey would rely on if he appeared had been firmly rejected by two of the highest courts in France. That reliance had been largely based on the DPP report which had been, as a result of bias and prejudice against the investigation team, ruled inadmissible in the High Court in Dublin, as well as its findings dismissed by the French appeal judges but still with the presumption of innocence of the accused in advance of a criminal trial, and the standard for conviction beyond all reasonable doubt.

Bailey knew well in an ironic twist that he could not use

the document that had kept him free in Ireland as a successful defence in the French criminal court, as all its failings of logic and prejudice had already been ruled on in other courts and would again be exposed in the Paris trial. The accused believed in the French system, as he proved in the appeals process, but he certainly did not believe in being found guilty in a criminal trial, especially while depending on the hugely devalued DPP report, and knew the evidence against him was overwhelming. This was the real reason why he did not travel.

The fact that there was no defence or defendant was Bailey's choice; it could or would have no effect on the validity of the proceedings. Irrespective of any differences between the Irish and French judicial systems in the matter of a criminal trial, the standard of proof was the same – beyond all reasonable doubt and the evidence must be sufficient and convincing for the three judges in this instance to convict. As would be the case in the three-judge Special Criminal Court in Ireland. Where witnesses could not attend, as obviously a lot of Irish were in that position, their statements would as in our system be read into the court record.

The Victor Hugo courtroom is a small, oak-panelled space with a corniced ceiling and the grandeur that comes with history. A brass chandelier hangs in the middle of a ceiling that is adorned with a sword, hatchet, scales of justice and an eye. The judges' bench is at the end of the room from the side entrance. Seating stretches on both sides, with an intervening aisle to about three quarters of the room. The last area of rows occupies the width of the room, resting against the back wall. On the left hand of the bench is the dock, in front of a lovely ornate clock. Directly opposite is the prosecutor's stand and chair, which was surrounded by the twenty-four volumes of evidence and procedure the French judicial process had gathered for the case.

Beside that was the space occupied by lawyers for the Bouniol family, Alain Spilliaert, Laurent Pettiti and Marie Dose. They represented as part of the *parties civiles* process relations of Sophie:

Pierre-Louis Baudey-Vignaud, son; Bertrand Bouniol, brother; Georges Bouniol, father; Stephane Bouniol, brother; Michel Gazeau, uncle; Jean-Pierre Gazeau, uncle; Marguerite Gazeau, mother; Marie Madeleine Opalka, aunt; and also ASSOPH. This is another superior aspect of the French system – the direct involvement of the family of the victim in the judicial process.

Close by, under the window overlooking the forecourt of the complex, two sets of benches accommodated just some of the thirty-one accredited journalists covering the case. In Ireland, as in Britain, there is an exaggerated emphasis on the rights of the accused, and the victim and relatives are after the verdict allowed recognition by means of a victim impact statement.

In France, the relatives are allowed an active role in the prosecution of the case right from the start, and legal representation. The lawyers for the family can make submissions at all stages of the investigation and prosecution, and most importantly during the trial itself, and relatives can also testify on the impact the murder has had on their lives.

Thirty-one witnesses, including French investigators and five experts, would be called or quoted. The proceedings would be overseen by Presiding Judge Frederique Aline, sitting with judges Didier Forton and Geraldine Detienne. Jean-Pierre Bonthoux, first advocate general, represented the public prosecutor. As the accused was absent, he would be tried according to the procedure called "criminal default", established by law on March 9, 2004. The previous year, the court made 149 decisions of conviction or acquittal out of which fourteen were rendered by default, equating to roughly ten per cent of all cases.

This illustrates the small number of what could be called the coward's gallery that Ian Bailey had just joined. Had he turned up to once more attempt to prove his innocence for the crime, the trial would have lasted six weeks in front of the three judges and six jurors. In the absence of the accused, the jurors are naturally dispensed with when no defence is in place and the trial would last four days when extra hours of daily hearings were added.

But whatever the outcome, one thing was certain, that the accused would for the first time be subjected to a criminal trial which over the long years of the case he had evaded for no good reason, and would either add or subtract to all the defeats he had in recent times been subjected to in court hearings and inquiries in Ireland, which was not even his native land. One thing Bailey had proved over the years was the propensity to initiate legal proceedings to "prove his innocence" and attempt to profit from the imagined results. This time there was little prospect of that, so he declined to get involved.

So, on any level of objectivity, this move could not be perceived in the light of his previous history as anything but pure bullshit. As Janet Malcolm so perfectly observed in *The Journalist and the Murderer*:

"The lawsuit functions as a powerful therapeutic agent ridding the subject of his humiliating powerlessness and restoring him to his cheer and amour propre.*"*

Not in this case, as the subject was far too scared to be exposed to the truth of his actions. He had already been provided with every opportunity by the French justice system to defend himself.

The trial opened on the afternoon of Monday, May 27, and in the main hall camera crews had gathered to give media attention to the comings and goings of the main protagonists, giving the impression on the outside of a high-profile celebrity trial. There were also several documentary crews, one under the cinematic baton of acclaimed film director Jim Sheridan, who would be a regular fixture in the courtroom.

The packed court rose at about 2.50 p.m. after the entry of the three judges. Presiding Judge Frederique Aline then, as her role demanded but redolent of a prosecuting counsel in our courts, read out the contents of the forty-two-page indictment document. This was a factual overview of the case and much of the evidence familiar to those who knew the details of the case, the reading of which took just over an hour and a half.

Ms Aline also reminded the court that just because the accused was not charged and brought to trial in Ireland, it did not mean he was innocent. It was a failure on the part of the Irish authorities (the DPP). Two French courts, she said, had decided that Bailey had a case to answer for the murder.

The presiding judge said that they considered Bailey was absent without a valid excuse and read a list of more than twenty Irish witnesses – whose statements would be read into the court record – with the exception of Bill Fuller and Amanda Reed who had travelled from West Cork their evidence would be read from the bench. The vast majority could not have afforded the cost of travel and accommodation in a city at the height of the tourist season. Expenses would be repaid but that would take a long time. The notice for the call of witnesses was also far too short.

The first witness called was Michel Larousse, a psychologist who had interviewed a number of people close to the victim and gave a profile of her character and details of her life. He said that she had a happy childhood and had as a young schoolgirl travelled to stay with a family in Dublin on an exchange basis. She studied law but did not complete the course and worked in arts-related jobs. "She hated being bored and did all sorts of things to keep busy. She was an open person but perhaps naïve."

She was independent; there were times she wanted to be with people and other times she preferred to be on her own. She was not afraid of much even in situations that carried risk. The witness gave an example of this, describing how she once allowed a homeless person to sleep in her car, and recalling another time when she invited a homeless person into her house for a meal. She would not have seen the attack coming that led to her death.

She was married and a son, Pierre Louis, was born in 1981, but the marriage did not last. She met Daniel Toscan du Plantier when he was head of the French film organisation UniFrance, where she had a job in the publicity department. He had already been married and divorced twice and he was more focused on his career than his relationships. She began an affair with an artist,

Bruno Carbonnet, but it turned sour when she wanted a child and he was not interested.

Around this time, she had rediscovered Ireland and bought a holiday home in West Cork, where she stayed regularly with friends and family members, and in 1993 with her then lover Carbonnet. After that ended, she was reconciled with Daniel. It was obvious that this backstory was important to the process, the contrast between the woman who had fallen on relatively hard times before her marriage to Daniel, whose cultural and financial influence could not be understated. Film was considered the jewel in the crown of French culture and her husband was the most powerful figure in the cinema industry of the country. And yet she maintained her solitary, independent and down-to-earth nature. This was, of course, to show the true human value of the living Sophie as opposed to the cipher of the dead victim, and to provide a contrast with the beastly, degenerate and violent character of the accused.

The prosecutor said that Mr Bailey had propagated a theory that Ms Toscan du Plantier had been murdered by a lover. He noted that she had asked several friends and members of her family to travel with her and she had called her husband repeatedly during her stay, which would have been unlikely had she been with a lover in West Cork.

Damien Roehrig, a French police officer assigned to the case, apart from his French investigation, had made a trip to Schull in 2011 to interview witnesses. He interviewed dozens of witnesses, who gave him statements. At least five of those stated that Bailey had made confessions to them about committing the crime. Helen Callanan, Bill Fuller, Malachi Reed, and Richie and Rosie Shelley had never altered their testimonies. Mr Reed, who was fourteen years of age at the time, was so traumatised by what Bailey had told him that he slept with an axe beside the bed.

The officer gave details of the statements of the witnesses and their reactions to being told by the accused that he had been responsible for the murder. This evidence demonstrated that the

French investigation and prosecution took those confessions and the accounts of them seriously, unlike the DPP, who brushed them off as a form of black humour and sarcasm, an assertion totally contradicted by the statements of the witnesses. Even more importantly, the confessions were not elicited under pressure in a police station but freely given without prompting in his own comfort zones by Bailey and therefore could only be interpreted as genuine admissions.

The following day, the testimony of three witnesses who heard confessions from Bailey was presented in court. The first witness, Helen Callanan, who had been the news editor of the *Sunday Tribune*, a newspaper which had published articles written by Bailey on the murder, could not be present and had written a letter to the court which was read out and was critical of the short notice given to Irish witnesses to appear. She was certainly correct about that, but it was also a fact that witnesses in Bailey's High Court action against the Irish State had to go through the same process and had been short-changed in terms of retrospective expenses. Not good, and worse for the French proceedings.

She made three statements to Gardai in 1997. She was subpoenaed by newspapers when Bailey sued them for defamation in 2003, and by the State in the context of Mr Bailey's High Court action in 2014. She also gave a statement to French investigators in Terenure Garda Station.

Judge Frederique Aline then read her testimony. Ms Callanan recounted that when working for the *Sunday Tribune*, she found out that Bailey – who was freelancing for the newspaper – was a suspect for the murder. When she confronted him, he replied, "Yes, I did it to resurrect my career." Shocked by the admission, she contacted the Gardai and made a statement.

Amanda Reed, who had travelled from West Cork, told the court how her then fourteen-year-old son Malachi came home from school on the evening of February 4, 1997, having been given a lift home by Bailey, who lived nearby. He said nothing that night but the following morning he was upset and told her that Bailey, who had been drinking, had suddenly announced to him while driving home the night before that he had killed Ms Toscan du Plantier: "I went up there with a rock and bashed her fucking brains in"

"Malachi was very upset, and I said that it was a very serious thing to say and we had to speak to the guards. He told me that when he heard what Bailey said he was terrified but could not get out of the car while it was moving."

She and her son gave statements to the Gardai shortly afterwards. She told the court that "the impact on our lives was huge; we felt that we were living close to a dangerous person. My son said he was a bad man."

Bill Fuller, who had at one time been a friend of the accused, also travelled from West Cork to give evidence of a third admission by Bailey. He recalled a conversation with Bailey in his house at the end of January 1997 during which Bailey showed him pictures of the turkey he had killed at Christmas and began to talk about the murder. He said, speaking in the second person, "You saw her in the shop with her tight arse and you fancied her, so you went up there to see what you could get. You tried to calm her but she was scared, she ran away screaming so you chased her to calm her down. You stove something into the back of her head, you realised you went too far and had to finish her off."

Fuller told him that this was the sort of thing he would do. "Funny you should say," replied Bailey, "that is how I met Jules. I saw her tight arse, but she let me in." Fuller added that it was common knowledge around the area that Bailey often talked of himself in the second or third person.

This was riveting and highly incriminating evidence from the two present witnesses; the absent one would be further corroborated by the entering into evidence later of Rosie and Richie Shelley's statements, who at a New Year's Eve gathering at Liscaha had been told by a highly emotional Bailey, who had tears streaming down his face, "I did it. I did it. I went too far."

Not one of the witnesses who heard the admissions detected

any sense of humour, black or otherwise. Malachi Reed and the Shelleys had been frightened, Helen Callanan shocked and Bill Fuller also shocked but not surprised. All were prompted to make statements about the events to members of the investigation team. In each case, Bailey was in his own comfort zone, in his car and in his house; there was no pressure on him to say anything other than that of the bursting thoughts in his head about what he did which needed release.

A stand-up comedian, a master of satire or sarcasm he was not, but rather a man with an overpowering need to unburden himself to anyone, even a fourteen-year-old schoolboy.

Earlier, a once high-profile figure in the French cinema world and former head of the Cannes Film Festival, Gilles Jacob, provided the court with further insight into the personality and life of Sophie. He had been a close friend of Daniel Toscan du Plantier and said that it was important to understand why a woman travelled to an isolated part of Ireland alone just before Christmas.

He testified that Daniel contributed a great deal to French cinema during the 1980s and 1990s as a roving ambassador for UniFrance, the film promotion board, and that he was brilliant at the job and well known.

The now eighty-eight-year-old Jacob, a slight and physically diminished figure, said that Daniel had been a great seducer of women whose conquests, as he put it – hardly politically correct at this time – included beautiful actresses Marie-Christine Barrault, Isabelle Huppert, Isabella Rossellini and Francesca Comencini. Sophie was a press attaché for UniFrance and for the Cannes Film Festival when he met her. "He was crazy about her ... it was difficult to resist his charm."

He had first met her at Daniel's manor in Ambax, Haute-Garonne in 1991, and he visited it so often that his friend found him a house to purchase nearby. "Daniel wanted to show Sophie off, but she did not want to be the wife of ... Daniel's world was exhausting; the phone was always ringing. Sometimes Sophie needed calm and silence."

Jacob said she needed to stand up to her husband to show that despite his conquests (relationships might have been a far more appropriate word) he had to pay attention to her. Sometimes she would just disappear, and Daniel would have to look for her all over Paris. She could stay with her friend Agnes Thomas, who had worked with her at UniFrance. He said he was close to Sophie for five years before her death and that they had communicated by fax.

Other people were obsessed by their dress and appearance when they walked up the red carpet in Cannes. "Not Sophie, for me she represented real life, she had remained herself, which is very difficult in that milieu." He was with Daniel in the house in Ambax on the day of the murder. They heard on the television news that a French woman had been murdered in Ireland and their first reaction was that it could not be Sophie. Then the French ambassador rang and confirmed that it was her.

"The image I remember of Sophie is her serene face with her beautiful dark eyes, always smiling. She lived in a luxurious milieu. It may be given to you, but it costs you dearly." Judge Frederique Aline questioned the witness and asked him if the victim tried to be seductive or provocative. "On the contrary, she had beautiful clothes but hers was an old-fashioned beauty. She was always discreet – she never spoke about sex or feelings. I cannot imagine the slightest trace of provocation or incitation. She had a sort of reserve."

The witness obviously knew his neighbour well and held her in the highest regard, and his account closely echoed Daniel's narrative in my interview with him. It was sad and emotive testimony for the observer, as it gave an accurate and affecting portrait of a woman of beauty and substance who was not seduced by the circles she moved in, who gloried in publicity while she craved simplicity and privacy.

One might be forgiven for thinking that this frail old man, who would have been anything but over two decades before, may have harboured an unrequited love just like Sophie's literary hero W.B. Yeats had for Maud Gonne.

Agnes Thomas, Sophie's best friend, described her as "joyous, lively with a sunny beauty and very generous. She was passionate about her work. She loved art, literature, music and wrote a great deal. She was really an exceptional person." Thomas to this day regrets that she declined the invitation to travel with her to West Cork in December 1996 because if she had gone, her best friend might still be alive.

Before the trip, she had spoken with her on the phone and Sophie had told her that a man had contacted her and wanted to meet her, but she did not want to meet him and was wary. "Sophie said that the man was a weird guy who wrote poetry. I told her to be careful about meeting such a man. She told the judge that she could not be sure if the man was Bailey." In response to a question of what she had told French investigators when making a statement in 2008, she had told them about the conversation of December 22, 1996 while Sophie was in Schull but had forgotten this earlier one.

Asked by a lawyer of the family's for the reason for the failure to remember the earlier conversation, Agnes Thomas explained, "The brain is a complex thing. I was working with the association. I had lost my best friend; it was so shocking something blocked in me. It took years. It came back to me when the film footage I saw about the murder had a mention of poetry. She told me about the man she found weird and I did advise her to be careful and not meet him."

There was little doubt in anyone's mind that the only weirdo in the area where Sophie visited who proclaimed to be a poet was none other than Ian Bailey, who read his excruciating verse regularly as well as thumping a bodhran in local pubs, and who had consistently lied under oath in Irish court proceedings that he did not know or have contact with the victim.

The third day, Wednesday, May 29, was taken up largely with the reading of witness statements, opening with those of the psychiatrist and psychologist who had provided a profile of Bailey garnered from the content of his diaries and history of violence against women, in particular his partner. There followed those of Jules Thomas, her three daughters, Detective Liam Leahy of the Irish Gardai and the statements of the accused while in custody. In the afternoon, members of the family gave the equivalent of victim impact statements and their lawyers made submissions to the court.

Sophie's son Pierre Louis Vignaud made an impassioned and highly affecting speech to the court. "I want to remember the love this person brought and that everyone who knew her had for her. I can recall my mother and the relationship I had with her. I remember the love she had for everyone, family, personally and professionally. There was a large part of my life when I was alone with her, we shared the same apartment, the same room – we knew each other well.

"She was someone who did not want only a life of ease. She was a woman who was passionate and intelligent. Her decision to buy the house in Ireland was about simplicity for her and reflected her personality. For her, Ireland was old and rugged and remote. The house was basic but comfortable and looked out on the landscape. That was what she was like. I kept the house the way it was. When I go back to Ireland, I don't go to a crime scene. It is how she left it and her heart and spirit lives on there.

"It is important to tell my children what sort of woman she was, intellectual but liked simple things. She and Daniel had a lust for life, they were vibrant and had a lovely, romantic, even literary relationship. Maman did not go to Ireland to flee Daniel Toscan du Plantier but to escape the public life she had with him in Paris. To recharge and take breath.

"I don't know what will come of this court case. But we have a duty to get justice, at least for my kids. What would I do if my daughter, when she grows up, was to go to Ireland alone? This court can help me feel secure, help me to decide whether to keep the house which is a big part of the soul of my mother."

Sophie's brother Bertrand said that Ireland mirrored his sister's spirit. She loved reading and working in the house and took her cooker there from France. His parents had put all their efforts into finding the truth about Sophie's killing and had been willing to do everything to help the case.

Her favourite aunt, Marie Madeleine, speaking from a wheelchair said that Sophie was beautiful, but it was despite herself; she wasn't trying to make herself so. One got a sense from her that she wanted to live a different way – be an Alice in Wonderland. She was the exact opposite of Daniel's other women. "It is important that justice be done. She should be here now in this city, walking free."

The court had already been given a great sense of who Sophie was, not the mere cipher of the murder case but a highly valued and valuable person. Now there was more an outpouring of love, but as always with the family, with the sense of dignity that made their testimonies even more gut-wrenching. I looked at the empty dock and wished we could all see what expression struggled from under the bloated, withered canvas of Bailey's visage when he had to witness what he had deprived the family of, the world of when he so brutally extinguished the life, the future of what another Irish literary giant O'Casey might have described as a darling woman.

We had all seen the ghost of Sophie resurrected, flesh added to her bones during the proceedings, but also heard and seen the horror of how she had been consigned prematurely to the darkness of the grave. The old familiar hate and rage bubbled in my bloodstream, coursing through my veins at the thought of the devil who quenched a life as well as a future and all hope and expectation. It had, over the years, woken me often in the hour of the wolf just between darkness and dawn, fresh from a dream in which a giant sparkling blade glistened in my hand:

"*Tis now the very witching time of night,
When churchyards yawn and hell itself breathes out
Contagion to this world. Now could I drink hot blood
And do such bitter business as the bitter day
Would quake to look on.*"

I was returned from my reverie by the familiar voice of Alain Spilliaert, the advocate for the family, making his submission on their behalf to the court as part of the *parties civiles* process.

"Mme President of the court, Mme Counsellor, Counsellor and First Advocate General. In the first fortnight of January 1997, my colleague Paul Haennig and I were appointed to represent Daniel Toscan du Plantier, Mme Marguerite and Mr Georges Bouniol relating to the murder of Sophie Toscan du Plantier in Ireland in December 1996. I then met the parents of the victim, who demonstrated dignity and courage in those terrible circumstances. We knew they were supported by their solid sons Bertrand and Stephane.

"My colleague Paul Haennig proposed to file a civil action complaint under the extra-territorial jurisdiction in the area of French justice. I was in agreement. Thus, on January 17, 1997, we deposited in the hands of judges a complaint about the murder of Sophie Toscan du Plantier." This was the genesis of the action that ended up in court that week. The lawyer then chronicled the narrative of the case in both France and Ireland over the decades both in great detail and admirable insight.

Laurent Pettiti attacked Frank Buttimer for criticising the French system and the cheek he had to call it a show trial. Bailey, his client, preferred to address himself to the television rather than do it in front of French judges and police.

His legal colleague Marie Dose attacked Bailey for the bestiality and savagery of the attack on the victim. She bemoaned the fact that there was no defence and was angry there was no lawyer there to act on the part of the accused. She provided an accurate and stinging portrait of the accused as an eccentric whose behaviour was bizarre. It was a picture of an elevated vagrant who would have been attracted to the beautiful and successful Sophie.

The vacuous and transparent excuse used by Bailey to explain the scratches on his arms, accepted by the DPP, could never have happened that way. The DPP report was all forgiving to Bailey's lies and contradictory versions of events. She assessed the evidence against Bailey in a dramatic and compelling fashion.

Wearing his ornate red robe with white collar and border, and black lower sleeves, the prosecutor Jean-Pierre Bonthoux cut a highly impressive figure as he entered his stand on Friday morning just after 10.30 a.m. to address the court. The sun suspended over Boulevard du Palais cast its rays through the window overlooking the Cour du Mai. The court was packed and the sense of anticipation that attends the final phase of every court hearing was palpable. Reminiscent of the hush that descends in the auditorium of the theatre as the lights start dimming and the curtain begins to slide back to reveal the stage and the players.

The prosecutor rose and the extended soliloquy began first with a firm but hushed tone. "To quote William Butler Yeats, a poet that Sophie Toscan du Plantier liked to read, 'the innocent and the beautiful have no enemy but time'. This proverb could be applied to the system of justice. During these three days, time stood still on the abominable crime committed which destroyed the life of Sophie Toscan du Plantier and her family.

"The paradox of destiny: this young woman was solitary, elegant, discreet; she did not like show, and she took refuge in this beautiful country that is Ireland. She was caught by a criminal who was the exact opposite to everything she was: obscure, barbaric, media attention-seeking. Her name should not be reduced to being a sole reference to this affair and today justice must be rendered to her."

Mr Bonthoux then addressed the absent accused and said that his lack of courage in not presenting himself to the court was an act of cowardice associated with the opportunity to denigrate the (French justice) system, contempt which was unacceptable. He enumerated the court cases in Ireland in which Bailey had suffered defeats, principally the libel case and his High Court action against the State. These were legal proceedings where the judges mattered and the DPP was not a judge, he said.

The prosecutor pointed out that this was not the trial of the Hound of the Baskervilles or the Beast of Gévaudan but Ian Bailey. "I am not accusing him of looking at the moon, being marginal, of writing thirty pages of obscenities in his journal which I read to the point of being nauseated. Of being an alcoholic, being violent with his partner, a failed journalist, a failed gardener, he is not the Beast of Gévaudan. There are serious charges against him which allowed for him to be brought before this court. The charges must be put in context of the place and time committed in 1996 in an isolated part of the Irish countryside. The evidence is there, an accumulation of proof which permits a trial and conviction."

He noted that in the libel trial of 2003, Judge Moran had commended the tenacity of the witnesses. But the DPP differed and then the prosecutor launched an attack on the DPP, saying the analysis made by him rested on a segmentation of the evidence which was supposedly considered invalid one by one. It fell short by not taking an overall approach to the case but rather piecemeal by taking each piece of evidence as stand alone.

"If you reduce every element to zero it does not take a mathematician to work out the sum will come to zero. The sum of zero is zero!" There is, he added, a global defect in the analysis as a result of the segmentation and a bias shown in the invalidation of the evidence.

"And the vocabulary used is instead always in the conditional for the accusation and in the affirmative for the discharge The confidential report, neither dated not signed, not on headed paper, like notes on a white page does not exist in any procedure other in that of the Supreme Court which dealt with the law not the substance (of the report)."

Mr Bonthoux dealt with the matter of how the DPP attempted to wrongly undermine evidence of witnesses like Malachi Reid, left terrified by the confession that Bailey made to him about bashing the brains out of the victim. "According to the DPP, he was agitated because he was summoned by the police. He was never summoned by the police. He did not want to discuss it with his mother because Bailey was drunk when he drove him home that evening."

On the matter of the scratches which were absent according to six witnesses on the evening of December 22 when Bailey was in the Galley pub and played the bodhran with his sleeves pulled up: "There were no scratches on the hands or forearms of Mr Bailey. It is not of interest to the DPP. The six people who were in ideal conditions remark nothing. Nothing was noticed. Therefore, they could not have been sustained earlier than the 23rd. For the DPP, one person saw a small scratch on one hand and this for the DPP is incontestable evidence."

He lacerated the DPP for declaring that Bailey never varied his evidence and proved that he did. He returned to the vital evidence of the scratches: "The scratches observed on Ian Bailey's hands and forearm are described by the police as 'straight lacerations' similar to those found on the body of Mme Toscan du Plantier and made by the briars according to the pathologist. The DPP had no samples of the briars in question. They are described [by him] as being thorns sharpened like razor blades. The DPP has never been to the scene of the crime. He only has the reports. The DPP disqualified himself by saying the briars are like razor blades."

The prosecutor was perfectly correct. I had examined the scene of the crime and paid special attention to the area of the thorn bushes from which the victim was dragged before the concrete block was dropped on her face and head. The thorns were of the ordinary variety that one would encounter in any domestic garden. Straight and spiky, nothing remotely resembling a razor blade. The pathologist noted injuries to the left arm and palm of the left hand, consistent with being sustained by the briars and thorns. No blade analogy appeared in his report.

The point made by the prosecutor that the DPP had not been to the scene of the crime so could not possibly make such judgements with accuracy was one made by counsel Luán O'Braonáin in the High Court action referring to the author of the report: "As far as the statements are concerned, this witness actually knows nothing about what happened in Schull, in Skibbereen other than going through materials that went to him." Both

French investigators and magistrates had been to the scene of the crime. The author of the DPP report had been invited by the Irish murder investigation team to view the scene of the crime but declined, saying he had maps. What map might expose the physical details of a crime scene? None.

Mr Bonthoux had the rapt and undivided attention of the court, including the judge and the magistrates, who were taking copious notes. His evisceration of the logic of the DPP's reasoning was both devastating and humiliating. One could only imagine how he would have dealt with the examination of Bailey had he been present. In my opinion, he would have matched Paul Gallagher in the libel action and Paul O'Higgins and Luán O'Braonáin in the High Court action cut for cut.

The DPP said that Bailey's version of the timetable, his movements in and around the time of the murder, did not vary. Not true, said the prosecutor. He first said he was in the Courtyard pub all night and then went home. Then he gave a second version stating that he was in the Galley pub all night with Jules Thomas, where he recited poetry and played his musical instrument in full view of the witnesses. On the way home, he stopped at the hill and said to Jules Thomas that there was a light on in Alfie Lyons's house. There was no light on in the house because Alfie Lyons and Shirley Foster were in bed.

There was a light on in Sophie's house which Bailey could clearly see. He asked Thomas when they got home, did she want to go out, and she said no. He did go out to write an article in the studio, he said – a cold, dilapidated space. But he did not deliver the article the next morning when it was due. Marie Farrell saw him not far from the scene of the crime sometime around 3 a.m. After that, Bailey went to her and made various threats to her.

So, Mr Bonthoux contended, the accused changed his versions to suit the circumstances, attempted to provide a false alibi and then threatened a principal witness. Stark and proven facts, the first from questionnaires and statements to the Gardai, the second from the multiple official complaints made by Farrell about being threatened by Bailey. None of which made any impression on the DPP.

Bailey, the prosecutor submitted, knew the place where the body was discovered and the nationality of the victim. He claimed he was having a rest on the morning of the murder, but a number of witnesses had him active from 10 a.m. He told some about the murder, he took photos at the scene of the crime, one in which the body of a woman lay on the ground in the exact spot where the victim was found, and was contacting newspapers at a time when nobody knew what had happened. When reporting on the crime, he did not tell his editor when he became a suspect.

He made confessions about his responsibility for the crime, the reason for which the DPP said was "black humour" or "sarcasm". "We are confronted by an atrocious crime. One would be peculiar to want to make smart jokes when one is the principal suspect. It is not even a psychological defence. He spoke to his editor in a professional conversation and he said, 'I did it,' and she went to the police. To the Shelley couple who are friends at a party, there is the subject of the murder, which is discussed all evening; he has only one desire – to confess to the murder. 'Yes, I did it.' The couple left petrified and went to the police."

What the prosecutor was arguing was simple. The words uttered by Bailey had the meaning that he intended and were not capable of being given an interpretation as done by the DPP, as the circumstances in which the admissions were delivered, and reaction of the witnesses could not possibly support such an assertion. There could be no irony or sarcasm involved in the act of confessing to a murder. It was what it was.

Malachi Reed was given a confession in the car. "According to the psychologist, he is in a 'comfort zone' in his car or in his home or with Bill Fuller, his friend who he trusts. A detailed confession which describes the scene of the crime and provides a sexual motivation."

Bonthoux then quoted Fuller's incriminating evidence as given to the court. It provided a motive (and the classical reaction of a sadistic sexual psychopath to rejection by a woman with whom he wished to have sex). He scared her and she ran.

"Whereas Sophie thought that opening her door, she was coming to help someone. It is natural and she knew him. She must then have noticed he was not in his normal state. For Sophie it did not work out well, she fled, he caught up with her, hit her with a slate and then with a concrete block. He has a personality that coincides with the crime, his assaults of Jules Thomas prove his violence towards women.

"There is a profusion of elements of accusation, objective elements, shameless lies on his part and justified evidence. It is an atrocious crime, barbaric against a lone woman. The motive is sexual and as his diaries show, he is a sexual predator … three minutes of terror and suffering. A nightmare for her family. The consequences of the crime are incalculable."

There was a pause. If the prosecutor had been a principal actor in a dramatic play in a large theatre, the skill, the tone, the use of sparing but cutting emphasis and above all the hugely impressive presence would have prompted an immediate standing ovation. It was in a criminal court, where any such display would have rather prompted instant recrimination from the bench. But I daresay that many supporters of the Bouniol family would have had such an internal reaction. I certainly did.

Jean-Pierre Bonthoux then said that he had the honour of asking the court for the maximum of what was provided for the crime, thirty years of criminal reclusion. He also requested that the court would pronounce in favour of a new EAW. He then delivered his last line. "This court case is a step. I hope one day to see Mr Bailey in this court, and see his lawyers defend him." The judge and the magistrates then retired for their deliberations.

Five long hours would pass before they, after the ringing of the court bell, returned at 5.25 p.m. Frederique Aline then read out the judgement of the court, her voice cutting through the silence in the Victor Hugo courtroom. In her opening remarks, before she settled down to the substance of the judgement, she said, "There has been no acquittal in Ireland. A decision by the DPP in Ireland does not have the value of a definitive judgement. Despite Mr Bailey's many denials and legal appeals, the absence of his implication does not stand up to examination."

The judge went through the list of horrific injuries found on the body by the initial post-mortem conducted by the Irish pathologist and then the one carried out by French pathologists after the exhumation of the body in 2008. Both findings were in complete agreement on the extreme violence of the blows struck and the considerable defence put up by the victim.

The extent and nature of the injuries inflicted, and other additional numerous wounds categorised as defensive as the victim struggled to protect herself from the onslaught proved that the purpose and intent of the perpetrator was to kill the victim and excludes an involuntary cause of death (manslaughter).

The culpability of Bailey was explored. The scratches and wounds on his hands and forearms described by up to a dozen witnesses most of whose depositions proved that he could not have sustained them either in the manner he described or the date nominated, December 22, on which night he was in the Galley pub with his sleeves up, hands and forearms exposed with no sign of the wounds. It was not until after the day of the murder they were noted by witnesses, some who recognised them as those typically suffered by contact with briars and thorns.

Bailey had said he did not know the victim but again witness evidence proved the contrary. Alfie Lyons, the victim's neighbour, testified that he had introduced Bailey to Sophie while the former was doing gardening work for him. The accused told others – including Yvonne Ungerer, Ann Cahalane, Helen Callanan – that he knew her. He was seen by witnesses on the main street of Schull close to where Sophie was on Saturday, December 21.

There were changes and contradictions in his statements about his movements on the night and day of the murder. The variations were designed to hide the fact that Bailey had left the house that night. Marie Farrell's evidence at the time of seeing him the night of the murder was still valid as the retraction of her evidence is to be considered in the light of the pressure and threats from Bailey confirmed by her former employee Geraldine O'Brien and his thesis of a conspiracy by the police had been completely rejected by the Irish High Court in 2015.

The following morning, in his interactions with local people and with journalists, he displayed knowledge of the crime and nationality of the victim long before it was in the public domain and before he claimed the time he had first heard of it from a call from Eddie Cassidy. The judge considered the credibility and veracity of witnesses who testified in relation to Bailey's confessions. None of them, she said, had been given in a joking or sarcastic context.

In relation to Bill Fuller's evidence: "The scenario described by Ian Bailey in which the victim fled her aggressor, and he threw something, striking her in the back of the head, to stop her before she got any further, is precisely and surprisingly compatible with the elements collected during the investigation and the conclusions of the medico-legal reports, the psycho-criminal analysis carried out by a clinical psychologist on this point remarks that it could be considered an admission, attributing to a third party, the negative sentiments which he refuses to recognise in himself.

"It is to be noted that all these witnesses took his confessions to be serious and cut off all relations with the accused and referred immediately to the police."

Judge Aline said that in the geography of the area, the place where the body was discovered is a short distance from the residence of Bailey, 4 miles by the longest route and 2.4 miles by the shorter one, both familiar routes to the accused. "The various night-time itineraries possible were measured in respect of distance and time and established that Ian Bailey could have gone there, even on foot, after the evening in the pub and return home with Thomas and then to the victim's home and back again to Jules Thomas, who would not see him until 9 a.m."

The various vicious assaults by Bailey on his partner were

narrated, his admission in his diary that he wanted to kill her and the alcoholic state that facilitated him to inflict the grievous violence which was present on the night of the murder. The psychological profile provided by the experts was quoted by the judge.

"These experts concluded that Ian Bailey was susceptible to having a narcissistic personality, psycho-rigid, impulsive, ego-centric and intolerant to frustration with an immense need for recognition and presenting the possibility of committing acts of violence under the disinhibiting effect of alcohol, he gets the satisfaction of being in the centre of attention, resorting to his imagination and cultivating ambiguity and provocation in an amused or playful tone or a defiant tone. The experts noted the characteristics of a split personality with a method of functioning which alternates between contradictory behaviour displaying a tendency to profound impulsive bouts while showing a perfect posture of control."

Judge Frederique Aline then briefly summed up the elements of the evidence that pointed to the guilt of the accused which the court had considered in its deliberations. "For all of these elements, the court considers it justified to sentence in absentia Ian Bailey to twenty-five years in jail. In addition, to deliver as the jurisdiction of the judgement a warrant for the arrest of Ian Bailey so as to ensure the execution of this judicial decision."

The French court and the prosecutor had brilliantly torn to pieces the Irish DPP's logic in deciding not to prosecute Bailey. A prosecution that would have on the evidence been pursued in any jurisdiction in Europe and indeed in the world.

The evidence that convicted Bailey in Paris was the same as presented in the Garda file in the main points. In relation to the confessions, the French court took them as what they were; there was no taking a questionable view as the DPP did that they were black jokes. Even if one leaves out the others, the confession to Richie Shelley during which Bailey cried and put his arms around him could not possibly be interpreted as a joke and would have been enough along with a lot of other incriminating evidence to charge him. Rosie Shelley had also witnessed the event and was in doubt that it was a confession.

The French court accepted the evidence of witnesses in the Galley pub on the evening of December 22, 1996, who stated that there were no scratches on Bailey on the day he nominated as having sustained them. The DPP took the view that this evidence was inconclusive. This was an opinion that could not stand up to any reasonable scrutiny given the facts.

The French also accepted the evidence proposed in the Garda file that Bailey had communicated foreknowledge of the murder to witnesses including Paul O'Colmain and Caroline Leftwich prior to the telephone call from Eddie Cassidy.

Also, the incontrovertible evidence of the threats and intimidation of Marie Farrell recorded by and investigated by the Gardai from seventeen official complaints made by her, but from which the DPP inexplicably made no inference. There was a simple question to be answered: why would the prime suspect of a brutal murder persistently attempt by threats to get a prime witness to change her statement? The answer was obvious to all but the DPP.

There was after the judge and magistrates vacated the bench a certain but muted jubilation among the family of Sophie, hugs and handshakes of which I indulged, considering this a victory. But all realised that the ultimate win was seeing Bailey once again in the court and consigned to a French prison. I hoped that Bailey, who knew well at this moment what had occurred, might consign something else into his pants.

Perhaps he was instead prancing around West Cork dressed like the clown he is, the joker, the killer, revelling in the attention. That, it would transpire, was exactly what he was doing. That was always part of his act, but whether he liked it or not, Ian Bailey had at last been given the status of a convicted murderer and if he imagined that it would not have any effect in the community of West Cork or anywhere else, he would be proved wrong.

He had been justifiably called a coward by the French

prosecutor, a man who had beaten his partner within an inch of her life and admitted in his diaries that he wanted to kill her, and had admitted to witnesses that he had come within an inch of strangling his former wife in England and then without mercy had murdered a defenceless French woman. And then had the gall to report on the murder. Coward with a capital C.

The boiling in my blood had receded like a retreating tide. I walked past the hordes of media interviewing anyone who came their way down the steps of the Palais de Justice into the beautiful sunshine of the Paris sky with the prospect of another three days in the city vacating my mind of all like a student who has completed exams but with the certainty that there was another one to face. One more chapter that every author must write but like the student will postpone until the final exam.

CHAPTER 25
THE FINAL CURTAIN

Dublin – 2019/20

There was of course huge coverage in both France and Ireland of both the trial and the verdict. One of the interesting articles was a statement issued by retired DPP James Hamilton in response to journalist Maeve Sheehan asking him to comment on the French criticism of the Irish failure to prosecute Bailey and published in the *Sunday Independent*.

He said that his predecessor, the late Eamon Barnes, had decided in 1997 that there was insufficient evidence to try Ian Bailey for the murder. He deferred the final decision to enable the Garda Síochána to conduct further enquiries. In 1999, when he was appointed DPP, he considered those further enquiries and he decided there was still insufficient evidence to prosecute Bailey. He had the benefit of senior counsel, who arrived at the same conclusion.

"In Irish law, it is possible to convict a person only on the basis of admissible and credible evidence given orally in court by witnesses which is relevant to the offence charged and a jury must be convinced of the case beyond all reasonable doubt. The evidence does not include material, which is merely prejudicial such as hearsay, rumour, innuendo, speculation, suspicion, gossip and evidence of bad character lacking any evidential link to the offence charged. The Irish courts will refuse to admit into evidence material which is prejudicial but lacking in evidential value."

He declined to talk further about the substance of the case alleged against Ian Bailey in the Garda file. "My reasons for the decision not to prosecute were fully set out in a memorandum prepared in my office and approved by me which was sent to the Garda Síochána and my decision was never challenged by the Garda to me."

But not to make too much of a fine point, James Hamilton had in his statement to Maeve Sheehan said that his decision not to prosecute Bailey for the crime was "never challenged by the Gardai *to me*". Emphasis added. But a challenge had been documented by the Gardai and sent to his office and for whatever reason would it not be?

But ultimately it did not matter that the challenge had not been made to any individual; the Garda challenge document had – and I confirmed this with three sources – been delivered to the office of the DPP, where presumably it still resides.

What Maeve Sheehan referred to in her article as the "now infamous forty-four-page critique of the Garda evidence" had been declared inadmissible in the High Court and had been robustly and successfully challenged at Bailey's appeals in two superior courts and a criminal court in France. While the DPP critique had been forwarded to the French authorities, the Garda rebuttal document had not. That would have been obviously far more valuable to the French investigation than the former.

It is late winter 2019 and there were a number of preliminary hearings at the High Court sitting in the Courts of Criminal Justice in Dublin in relation to the extradition proceedings attempting to bring Ian Bailey to face further justice in France in the wake of his conviction for the murder of Sophie Toscan du Plantier the previous May in the Criminal Court of Paris.

At the first hearing it was abundantly obvious there had been a remarkable physical transformation of Bailey. The once powerful physique had shrunk, his upper back had acquired a hump which caused him to stoop and he walked with the familiar shuffle of extreme old age despite the fact he is only in his early sixties.

His once lush hair had disintegrated into patches of wisps, barely concealing encroaching baldness. Wrinkles had spread across his forehead and face like a spider's web. His skin had the grey-green pallor like that of a vampire suddenly caught by the rays of dawn. Large pouches hung under his deadened eyes atop a bloated visage adorned by a grey moustache and goatee which only served to increase the general impact of decrepitude.

All is reminiscent to me of the hideous portrait in the attic of his Victorian counterpart, the murderous protagonist and narcissist Dorian Gray in Oscar Wilde's famous novella – *The Picture of Dorian Gray*. The excesses of a life badly led is all there to see. I had received plenty of notice on the subject from my contacts in West Cork to expect the sight of the human shipwreck, but in the cold light of the court there was no merciful or flattering relief for the man I now saw.

On that day, the court was packed with lawyers, reporters and relatives or friends of the bailed accused and those in prison, most of whom were of Eastern European nationality, appearing before Mr Justice Binchy. When called, Bailey left the body of the court and sat in the dock, which is automatically occupied by the subjects of the extradition proceedings.

Heading for a subsequent hearing, I alighted from the 145 bus at Heuston Station minus my glasses and almost bumped into a dishevelled figure exiting the side entrance and sucking on the butt of a cigarette. His face was hardly visible as the side features were covered by a fur contraption that looked like it had been acquired in a raid on a taxidermist.

I was about to reach into my pocket for some small change I could offer the indigent when the man stepped off the footpath facing me. With a shock, I realised it was Ian Bailey, who had just got off the Cork train and was now shuffling across the bridge towards the court complex. I followed him at a distance and later sat opposite him in the court. This time, he remained in the seat at the back of the court and when called stood up, making no effort to go to the dock.

Obviously, the West Cork respondent thought he was a cut above the rest of the miscreants, some of whom were being sought by other jurisdictions for drug dealing and murder, and all of whom sat in the dock when being addressed by the judge.

Subsequently, the court endorsed the warrant and Bailey was arrested and bailed. Mr Justice Binchy, who conducted most of the proceedings, was promoted to the Court of Appeal and was replaced by Mr Justice Paul Burns. A full hearing was set for July 15–17, 2020. As the judge rightly observed on the second day, extradition hearings are particularly dry affairs and the opening day proved that without a doubt.

This was because the main legal battleground would be fought on not just the facts of the previous history of the case in terms of judgements but also on the interpretation of European and Irish legislation in relation to the European Arrest Warrant. Of course, the legal landscape had changed, as State counsel Robert Barron pointed out early on by the fact that Bailey was now a convicted murderer, and there also had been an amendment in 2019 to the Irish EAW legislation. That is dry stuff, for sure.

However, Bailey's counsel Ronan Munro in his opening submissions did read out an affidavit from his client which was as remarkable for its omissions as for its contents, which amounted to an elongated whinge of self-pity. He stated he had been in a relationship with Jules Thomas for twenty-seven years, as if the longevity suggested some quality and stability.

He said he could not get work as a journalist as a result of false allegations made against him in relation to the crime. He omitted to say that the real reason was that he had reported on the murder for several media outlets, had invented sources and quotes, fabricated stories and carried out a monstrous act of deception on the newspapers who had hired him.

He stated that he suffered from depressive episodes and breakouts on his skin and panic attacks as a result of unwelcome attention on him and his family. He omitted to say that over the years he had a serious problem with drugs and alcohol, which can and does produce the effects he had just outlined quite independent of any "unwelcome attention".

His standing, he said, had suffered greatly in the small rural community where he lived. He might have reflected more accurately that the standing and status that he claimed had been a long time before affected by virtue of his three brutal assaults on his partner Jules Thomas and his slandering of local members of that community in the libel and High Court trials and in addition members of the murder investigation team.

He tries, he stated, not to dwell on being "hunted", and his writing of poetry had a cathartic effect on him. His sleep patterns had been disturbed and he had a recurring dream of being re-arrested and confined in a cell. This self-portrait as presented in his affidavit was as close to reality as the distance between the Earth and the moon.

Mr Munro then got on with the submission contending that the Supreme Court appeal in 2012 gave his client absolute protection from surrender and allied to Mr Justice Hunt's judgement of 2017 that the French issue of a further EAW warrant had been an abuse of process backed by the Supreme Court judgement in another case in relation to Tobin. All good defence strategy.

All through Bailey looking the worse for wear, skulking as usual on a backbench instead of taking his rightful place in the dock. He was dishevelled in dress, the sartorial elegance adopted in previous court hearings abandoned. He appeared like an actor who had come from an audition for one of the tramps in *Waiting for Godot*. Not content to wear the conventional face mask that Covid required, he adorned his decrepit features with a colourful scarf which seemed to be more appropriate for a member of the opposite sex.

During this important hearing and despite his physical degeneration, there was still evidence of his long-held need for attention. But it was a muted gesture, almost pathetic combined with an expanding midriff spilling over his trousers, a figure that could never now attract the sort of attention he had long sought.

None of that was of concern to the counsels involved in this extradition case. Nonetheless, counsel for either side present argue as if it is a certainty, knowing full well that anything in a legal battle is anything but that, as it will be up to the judge to decide. One counsel may say I am right on this point and the other will naturally disagree. Case law quoted by one or the other may or may not apply.

On the second day, Mr Justice Burns enquired if there was any representative of the family of the victim present. A woman who had been recording the proceedings on her computer for a Dublin firm of solicitors on behalf of the family answered in the affirmative. The judge said that court hearings of any kind are distressing but given the dry nature of extradition proceedings, it should not be taken that anyone had forgotten the tragic nature of Sophie Toscan du Plantier's death. It was a kind and poignant gesture from the court.

Mr Munro continued with the dry business, submitting that the EAWs against his client would never stop and had a prejudicial effect on him. This was the third warrant for his extradition and the amendment to the act in 2019 would have made no difference to his client had it applied in the mid-1990s. The French authorities he claimed had lost entitlement to a further warrant when the second was dismissed by the High Court in 2017.

The second warrant was effectively saying that the Supreme Court in 2012 had got it wrong when refusing surrender after the High Court had ordered it in 2011. The dismissal of the second closed the door on further warrants and the French had lost the right to issue any more. The third was an abuse of process which was getting worse. The court should put a stop to it.

On the morning of the third day, as I and barristers for both sides, journalists and any onlookers that might be admitted gathered outside the court doors while in conversation, I was approached by an onrushing Bailey – in his crumpled attire with his finger pointing towards my face and thumb cocked in the manner of an imaginary gun – who began to roar with what resembled a strangulated squawk, "You stop your slandering of me. You stop slandering me."

I replied with as much restraint as I could muster, "I advise you to stop threatening me."

He retreated towards the assembled audience as if to take a bow and then whirled around and rushed towards me again, with the index finger pointed just inches from my face, and roared, "You will stop this slander or there will be consequences."

I replied more forcefully this time, "If you issue one more threat, the consequences will find them on your account."

His mottled skin went a greyer shade and the raging old bull pushed by me into the court. Calmly, I followed, thinking this might be the end of it, but I was wrong. As soon as I entered the court, he was there again and rushed towards me, his arms askew, and squawked once more: "Social distancing. Social distancing."

My patience was now waning, so I reminded him that he was the one breaking the rule: "So, get the fuck out of my way."

He did just that and slunk off to his usual perch in the court.

Once a bully, always a bully. Always a bully, always a coward.

As we all know, the greatest lines of response in such interactions always revisit us in retrospect. I might have reminded the thundering Bailey that a man who had beaten his partner three times and admitted in his diaries an intent to kill her; who had stalked women and made recordings of his observations of them for his own sexual gratification; had forged a life insurance policy with the signature of his then wife; who had waged a campaign of vile intimidation against the principal witness in the murder case; who had attempted unsuccessfully to ruin the reputation of the murder investigators; who had lied repeatedly in his statements and under oath in court and was now a convicted murderer; was hardly in a position to accuse me in an intimidating manner of slander. But then, he knew all that and I would have been wasting my time bringing it to his attention.

In court, Mr Robert Barron for the Minister for Justice got on quietly and efficiently with the business of dealing with the legal contentions of the defence in relation to the Supreme Court decision and the High Court decision of 2017, which he argued did not have the finality as suggested by the defence that would provide a bar for surrender.

Nor could the issuing of a third warrant be considered an abuse of process, as both the factual and legal situation had changed since the issuing of the second, as the respondent Bailey had been convicted of the murder and there had been a change in legislation in 2019. So, it did not fit what was the traditional law in relation to abuse of process.

There was much speculation by the opposing counsel about what would happen if Bailey surrendered in terms of a retrial. It was his view that they just did not know and therefore it was impossible to make submissions on the subject without knowing, and any criticism of the French criminal procedure was inappropriate. In relation to the matter of an elongated timescale, there were no statute of limitations.

Robert Barron S.C. pointed out that a document produced by the defence from a French source in relation to criminal law and procedures was but a partial expression of French law and contained opinion, which suggested unfairness and was of no evidential value or assistance to the court. There was a lot of second-guessing by the defence about procedures in France and they could not go down that road as they knew nothing about those procedures or what evidence might be available.

Mr Justice Burns reminded the parties that the court must have respect for French criminal procedures and in relation to a defence submission that it appeared that it was inviting this court to act as a court of appeal and that could not happen. After the submissions were complete, Mr Justice Burns reserved judgement, which he said he would deliver on October 12, 2020.

On that day, the court was sparsely populated due to Covid-19 restrictions. Speaking with journalists before the proceedings, we agreed that Bailey would not be surrendered. There had been nothing in the hearings on the extradition to suggest otherwise. The Supreme Court in 2011 and the High Court in 2017 had refused his surrender in the wake of the first judgment in 2011 in which Judge Michael Peart had rejected all objections and ordered the respondent to be extradited.

Bailey took his usual position at the back seat of the court instead of the dock. His physical appearance showed dramatic signs of deterioration, and he wore a scarf around his nose and mouth instead of the usual face mask. Just after 2 p.m. Mr Justice Burns began his judgement and it quickly became apparent that there would be no surrender granted even though the respondent was now a convicted murderer. Extradition proceedings are all based on legislative and judicial technicalities – whether the respondent is guilty or innocent is simply irrelevant. I have seen and read the extradition proceedings in which the respondent, from the details of the offence, was clearly guilty of that crime, but his surrender was refused because certain rules and regulations were not observed in the issuing or execution of the arrest warrant.

The interpretation of those rules is often problematic. In this instance, the wording of Section 44 of the Irish legislation is not just obscure but impenetrable and virtually impossible to interpret in any meaningful way. A long time ago, it should have been referred to the European Court in Luxembourg for clarification. Mr Justice Peart disagreed with Mr Justice Burns on the interpretation that it provided a bar to surrender.

Mr Justice Burns also ruled that the Supreme Court decision of 2012 and the Hight Court decision of 2017 – not to surrender – gave Bailey an immunity or an accrued right to further being extradited on this application. This was even though Bailey's criminal status had in the meantime changed to one of a convicted murderer and there had been an amendment to the Irish legislation in 2019.

So, no drama here, it was like watching paint dry, and the tension of expectation was completely absent. It was no surprise when at the end of a lengthy reading the extradition was refused. The judge makes his or her own decision based on the facts and interpretation of those facts. The question was: would the essence of the judgment be worthy of appeal by the State?

This would be decided at a further hearing marked for October

27. I confirmed in advance from two highly placed sources that the State would not in fact appeal, which meant that the final curtain had fallen on the case and that the respondent would not face the punishment for the crime of murder for which he had been convicted by the Criminal Courts in Paris in May 2019.

However, Ian Bailey dare not set foot outside of Ireland. The 27 European countries who are signatories to the EAW legislation would have no hesitation in arresting him while awaiting an extradition warrant from France. There is little doubt that it would be unencumbered by defective Irish law on the matter and the complete absence of the accrued right of the respondent not to be surrendered. There is no safe haven for a person legitimately convicted for the brutal murder of a French citizen in any of the signatories other than Ireland, where the refusal to charge him or surrender him bestows no status of innocence of the crime.

But the net effect is that another legal stake has been driven into the heart of the Bouniol family whose elderly parents Georges and Marguerite will now not live to see the killer of their daughter serve any time. They have endured great suffering over the years by the denial of justice, but not until now had they been deprived of any hope, finally torn from them by the machinations and failings of the Irish criminal justice system.

The Bouniol family's ASSOPH chronicle of their previous experience of that system was presciently titled Justice Denied because when it was written the authors had hoped that the title in the future could be Justice Delivered. It was not to be. The former title is even more apt now. In essence, it's a tragedy of Shakespearean proportion replete with the poisoning of innocence, protection of the guilty, the destruction of faith and hope, insult to human decency and the undermining of the whole foundation of criminal law, which is to punish the perpetrator and make amends to the victim.

Every murder has dire consequences and multiple victims such as the friends and family of the immediate victim, which have a huge and lasting impact beyond the crime itself. Some of the wider victims never get the capacity to recover from the event even with the benefit of support and the passage of time. The cruelty of depriving any human of the most precious gift of life is bad enough, but the manner employed can add another layer of pain and grief.

It is simply impossible to avoid imagining the final terrifying moments of the victim. There may be some consolation, however scant, if and when the perpetrator receives fitting legal punishment for the crime. This is the cold retribution for the violation of the outer law. There could be further comfort for the loved ones of the victim if the killer sought some redemption from the act from the inner moral law by apology and genuine self-renunciation.

That, however, rarely happens, as among other things, murder is a sin of pride, which goes some way in explaining why in the face of evidence to the contrary, killers in general and psychopathic killers in particular will continue to deny their crimes. In the latter category, when as evidenced by MacDonald and Bailey, possessed of boundless confidence of their innocence accompanied by the self-idolatry that provided them with an immunity to the meaning and consequences of their acts of human desecration and destruction.

Their capacity for self-deception and spiritual bankruptcy is infinite. They refuse to recognise both the laws of humankind and nature. They travel in the dark night of a soulless universe where bright stars never shine, where grief, sin and punishment have no place and occupy a cramped mental tomb, feeding from their vile thoughts like rats preying on garbage.

In this cerebral hellhole, they are deaf to the biblical admonition of God to Cain that blood spilled cries out from the soil and so cursed shall the murderer be for all time and beyond. Or Ecclesiastes written by the unknown teacher between 450–200 BCE, who punches far beyond his biblical weight, telling us that fools walk in darkness, fold their hands and consume their own flesh:

"*What has been is what will be*
And what has been done is what will be done
There is nothing new under the sun."

EPILOGUE
SOPHIE'S CHOICE

Prosecutor Jean-Pierre Bonthoux, in a speech to the Paris Criminal Court, mentioned the paradox of destiny referring to Sophie's choice of finding the house in Toormore, which fulfilled her desire to find peace and contentment far away from the pressures of her life in the French capital in a country which she had fallen in love with from the time she had first encountered it as a teenager on a student exchange programme with the McKiernan family in Dublin.

Fourteen-year-old Sophie and her brother Bertrand two years younger had in July 1971 travelled to Dublin for a month's stay with the McKiernan family who lived in Sutton on the northside of Dublin. In August, Patricia McKiernan, the same age as Sophie, came to stay for a month with the Bouniol family in Paris.

Nothing more poignantly expresses the spiritual connection Sophie forged with Ireland than the diary she kept of her search for a house in the more remote regions of the country, accompanied by her cousin Alexandra. She expressed her feelings in these excerpts provided by her family:

"I think a lot about the house in Ireland. Daniel has told everybody and people are happy for me! I am going to go there very soon with Alexandra. We will visit the south western and western regions to see which area I would prefer and also to get some information about prices.

"I don't know if it is a good idea to go over there to thinking about the views of others on my crazy enterprise. Well, we will see! I have

always dreamed of putting down roots in a country like that! But why would I like to find a country like that? But why would I like to find a country? I already have one. But I am looking for another that would be mine, that I would make my own, somewhere I would be happy and that would be happy to have me.

"Yesterday we visited two houses, one smaller than the other. The larger of the houses is situated in a very wild, very beautiful corner of the country, but it is a rather strange house, two rooms downstairs, three rooms upstairs, a little bleak, but with potential for renovation.

"I have to step back a little. I have such a vision of Ireland when I close my eyes. I see a countryside of mountains, sea, bogs and other combinations of features. Everything changes so quickly here: the scenery, the vegetation, nature! Everything goes by so quickly. Travel a few kilometres in the car and you are in another country!

"The people are genuinely very nice, very obliging and somewhat amused to see two young French women coming to choose a house!

"It is a country of endurance, of resistance, of pride in the flag more than mere roots! There is simultaneously, pride and concern in the attachment of an Irishman to his country, no resignation despite the clarity of their thoughts, their sayings and their proverbs. They speak earnestly and with great interest about the weather and constantly assure us that the weather we are having is not normal.

"I really love this country. I am adapting to it and at the same time my body, more or less is, getting used to the cold. I am getting used to it. I am becoming hardened to it and I feel at ease here, with the people, their language and their thoughts. To adapt oneself to a country and a people you must also follow the same rhythm, with the same easiness and kindness. I would love to find a house and to stay there for a time. Perhaps it does not need to be too isolated for me to find serenity.

"The scenery is to die for, it changes all the time going from English type countryside with Swiss chalet-like houses. Sometimes strands of fir trees appear on the horizon, but rarely trees grow badly here.

"Tomorrow we are going to John Casey's, a property and insurance agent, we wait there while he goes in search of the key for the house we want to view again. I like this area and the choice I must make between the two houses that I prefer is also a choice between two climates. On the one hand, a gentle climate, sweet scenery and a house that is not so pretty, on the other there is a more isolated house on the cliffs above rocks, a strong and windy landscape, where the sky and the sea share the horizon; a more comfortable house."

It was the second house she chose. The paradox of destiny. But how was this beautiful human to know that nearby lived a violent, barbaric murderous beast who would bide his time and then set a trap for her and extinguish her life of worth in exchange for the poverty of his useless existence? A pariah, a perverted stalker of young women, a recorder of filth and violence in his diaries, a perpetrator of horrendous abuse towards and coercion of his partner.

"Ireland, the sky and the sea and the land as far as the eye can see. Furrows in the earth from cutting and harvesting the turf, autumn when everything is red and green like the hair and eyes of the Irish people. Every description seems to me to be inadequate to capture the reality of the country."

Sophie's mortal remains had first been interred in the graveyard near the church where her funeral had taken place in Mauvezin-de L'Isle near her husband's country house in Ambax. After Daniel's death in 2003, the coffin had been disinterred and reinterred in the Bouniol family plot in the cemetery of Saint Germain-du-Tell. Five years later her body was exhumed as part of the French investigation of her murder.

Finally, her body is resting in the Combret family cemetery in Saint-Germain-du-Tell in Lozère. The seasons fall upon her tomb as they did so many years ago as she lay exposed down the laneway from her home in Toormore – the cold, the wind and the sun on the thorns, laneway, field and far beyond.

But there is a light emanating from and to that grave. It is the light of love and justice, a more powerful shaft than the forces of foolish legal imperatives or the evil act of a killer.

To contact the author, Michael Sheridan, please email Gadfly
Press at gadflypress@outlook.com

If you have enjoyed this book, we would appreciate you leaving a
review on Amazon or Goodreads.

ACKNOWLEDGEMENTS

People imagine that the author does all the work – the loneliness of the long-distance writer. In reality, there is a supporting cast, many of whose members would never dream of requesting a credit. The publisher leads the cast, so my gratitude to Shaun Atwood for his faith in the project. Agent Isabel Atherton, who toiled ceaselessly when the time was not right. Sheridan family members Cian, Fionn, Sarah and Geraldine Norton for their tolerance.

Fionnuala Dwyer for her mastery of scanning highly important material, Sam, Freddy and Tommy of Copy Graphics for their trustworthy handling of confidential documents from both jurisdictions. Journalists Ann Mooney and Senan Molony for their constant co-operation and insights, and Sarah Collins and Sharon Gaffney for their assistance at the trial in Paris. Nick Foster for our valuable ruminations on the case mutually beneficial.

John Coleman, the concierge without compare of the Metropole Hotel in Cork, Tricia Daly, Donal Gaffney, Liam le taxi, Jean, Dr Patricia Comer, Alain Spilliaert, Jean-Pierre Gazeau and Jean-Antoine Bloc for their unfailing support and advice and comments on the manuscript. Roisin Moran of the Old Rectory writer's retreat in Westport, Dave, Cecilia, Bea and the staff of the 105 Café for providing a working haven away from home, and for the same of staff members Jodi and Diana of The Natural Bakery in Stillorgan. The muse Fedelma.

The late Danny McCarthy of Mentor Books, who championed me in the early stages of writing true crime books.

The named and unnamed sources without whose participation no book of this nature could be written.

BIBLIOGRAPHY

Books

Cameron, Deborah, *The Lust to Kill*,
New York University Press, 1987

Cleckley, Hervey M., *The Mask of Sanity*,
Mosby Medical Library, 1982

Cros, Julien, Bloc, Jean-Antoine, *Justice Denied*, ASSOPH, 2014

Dostoyevsky, Fyodor, *Crime And Punishment*,
Penguin Books, 1991

Douglas, John; Olshaker, Mark, *Mindhunter*, Arrow Books, 2017

Malcolm, Janet, *The Journalist and the Murderer*, Granta, 1997

Meloy, J. Reid, *The Psychopathic Mind: Origins, Dynamics,
Treatment*, Jason Aronson Inc., 1988

Morris, Errol, *A Wilderness of Error*, Penguin Books, 2012

McGinnis, Joe, *Fatal Vision*, Signet Books, 1983

McNamara, Michelle, *I'll Be Gone in the Dark*,
Faber and Faber, 2018

Somerville-Large, Peter, *The Coast of West Cork*,
Appletrec Press, 1991

Sheridan, Michael, *Death in December*, O'Brien Press, 2002

Sheridan, *Michael*, *Frozen Blood: Serial Killers in Ireland*, Mentor Books, 2003

Reports

2000 DPP's Analysis of Evidence in the STP Case: An Opposing Point of View, Jean-Pierre Gazeau, Jean-Antoine Bloc, Daude, Frances Lefevre, ASSOPH, 2012

Annual Report EAW, 2016

Crime Scene Awareness for Non-Forensic Personnel, United Nations, New York, 2009

The Role and Impact of Forensic Evidence in the Criminal Justice Process, Peterson, Joseph; Sommers, Ira; Baskin, Deborah; Johnson, Donald, U.S. Dept of Justice, 2010

Garda Ombudsman's Report, July 2018

Fenelley Commission Report, March 2017

Office of the Director of Equality Investigations

Employment Equality Act 1998, Equality Officer's Decision, Dec-E2002-047

Parties: Sheehan and the DPP

Journals

Meloy, J. Reid, *The Psychology of Wickedness and Sadism*, Psychiatric Annals, September 1997

Vitacu, M.J., *Psychopathy*, The British Journal of Psychiatry, 2007

Woodworth M. and Porter S., *Historical Foundation and Current*

Applications of Criminal Profiling in Violent Crime Investigations, Kluwer Academic Publishers, 2001

Hold, Meloy, Strack, *Sadism and Psychopathy in Violent and Sexually Violent Offenders*, J Am ACAD Psychiatry Law Vol. 27, No. 1, 1999.

Magazines

Montague, J, *A Devil in the Hills*, *New Yorker*, January 10, 2000

Paris Match, various editions

Newspapers

Irish Examiner, Irish Times, Irish Independent, Irish Star, Irish Daily Mirror, The Sunday Times, The Daily Telegraph, Sunday Independent, The Echo, Sunday Tribune, Le Figaro, Le Monde, Le Parisien

OTHER BOOKS BY
GADFLY PRESS

By Steve Wraith:
The Krays' Final Years:
My Time with London's Most Iconic Gangsters

By Natalie Welsh:
Escape from Venezuela's Deadliest Prison

By Shaun Attwood:

English Shaun Trilogy
Party Time
Hard Time
Prison Time

War on Drugs Series
Pablo Escobar: Beyond Narcos
American Made: Who Killed Barry Seal? Pablo Escobar
or George HW Bush
The Cali Cartel: Beyond Narcos
Clinton Bush and CIA Conspiracies:
From the Boys on the Tracks to Jeffrey Epstein

Un-Making a Murderer:
The Framing of Steven Avery and Brendan Dassey
The Mafia Philosopher: Two Tonys
Life Lessons
Pablo Escobar's Story (4-book series)

By Steve Wraith:

The Krays' Final Years: My Time with London's Most Iconic Gangsters

Britain's most notorious twins – Ron and Reg Kray – ascended the underworld to become the most feared and legendary gangsters in London. Their escalating mayhem culminated in murder, for which they received life sentences in 1969.

While incarcerated, they received letters from a schoolboy from Tyneside, Steve Wraith, who was mesmerised by their story. Eventually, Steve visited them in prison and a friendship formed. The Twins hired Steve as an unofficial advisor, which brought him into contact with other members of their crime family. At Ron's funeral, Steve was Charlie Kray's right-hand man.

Steve documents Ron's time in Broadmoor – a high-security psychiatric hospital – where he was battling insanity and heavily medicated. Steve details visiting Reg, who served almost 30 years in a variety of prisons, where the gangster was treated with the utmost respect by the staff and the inmates.

By Natalie Welsh:

Escape from Venezuela's Deadliest Prison

After getting arrested at a Venezuelan airport with a suitcase of cocaine, Natalie was clueless about the danger she was facing. Sentenced to 10 years, she arrived at a prison with armed men on the roof, whom she mistakenly believed were the guards, only to find out they were homicidal gang members. Immediately, she was plunged into a world of unimaginable horror and escalating violence, where murder, rape and all-out gang warfare were carried out with the complicity of corrupt guards. Male prisoners often entered the females' housing area, bringing gunfire with them and leaving corpses behind. After 4.5 years, Natalie risked everything to escape and flee through Colombia, with the help of a guard who had fallen deeply in love with her.

By Shaun Attwood:

Pablo Escobar: Beyond Narcos

War on Drugs Series Book 1

The mind-blowing true story of Pablo Escobar and the Medellín Cartel beyond their portrayal on Netflix.

Colombian drug lord Pablo Escobar was a devoted family man and a psychopathic killer; a terrible enemy, yet a wonderful friend. While donating millions to the poor, he bombed and tortured his enemies – some had their eyeballs removed with hot spoons. Through ruthless cunning and America's insatiable appetite for cocaine, he became a multi-billionaire, who lived in a $100-million house with its own zoo.

Pablo Escobar: Beyond Narcos demolishes the standard good versus evil telling of his story. The authorities were not hunting Pablo down to stop his cocaine business. They were taking over it.

American Made: Who Killed Barry Seal? Pablo Escobar or George HW Bush

War on Drugs Series Book 2

Set in a world where crime and government coexist, *American Made* is the jaw-dropping true story of CIA pilot Barry Seal that the Hollywood movie starring Tom Cruise is afraid to tell.

Barry Seal flew cocaine and weapons worth billions of dollars into and out of America in the 1980s. After he became a government informant, Pablo Escobar's Medellin Cartel offered a million for him alive and half a million dead. But his real trouble began after he threatened to expose the dirty dealings of George HW Bush.

American Made rips the roof off Bush and Clinton's complicity in cocaine trafficking in Mena, Arkansas.

"A conspiracy of the grandest magnitude." Congressman Bill Alexander on the Mena affair.

The Cali Cartel: Beyond Narcos

War on Drugs Series Book 3

An electrifying account of the Cali Cartel beyond its portrayal on Netflix.

From the ashes of Pablo Escobar's empire rose an even bigger and more malevolent cartel. A new breed of sophisticated mobsters became the kings of cocaine. Their leader was Gilberto Rodríguez Orejuela – known as the Chess Player due to his foresight and calculated cunning.

Gilberto and his terrifying brother, Miguel, ran a multi-billion-dollar drug empire like a corporation. They employed a politically astute brand of thuggery and spent $10 million to put a president in power. Although the godfathers from Cali preferred bribery over violence, their many loyal torturers and hit men were never idle.

Clinton Bush and CIA Conspiracies: From the Boys on the Tracks to Jeffrey Epstein

War on Drugs Series Book 4

In the 1980s, George HW Bush imported cocaine to finance an illegal war in Nicaragua. Governor Bill Clinton's Arkansas state police provided security for the drug drops. For assisting the CIA, the Clinton Crime Family was awarded the White House. The #clintonbodycount continues to this day, with the deceased including Jeffrey Epstein.

This book features harrowing true stories that reveal the insanity of the drug war. A mother receives the worst news about her son. A journalist gets a tip that endangers his life. An unemployed man becomes California's biggest crack dealer. A DEA agent in Mexico is sacrificed for going after the big players.

The lives of Linda Ives, Gary Webb, Freeway Rick Ross and Kiki Camarena are shattered by brutal experiences. Not all of them will survive.

Pablo Escobar's Story (4-book series)

"Finally, the definitive book about Escobar, original and up-to-date" – UNILAD

"The most comprehensive account ever written" – True Geordie

Pablo Escobar was a mama's boy who cherished his family and sang in the shower, yet he bombed a passenger plane and formed a death squad that used genital electrocution.

Most Escobar biographies only provide a few pieces of the puzzle, but this action-packed 1000-page book reveals everything about the king of cocaine.

Mostly translated from Spanish, Part 1 contains stories untold in the English-speaking world, including:

The tragic death of his youngest brother Fernando.

The fate of his pregnant mistress.

The shocking details of his affair with a TV celebrity.

The presidential candidate who encouraged him to eliminate their rivals.

The Mafia Philosopher

"A fast-paced true-crime memoir with all of the action of Goodfellas" – UNILAD

"Sopranos v Sons of Anarchy with an Alaskan-snow backdrop" – True Geordie Podcast

Breaking bones, burying bodies and planting bombs became second nature to Two Tonys while working for the Bonanno Crime Family, whose exploits inspired The Godfather.

After a dispute with an outlaw motorcycle club, Two Tonys left a trail of corpses from Arizona to Alaska. On the run, he was pursued by bikers and a neo-Nazi gang blood-thirsty for revenge, while a homicide detective launched a nationwide manhunt.

As the mist from his smoking gun fades, readers are left with an unexpected portrait of a stoic philosopher with a wealth of charm, a glorious turn of phrase and a fanatical devotion to his daughter.

Party Time

An action-packed roller-coaster account of a life spiralling out of control, featuring wild women, gangsters and a mountain of drugs.

Shaun Attwood arrived in Phoenix, Arizona, a penniless business graduate from a small industrial town in England. Within a decade, he became a stock-market millionaire. But he was leading a double life.

After taking his first Ecstasy pill at a rave in Manchester as a shy student, Shaun became intoxicated by the party lifestyle that would change his fortune. Years later, in the Arizona desert, he became submerged in a criminal underworld, throwing parties for thousands of ravers and running an Ecstasy ring in competition with the Mafia mass murderer Sammy 'The Bull' Gravano.

As greed and excess tore through his life, Shaun had eye-watering encounters with Mafia hit men and crystal-meth addicts, enjoyed extravagant debauchery with superstar DJs and glitter girls, and ingested enough drugs to kill a herd of elephants. This is his story.

Hard Time

"Makes the Shawshank Redemption look like a holiday camp" – NOTW

After a SWAT team smashed down stock-market millionaire Shaun Attwood's door, he found himself inside of Arizona's deadliest jail and locked into a brutal struggle for survival.

Shaun's hope of living the American Dream turned into a nightmare of violence and chaos, when he had a run-in with Sammy the Bull Gravano, an Italian Mafia mass murderer.

In jail, Shaun was forced to endure cockroaches crawling in his ears at night, dead rats in the food and the sound of skulls getting cracked against toilets. He meticulously documented the conditions and smuggled out his message.

Join Shaun on a harrowing voyage into the darkest recesses of human existence.

Hard Time provides a revealing glimpse into the tragedy, brutality, dark comedy and eccentricity of prison life.

Featured worldwide on Nat Geo Channel's Locked-Up/ Banged-Up Abroad Raving Arizona.

Prison Time

Sentenced to 9½ years in Arizona's state prison for distributing Ecstasy, Shaun finds himself living among gang members, sexual predators and drug-crazed psychopaths. After being attacked by a Californian biker in for stabbing a girlfriend, Shaun writes about the prisoners who befriend, protect and inspire him. They include T-Bone, a massive African American ex-Marine who risks his life saving vulnerable inmates from rape, and Two Tonys, an old-school Mafia murderer who left the corpses of his rivals from Arizona to Alaska. They teach Shaun how to turn incarceration to his advantage, and to learn from his mistakes.

Shaun is no stranger to love and lust in the heterosexual world, but the tables are turned on him inside. Sexual advances come at him from all directions, some cleverly disguised, others more sinister – making Shaun question his sexual identity.

Resigned to living alongside violent, mentally-ill and drug-addicted inmates, Shaun immerses himself in psychology and philosophy to try to make sense of his past behaviour, and begins applying what he learns as he adapts to prison life. Encouraged by Two Tonys to explore fiction as well, Shaun reads over 1000 books which, with support from a brilliant psychotherapist, Dr Owen, speed along his personal development. As his ability to deflect daily threats improves, Shaun begins to look forward to his release with optimism and a new love waiting for him. Yet the words of Aristotle from one of Shaun's books will prove prophetic: "We cannot learn without pain."

Un-Making a Murderer: The Framing of Steven Avery and Brendan Dassey

Innocent people do go to jail. Sometimes mistakes are made. But even more terrifying is when the authorities conspire to frame them. That's what happened to Steven Avery and Brendan Dassey, who were convicted of murder and are serving life sentences.

Un-Making a Murderer is an explosive book which uncovers the illegal, devious and covert tactics used by Wisconsin officials, including:

– Concealing Other Suspects

– Paying Expert Witnesses to Lie

– Planting Evidence

– Jury Tampering

The art of framing innocent people has been in practice for centuries and will continue until the perpetrators are held accountable. Turning conventional assumptions and beliefs in the justice system upside down, *Un-Making a Murderer* takes you on that journey.

Hard Time by Shaun Attwood

Chapter 1

Sleep deprived and scanning for danger, I enter a dark cell on the second floor of the maximum-security Madison Street jail in Phoenix, Arizona, where guards and gang members are murdering prisoners. Behind me, the metal door slams heavily. Light slants into the cell through oblong gaps in the door, illuminating a prisoner cocooned in a white sheet, snoring lightly on the top bunk about two thirds of the way up the back wall. Relieved there is no immediate threat, I place my mattress on the grimy floor. Desperate to rest, I notice movement on the cement-block walls. *Am I hallucinating?* I blink several times. The walls appear to ripple. Stepping closer, I see the walls are alive with insects. I flinch. So many are swarming, I wonder if they're a colony of ants on the move. To get a better look, I put my eyes right up to them. They are mostly the size of almonds and have antennae. American cockroaches. I've seen them in the holding cells downstairs in smaller numbers, but nothing like this. A chill spread over my body. I back away.

Something alive falls from the ceiling and bounces off the base of my neck. I jump. With my night vision improving, I spot cockroaches weaving in and out of the base of the fluorescent strip light. Every so often one drops onto the concrete and resumes crawling. Examining the bottom bunk, I realise why my cellmate is sleeping at a higher elevation: cockroaches are pouring from gaps in the decrepit wall at the level of my bunk. The area is thick with them. Placing my mattress on the bottom bunk scatters them. I walk towards the toilet, crunching a few under my shower sandals. I urinate and grab the toilet roll. A cockroach darts from the centre of the roll onto my hand, tickling my fingers. My arm jerks as if it has a mind of its own, losing the cockroach and the toilet roll. Using a towel, I wipe the bulk of them off the bottom bunk, stopping only to shake the odd one off my hand. I unroll my mattress. They begin to regroup and inhabit my mattress. My adrenaline is pumping so much, I lose my fatigue.

Nauseated, I sit on a tiny metal stool bolted to the wall. *How will I sleep? How's my cellmate sleeping through the infestation and my arrival?* Copying his technique, I cocoon myself in a sheet and lie down, crushing more cockroaches. The only way they can access me now is through the breathing hole I've left in the sheet by the lower half of my face. Inhaling their strange musty odour, I close my eyes. I can't sleep. I feel them crawling on the sheet around my feet. *Am I imagining things?* Frightened of them infiltrating my breathing hole, I keep opening my eyes. Cramps cause me to rotate onto my other side. Facing the wall, I'm repulsed by so many of them just inches away. I return to my original side.

The sheet traps the heat of the Sonoran Desert to my body, soaking me in sweat. Sweat tickles my body, tricking my mind into thinking the cockroaches are infiltrating and crawling on me. The trapped heat aggravates my bleeding skin infections and bedsores. I want to scratch myself, but I know better. The outer layers of my skin have turned soggy from sweating constantly in this concrete oven. Squirming on the bunk fails to stop the relentless itchiness of my skin. Eventually, I scratch myself. Clumps of moist skin detach under my nails. Every now and then I become so uncomfortable, I must open my cocoon to waft the heat out, which allows the cockroaches in. It takes hours to drift to sleep. I only manage a few hours. I awake stuck to the soaked sheet, disgusted by the cockroach carcasses compressed against the mattress.

The cockroaches plague my new home until dawn appears at the dots in the metal grid over a begrimed strip of four-inch-thick bullet-proof glass at the top of the back wall – the cell's only source of outdoor light. They disappear into the cracks in the walls, like vampire mist retreating from sunlight. But not all of them. There were so many on the night shift that even their vastly reduced number is too many to dispose of. And they act like they know it. They roam around my feet with attitude, as if to make it clear that I'm trespassing on their turf.

My next set of challenges will arise not from the insect world, but from my neighbours. I'm the new arrival, subject to scrutiny about my charges just like when I'd run into the Aryan Brotherhood prison gang on my first day at the medium-security Towers jail a year ago. I wish my cellmate would wake up, brief me on the mood of the locals and introduce me to the head of the white gang. No such luck. Chow is announced over a speaker system in a crackly robotic voice, but he doesn't stir.

I emerge into the day room for breakfast. Prisoners in black-and-white bee-striped uniforms gather under the metal-grid stairs and tip dead cockroaches into a trash bin from plastic peanut-butter containers they'd set as traps during the night. All eyes are on me in the chow line. Watching who sits where, I hold my head up, put on a solid stare and pretend to be as at home in this environment as the cockroaches. It's all an act. I'm lonely and afraid. I loathe having to explain myself to the head of the white race, who I assume is the toughest murderer. I've been in jail long enough to know that taking my breakfast to my cell will imply that I have something to hide.

The gang punishes criminals with certain charges. The most serious are sex offenders, who are KOS: Kill On Sight. Other charges are punishable by SOS – Smash On Sight – such as drive-by shootings because women and kids sometimes get killed. It's called convict justice. Gang members are constantly looking for people to beat up because that's how they earn their reputations and tattoos. The most serious acts of violence earn the highest-ranking tattoos. To be a full gang member requires murder. I've observed the body language and techniques inmates trying to integrate employ. An inmate with a spring in his step and an air of confidence is likely to be accepted. A person who avoids eye contact and fails to introduce himself to the gang is likely to be preyed on. Some of the failed attempts I saw ended up with heads getting cracked against toilets, a sound I've grown familiar with. I've seen prisoners being extracted on stretchers who looked dead – one had yellow fluid leaking from his head. The constant violence gives me nightmares, but the reality is that I put myself in here, so I force myself to accept it as a part of my punishment.

It's time to apply my knowledge. With a self-assured stride, I take my breakfast bag to the table of white inmates covered in neo-Nazi tattoos, allowing them to question me.

"Mind if I sit with you guys?" I ask, glad exhaustion has deepened my voice.

"These seats are taken. But you can stand at the corner of the table."

The man who answered is probably the head of the gang. I size him up. Cropped brown hair. A dangerous glint in Nordic-blue eyes. Tiny pupils that suggest he's on heroin. Weightlifter-type veins bulging from a sturdy neck. Political ink on arms crisscrossed with scars. About the same age as me, thirty-three.

"Thanks. I'm Shaun from England." I volunteer my origin to show I'm different from them but not in a way that might get me smashed.

"I'm Bullet, the head of the whites." He offers me his fist to bump. "Where you roll in from, wood?"

Addressing me as wood is a good sign. It's what white gang members on a friendly basis call each other.

"Towers jail. They increased my bond and re-classified me to maximum security."

"What's your bond at?"

"I've got two $750,000 bonds," I say in a monotone. This is no place to brag about bonds.

"How many people you kill, brother?" His eyes drill into mine, checking whether my body language supports my story. My body language so far is spot on.

"None. I threw rave parties. They got us talking about drugs on wiretaps." Discussing drugs on the phone does not warrant a $1.5 million bond. I know and beat him to his next question. "Here's my charges." I show him my charge sheet, which includes conspiracy and leading a crime syndicate – both from running an Ecstasy ring.

Bullet snatches the paper and scrutinises it. Attempting to pre-empt his verdict, the other whites study his face. On edge, I wait for him to respond. Whatever he says next will determine whether I'll be accepted or victimised.

"Are you some kind of jailhouse attorney?" Bullet asks. "I want someone to read through my case paperwork." During our few minutes of conversation, Bullet has seen through my act and concluded that I'm educated – a possible resource to him.

I appreciate that he'll accept me if I take the time to read his case. "I'm no jailhouse attorney, but I'll look through it and help you however I can."

"Good. I'll stop by your cell later on, wood."

After breakfast, I seal as many of the cracks in the walls as I can with toothpaste. The cell smells minty, but the cockroaches still find their way in. Their day shift appears to be collecting information on the brown paper bags under my bunk, containing a few items of food that I purchased from the commissary; bags that I tied off with rubber bands in the hope of keeping the cockroaches out. Relentlessly, the cockroaches explore the bags for entry points, pausing over and probing the most worn and vulnerable regions. *Will the nightly swarm eat right through the paper?* I read all morning, wondering whether my cellmate has died in his cocoon, his occasional breathing sounds reassuring me.

Bullet stops by late afternoon and drops his case paperwork off. He's been charged with Class 3 felonies and less, not serious crimes, but is facing a double-digit sentence because of his prior convictions and Security Threat Group status in the prison system. The proposed sentencing range seems disproportionate. I'll advise him to reject the plea bargain – on the assumption he already knows to do so, but is just seeking the comfort of a second opinion, like many un-sentenced inmates. When he returns for his paperwork, our conversation disturbs my cellmate – the cocoon shuffles – so we go upstairs to his cell. I tell Bullet what I think. He is excitable, a different man from earlier, his pupils almost non-existent.

"This case ain't shit. But my prosecutor knows I done other shit, all kinds of heavy shit, but can't prove it. I'd do anything to get that sorry bitch off my fucking ass. She's asking for something bad to happen to her. Man, if I ever get bonded out, I'm gonna chop that bitch into pieces. Kill her slowly though. Like to work her over with a blowtorch."

Such talk can get us both charged with conspiring to murder a prosecutor, so I try to steer him elsewhere. "It's crazy how they can catch you doing one thing, yet try to sentence you for all of the things they think you've ever done."

"Done plenty. Shot some dude in the stomach once. Rolled him up in a blanket and threw him in a dumpster."

Discussing past murders is as unsettling as future ones. "So, what's all your tattoos mean, Bullet? Like that eagle on your chest?"

"Why you wanna know?" Bullet's eyes probe mine.

My eyes hold their ground. "Just curious."

"It's a war bird. The AB patch."

"AB patch?"

"What the Aryan Brotherhood gives you when you've put enough work in."

"How long does it take to earn a patch?"

"Depends how quickly you put your work in. You have to earn your lightning bolts first."

"Why you got red and black lightning bolts?"

"You get SS bolts for beating someone down or for being an enforcer for the family. Red lightning bolts for killing someone. I was sent down as a youngster. They gave me steel and told me who to handle and I handled it. You don't ask questions. You just get blood on your steel. Dudes who get these tats without putting work in are told to cover them up or leave the yard."

"What if they refuse?"

"They're held down and we carve the ink off them."

Imagining them carving a chunk of flesh to remove a tattoo, I cringe. He's really enjoying telling me this now. His volatile nature is clear and frightening. *He's accepted me too much. He's trying to impress me before making demands.*

At night, I'm unable to sleep. Cocooned in heat, surrounded by cockroaches, I hear the swamp-cooler vent – a metal grid at the top of a wall – hissing out tepid air. Giving up on sleep, I put my earphones on and tune into National Public Radio. Listening to a Vivaldi violin concerto, I close my eyes and press my tailbone down to straighten my back as if I'm doing a yogic relaxation. The playful allegro thrills me, lifting my spirits, but the wistful adagio provokes sad emotions and tears. I open my eyes and gaze into the gloom. Due to lack of sleep, I start hallucinating and hearing voices over the music whispering threats. I'm at breaking point. Although I have accepted that I committed crimes and deserve to be punished, no one should have to live like this. I'm furious at myself for making the series of reckless decisions that put me in here and for losing absolutely everything. As violins crescendo in my ears, I remember what my life used to be like.

Prison Time by Shaun Attwood

Chapter 1

"I've got a padlock in a sock. I can smash your brains in while you're asleep. I can kill you whenever I want." My new cellmate sizes me up with no trace of human feeling in his eyes. Muscular and pot-bellied, he's caked in prison ink, including six snakes on his skull, slithering side by side. The top of his right ear is missing in a semi-circle.

The waves of fear are overwhelming. After being in transportation all day, I can feel my bladder hurting. "I'm not looking to cause any trouble. I'm the quietest cellmate you'll ever have. All I do is read and write."

Scowling, he shakes his head. "Why've they put a fish in with me?" He swaggers close enough for me to smell his cigarette breath. "Us convicts don't get along with fresh fish."

"Should I ask to move then?" I say, hoping he'll agree if he hates new prisoners so much.

"No! They'll think I threatened you!"

In the eight by twelve feet slab of space, I swerve around him and place my property box on the top bunk.

He pushes me aside and grabs the box. "You just put that on my artwork! I ought to fucking smash you, fish!"

"Sorry, I didn't see it."

"You need to be more aware of your fucking surroundings! What you in for anyway, fish?"

I explain my charges, Ecstasy dealing and how I spent twenty-six months fighting my case.

"How come the cops were so hard-core after you?" he asks, squinting.

"It was a big case, a multi-million-dollar investigation. They raided over a hundred people and didn't find any drugs. They were pretty pissed off. I'd stopped dealing by the time they caught up with me, but I'd done plenty over the years, so I accept my punishment."

"Throwing raves," he says, staring at the ceiling as if remembering something. "Were you partying with underage girls?" he asks, his voice slow, coaxing.

Being called a sex offender is the worst insult in prison. Into my third year of incarceration, I'm conditioned to react. "What you trying to say?" I yell angrily, brow clenched.

"Were you fucking underage girls?" Flexing his body, he shakes both fists as if about to punch me.

"Hey, I'm no child molester, and I'd prefer you didn't say shit like that!"

"My buddy next door is doing twenty-five to life for murdering a child molester. How do I know Ecstasy dealing ain't your cover story?" He inhales loudly, nostrils flaring.

"You want to see my fucking paperwork?"

A stocky prisoner walks in. Short hair. Dark eyes. Powerful neck. On one arm: a tattoo of a man in handcuffs above the word OMERTA – the Mafia code of silence towards law enforcement. "What the fuck's going on in here, Bud?" asks Junior Bull – the son of "Sammy the Bull" Gravano, the Mafia mass murderer who was my biggest competitor in the Ecstasy market.

Relieved to see a familiar face, I say, "How're you doing?"

Shaking my hand, he says in a New York Italian accent, "I'm doing alright. I read that shit in the newspaper about you starting a blog in Sheriff Joe Arpaio's jail."

"The blog's been bringing media heat on the conditions."

"You know him?" Bud asks.

"Yeah, from Towers jail. He's a good dude. He's in for dealing Ecstasy like me."

"It's a good job you said that 'cause I was about to smash his ass," Bud says.

"It's a good job Wild Man ain't here 'cause you'd a got your ass thrown off the balcony," Junior Bull says.

I laugh. The presence of my best friend, Wild Man, was partly the reason I never took a beating at the county jail, but with Wild Man in a different prison, I feel vulnerable. When Bud casts a death stare on me, my smile fades.

"What the fuck you guys on about?" Bud asks.

"Let's go talk downstairs." Junior Bull leads Bud out.

I rush to a stainless-steel sink/toilet bolted to a cement-block wall by the front of the cell, unbutton my orange jumpsuit and crane my neck to watch the upper-tier walkway in case Bud returns. I bask in relief as my bladder deflates. After flushing, I take stock of my new home, grateful for the slight improvement in the conditions versus what I'd grown accustomed to in Sheriff Joe Arpaio's jail. No cockroaches. No blood stains. A working swamp cooler. Something I've never seen in a cell before: shelves. The steel table bolted to the wall is slightly larger, too. *But how will I concentrate on writing with Bud around?* There's a mixture of smells in the room. Cleaning chemicals. Aftershave. Tobacco. A vinegar-like odour. The slit of a window at the back overlooks gravel in a no-man's-land before the next building with gleaming curls of razor wire around its roof.

From the doorway upstairs, I'm facing two storeys of cells overlooking a day room with shower cubicles at the end of both tiers. At two white plastic circular tables, prisoners are playing dominoes, cards, chess and Scrabble, some concentrating, others yelling obscenities, contributing to a brain-scraping din that I hope to block out by purchasing a Walkman. In a raised box-shaped Plexiglas control tower, two guards are monitoring the prisoners.

Bud returns. My pulse jumps. Not wanting to feel like I'm stuck in a kennel with a rabid dog, I grab a notepad and pen and head for the day room.

Focussed on my body language, not wanting to signal any weakness, I'm striding along the upper tier, head and chest elevated, when two hands appear from a doorway and grab me. I drop the pad. The pen clinks against grid-metal and tumbles to the day room as I'm pulled into a cell reeking of backside sweat and masturbation, a cheese-tinted funk.

"I'm Booga. Let's fuck," says a squat man in urine-stained boxers, with WHITE TRASH tattooed on his torso below a mobile home, and an arm sleeved with the Virgin Mary.

Shocked, I brace to flee or fight to preserve my anal virginity. I can't believe my eyes when he drops his boxers and waggles his penis.

Dancing to music playing through a speaker he has rigged up, Booga smiles in a sexy way. "Come on," he says in a husky voice. "Drop your pants. Let's fuck." He pulls pornography faces. I question his sanity. He moves closer. "If I let you fart in my mouth, can I fart in yours?"

"You can fuck off," I say, springing towards the doorway.

He grabs me. We scuffle. Every time I make progress towards the doorway, he clings to my clothes, dragging me back in. When I feel his penis rub against my leg, my adrenalin kicks in so forcefully I experience a burst of strength and wriggle free. I bolt out as fast as my shower sandals will allow and snatch my pad. Looking over my shoulder, I see him stood calmly in the doorway, smiling. He points at me. "You have to walk past my door every day. We're gonna get together. I'll lick your ass and you can fart in my mouth." Booga blows a kiss and disappears.

I rush downstairs. With my back to a wall, I pause to steady my thoughts and breathing. In survival mode, I think, *What's going to come at me next?* In the hope of reducing my tension, I borrow a pen to do what helps me stay sane: writing. With the details fresh in my mind, I document my journey to the prison for my blog readers, keeping an eye out in case anyone else wants to test the new prisoner. The more I write, the more I fill with a sense of purpose. Jon's Jail Journal is a connection to the outside world that I cherish.

Someone yells, "One time!" The din lowers. A door rumbles

open. A guard does a security walk, his every move scrutinised by dozens of scornful eyes staring from cells. When he exits, the din resumes, and the prisoners return to injecting drugs to escape from reality, including the length of their sentences. This continues all day with "Two times!" signifying two approaching guards, and "Three times!" three and so on. Every now and then an announcement by a guard over the speakers briefly lowers the din.

Before lockdown, I join the line for a shower, holding bars of soap in a towel that I aim to swing at the head of the next person to try me. With boisterous inmates a few feet away, yelling at the men in the showers to "Stop jerking off," and "Hurry the fuck up," I get in a cubicle that reeks of bleach and mildew. With every nerve strained, I undress and rinse fast.

At night, despite the desert heat, I cocoon myself in a blanket from head to toe and turn towards the wall, making my face more difficult to strike. I leave a hole for air, but the warm cement block inches from my mouth returns each exhalation to my face as if it's breathing on me, creating a feeling of suffocation. For hours, my heart drums so hard against the thin mattress I feel as if I'm moving even though I'm still. I try to sleep, but my eyes keep springing open and my head turning towards the cell as I try to penetrate the darkness, searching for Bud swinging a padlock in a sock at my head.

ABOUT THE AUTHOR

Michael Sheridan was the main screenwriter and co-producer of the Sky Pictures/Irish Film Board feature film *When the Sky Falls*, the story of the life and death of assassinated Irish crime reporter Veronica Guerin. He wrote and directed *Neil Jordan: A Profile* broadcast by RTE and WNET. He was a storyline consultant on the documentary *Sinatra and the Jack Pack* produced by David Harvey, and broadcast on one of the biggest cable channels in the US. He is working as a consultant on a five-part series for Sky, *Murder at the Cottage: The Search for Justice for Sophie*, directed by Jim Sheridan and produced by Donal McIntyre.

He adapted and directed a musical version of his best-selling Victorian true crime book *Murder at Shandy Hall*, which was a sell-out production at the Cork Opera House.

In addition, he is Ireland's most successful non-fiction author with combined sales of over 700,000 copies. He has been writing on the Sophie Toscan Du Plantier case as a journalist and author for seventeen years and his book published in 2002 on the subject, *Death in December* was a best seller. He was co-author and ghost-writer of the story of the Magdalen Laundry survivor Kathy O Beirne, *Don't Ever Tell* which spent 22 weeks in the UK's top ten and was an international hit published in twenty countries. Among his other best-selling books are *Murder at Shandy Hall*, *Frozen Blood* and *Sinatra and The Jack Pack*.

His second book on the Du Plantier case, *The Murder of Sophie: How I Hunted and Haunted the West Cork Killer* was researched and written with the exclusive and full backing and co-operation of the victim's family, the chief murder investigator and many witnesses.

Lightning Source UK Ltd.
Milton Keynes UK
UKHW052247060821
388368UK00019B/1007